The Internet

Opposing Viewpoints®

Other Books of Related Interest

The Internet

Opposing Viewpoints®

James D. Torr, *Book Editor*

Bruce Glassman, *Vice President*
Bonnie Szumski, *Publisher*
Helen Cothran, *Managing Editor*

OPPOSING
VIEWPOINTS®
SERIES

GREENHAVEN PRESS
An imprint of Thomson Gale, a part of The Thomson Corporation

THOMSON
—★—
GALE

Detroit • New York • San Francisco • San Diego • New Haven, Conn.
Waterville, Maine • London • Munich

THOMSON
GALE

LIBRARY OF CONGRESS CATALOGING-IN-PUBLICATION DATA

The Internet : opposing viewpoints / James D. Torr, book editor.
     p. cm. — (Opposing viewpoints series)
Includes bibliographical references and index.
ISBN 0-7377-2941-4 (lib. : alk. paper) — ISBN 0-7377-2942-2 (pbk. : alk. paper)
     1. Internet—Social aspects. 2. World Wide Web—Social aspects. I. Torr, James
D., 1974– . II. Opposing viewpoints series (Unnumbered)
HM851.I575 2005
303.48'33—dc22   2004059699

Printed in the United States of America

"Congress shall make no law...abridging the freedom of speech, or of the press."

First Amendment to the U.S. Constitution

The basic foundation of our democracy is the First Amendment guarantee of freedom of expression. The Opposing Viewpoints Series is dedicated to the concept of this basic freedom and the idea that it is more important to practice it than to enshrine it.

Contents

Why Consider Opposing Viewpoints?

"The only way in which a human being can make some approach to knowing the whole of a subject is by hearing what can be said about it by persons of every variety of opinion and studying all modes in which it can be looked at by every character of mind. No wise man ever acquired his wisdom in any mode but this."

John Stuart Mill

In our media-intensive culture it is not difficult to find differing opinions. Thousands of newspapers and magazines and dozens of radio and television talk shows resound with differing points of view. The difficulty lies in deciding which opinion to agree with and which "experts" seem the most credible. The more inundated we become with differing opinions and claims, the more essential it is to hone critical reading and thinking skills to evaluate these ideas. Opposing Viewpoints books address this problem directly by presenting stimulating debates that can be used to enhance and teach these skills. The varied opinions contained in each book examine many different aspects of a single issue. While examining these conveniently edited opposing views, readers can develop critical thinking skills such as the ability to compare and contrast authors' credibility, facts, argumentation styles, use of persuasive techniques, and other stylistic tools. In short, the Opposing Viewpoints Series is an ideal way to attain the higher-level thinking and reading skills so essential in a culture of diverse and contradictory opinions.

In addition to providing a tool for critical thinking, Opposing Viewpoints books challenge readers to question their own strongly held opinions and assumptions. Most people form their opinions on the basis of upbringing, peer pressure, and personal, cultural, or professional bias. By reading carefully balanced opposing views, readers must directly confront new ideas as well as the opinions of those with whom they disagree. This is not to simplistically argue that everyone who reads opposing views will—or should—change his or her opinion. Instead, the series enhances readers' understanding of their own views by encouraging confrontation with opposing ideas. Careful examination of others' views can lead to the readers' understanding of the logical inconsistencies in their own opinions, perspective on why they hold an opinion, and the consideration of the possibility that their opinion requires further evaluation.

Evaluating Other Opinions

To ensure that this type of examination occurs, Opposing Viewpoints books present all types of opinions. Prominent spokespeople on different sides of each issue as well as well-known professionals from many disciplines challenge the reader. An additional goal of the series is to provide a forum for other, less known, or even unpopular viewpoints. The opinion of an ordinary person who has had to make the decision to cut off life support from a terminally ill relative, for example, may be just as valuable and provide just as much insight as a medical ethicist's professional opinion. The editors have two additional purposes in including these less known views. One, the editors encourage readers to respect others' opinions—even when not enhanced by professional credibility. It is only by reading or listening to and objectively evaluating others' ideas that one can determine whether they are worthy of consideration. Two, the inclusion of such viewpoints encourages the important critical thinking skill of objectively evaluating an author's credentials and bias. This evaluation will illuminate an author's reasons for taking a particular stance on an issue and will aid in readers' evaluation of the author's ideas.

It is our hope that these books will give readers a deeper understanding of the issues debated and an appreciation of the complexity of even seemingly simple issues when good and honest people disagree. This awareness is particularly important in a democratic society such as ours in which people enter into public debate to determine the common good. Those with whom one disagrees should not be regarded as enemies but rather as people whose views deserve careful examination and may shed light on one's own.

Thomas Jefferson once said that "difference of opinion leads to inquiry, and inquiry to truth." Jefferson, a broadly educated man, argued that "if a nation expects to be ignorant and free . . . it expects what never was and never will be." As individuals and as a nation, it is imperative that we consider the opinions of others and examine them with skill and discernment. The Opposing Viewpoints Series is intended to help readers achieve this goal.

David L. Bender and Bruno Leone,
Founders

Greenhaven Press anthologies primarily consist of previously published material taken from a variety of sources, including periodicals, books, scholarly journals, newspapers, government documents, and position papers from private and public organizations. These original sources are often edited for length and to ensure their accessibility for a young adult audience. The anthology editors also change the original titles of these works in order to clearly present the main thesis of each viewpoint and to explicitly indicate the opinion presented in the viewpoint. These alterations are made in consideration of both the reading and comprehension levels of a young adult audience. Every effort is made to ensure that Greenhaven Press accurately reflects the original intent of the authors included in this anthology.

Introduction

"The notion of a truly interconnected world that had already begun with broadcasting and telephone technologies appears likely to blossom via the Internet."[1]

"If the phrase 'Internet revolution' sounds familiar, that's because technology talk these days is suffused with references to revolution,"[2] writes Andrew L. Shapiro in his book *The Control Revolution: How the Internet Is Putting Individuals in Charge and Changing the World We Know.* "We speak of a communications revolution, an information revolution, a digital revolution," he adds, "Certainly, we are communicating in ways that are different from before. And we have a whole new way to access and manipulate information. These are, no doubt, major developments. But in an age of unchecked hyberbole, it makes sense to ask: Are these changes really *revolutionary?*"[3]

Many people believe they are. Since the creation of the World Wide Web in the early 1990s, countless writers have described the Internet as part of a broader revolution that includes the telephone, radio, and the television. For example, in *The Death of Distance: How the Communications Revolution Is Changing Our Lives*, author Francis Cairncross argues that "the new century will be dominated by the transformation in the cost of transporting knowledge and ideas. That revolution began long ago with the mail, proceeded through the telegraph, the telephone, and broadcasting, and has culminated in a group of innovations that are racing forward with amazing speed."[4]

There are countless predictions about how this revolution will change the world. In his 1999 book *E-topia*, William J. Mitchell offers a typical portrait of where the information revolution is headed:

> Eventually, information of every kind will collect in a planetful of computers, will be delivered wherever you want to through a single digital channel. Everyday objects—from wristwatches to a wallboard will become smarter and smarter, and will serve as our interfaces to the ubiquitous digital world. And paradoxically, wherever you happen to

come in contact with this immense collective construction, it will seem to have the intimacy of underwear.

Instead of forming new relationships of people and agricultural production sites as in the agricultural revolution, or of people and machines in the industrial revolution, this global digital network will reconstitute relationships of people with *information*.[5]

There is a great deal of disagreement over what the long-term effects of so much information will be. A common theme in the discussion is that information is empowering. For example, many Internet optimists believe that free, easily accessible information and communication via the Internet will make it impossible for authoritarian governments to prevent their citizens from organizing or to control the news they get. At the other end of the spectrum, some Internet pessimists worry that virtually free and instantaneous worldwide communications will lead to the breakdown of national barriers which could result in collapsing governments and chaos. The tendency for discussions about the Internet to be dominated by either wonderful or dire predictions has led Century Foundation president Richard C. Leone to remark in 1999 that "it is apparently impossible for someone to write about the 'Net' with restraint or understatement."[6]

Contrary to Leone's observation, beginning in 2000, restraint did begin to color discussions about the Internet. The late 1990s was characterized by "dot-com mania," in which many people invested in newly founded Internet companies. The value of technology stocks soared, until the "tech bubble" burst as investors began abandoning Internet companies that had failed to show a profit. Overexuberance about the potential of the Internet had cost a lot of people a lot of money, and some writers questioned whether all the talk of an information revolution had been merely hype.

In one example, reporter Phillip J. Longman argued in a December 2000 issue of *U.S. News & World Report* that the Internet had not improved people's lives nearly as much as previous advances such as mass production of the automobile or the discovery of antibiotics. "There is a distinction to be made between inventions that are merely sophisticated—such as, say, personal digital assistants—and those that fundamentally alter the human condition," he writes:

> The invention of the light bulb created more useful hours in each day for virtually every human being. . . . The internal combustion engine allowed for mass, high-speed transportation of both people and freight while also opening up vast regions of cheap land to suburban development. The materials revolution that brought us petroleum refining, synthetic chemicals, and pharmaceuticals involved learning to rearrange molecules in ways that made raw materials fundamentally more valuable. Without the genetically improved seeds that brought us the "Green Revolution" of the late 1960s and '70s there would be mass starvation.
>
> Can we make any parallel claim about the single greatest technology of our own time?[7]

In short, Longman suggests that the Internet may not be all that revolutionary, after all.

On the other hand, it may be that the information revolution is just beginning. According to Internet pioneer Jake Winebaum, "The Internet is just 20% invented. . . . That last 80% is happening now."[8] Information technology is certainly still evolving at an incredibly rapid rate: As Alex Lightman writes in *Brave New Unwired World*, "As recently as 1980 phone conversations only traveled on copper wires and were capable of carrying less than a page of information per second. Today, a strand of optical fiber as thin as a human hair can transmit in a single second the equivalent of over 90,000 volumes of an encyclopedia."[9] Furthermore, it can take years for the effects of a technological innovation to emerge. For example, Cairncross notes that a decline in air-transport drove the rise of mass tourism, but it took fifteen years for tourism to become one of the world's largest industries. The World Wide Web was created in the 1990s, but the Internet revolution may continue for decades to come.

The Internet: Opposing Viewpoints explores the key issues involving the Internet in the following chapters: How Does the Internet Affect Society? How Serious Is the Problem of Illegal Activity on the Internet? How Should the Internet Be Regulated? What Will Be the Future of the Internet? There is no question that technology can change the world. In assessing the Internet revolution, the question is not whether the Internet is having an impact on society, but exactly what that impact is—and how the technology can be harnessed for the better.

Notes

1. Bruce C. Klopfenstein, "The Internet Phenomenon," in Alan B. Albarran and David H. Goff, eds., *Understanding the Web: Social, Political, and Economic Dimensions of the Internet*. Ames: Iowa State University Press, 2000, p. 19.

2. Andrew L. Shapiro, *The Control Revolution: How the Internet Is Putting Individuals in Charge and Changing the World We Know*. New York: Perseus, 1999, p. 9.

3. Shapiro, *The Control Revolution*, p. 9.

4. Francis Cairncross, *The Death of Distance: How the Communications Revolution Is Changing Our Lives*. Boston: Harvard Business School Press, 2001, p. 2.

5. William J. Mitchell, *E-topia: "Urban Life, Jim—but Not as We Know It."* Cambridge, MA: MIT Press, 1999.

6. Richard C. Leone, foreword to Shapiro, *The Control Revolution*, p. x.

7. Phillip J. Longman, "The Slowing Pace of Progress," *U.S. News & World Report*, December 25, 2000, p. 68.

8. Quoted in Carter Henderson, "How the Internet Is Changing Our Lives," *Futurist*, July 2000, p. 38.

9. Alex Lightman, with William Rojas, *Brave New Unwired World: The Digital Big Bang and the Infinite Internet*. New York: John Wiley & Sons, 2002, p. 9.

CHAPTER 1

How Does the Internet Affect Society?

Chapter Preface

Internet optimists—who are sometimes referred to as technophiles or cyberutopians—believe that technologies which enhance people's ability to learn and communicate are inherently beneficial to society. For example, writer Carter Henderson avers that the world is entering a new "Cyber Age," whose hallmark is "connectivity and the sharing of information. The assertion that 'information is meant to be free' is an increasing reality since it can be moved from those who have it to those who need it in the blink of an eye—and at virtually no cost. . . . The onrushing Cyber Age has given newfound power to us all."

At the other end of the spectrum are Internet skeptics. Author Deborah C. Sawyer, for example, argues that "more and more information of dubious merit proliferates on the Internet." She believes that Internet communication often serves as "an excuse to dodge person-to-person interaction," and that discourtesy and dishonesty are common on the Internet. Others argue that the anonymity of the Internet allows people to engage in antisocial or immoral activities, such as viewing child pornography.

According to the Pew Internet and American Life Project, which seeks to measure Americans' use of and perceptions about the Internet, most Americans are somewhat ambivalent about the Internet's effect on society. As Pew researcher Lee Rainie explains, "Internet users have finessed the question of whether the Internet is a good or bad thing. Their attitude can be summed up as follows: 'I'm okay, they're not.' Wired Americans believe that their own use of the Internet benefits them and is socially enhancing, although they worry that others may be doing ugly, criminal, perverted, or self-destructive things online."

The question of how the Internet affects society will become increasingly complex as new uses for the Internet proliferate. The authors in the following chapter debate the issue in two specific areas: interpersonal relationships and politics.

"In this new social clearing [the Web], types of associations are being created with a rapidity unequalled in our history."

The Internet Increases Social Interaction

David Weinberger

David Weinberger is a technology writer and the author of *Small Pieces Loosely Joined*, from which the following viewpoint is excerpted. In it, he maintains that the World Wide Web is bringing people together in unprecedented ways. Weinberger views the Web as a vast collection of relatively small groups that are formed around common interests ranging from crossword puzzles to politics. According to the author, these groups are very different from real-world groups—in particular, he argues that the Web allows people to maintain their individuality when interacting with large masses in a way that is not possible offline. Weinberger views the Web as a gathering place, one that is constantly evolving and completely unconstrained by geography. The Web benefits society, he concludes, by empowering people to socialize in new ways.

As you read, consider the following questions:
1. What "simple formula" characterizes traditional social interactions, in Weinberger's view?
2. What example does the author use to illustrate the "rapid mutation of social forms" on the Web?
3. According to the author, what makes humans social?

We know everyone in our monthly book club, we know most of the people at the Parent-Teachers Association meeting, we know some people and recognize a few more at the annual town picnic, and each of us is just a face in the crowd at the mass rally. The bigger the crowd, the more faceless we each become, mirroring socially the physical fact that faces become smaller and smaller the farther back in the crowd they are. We have a rich set of terms to describe the relationships among people in groups: I *know* the friend I came to the march with, I *recognize* some people from my home town, I've *heard* of the person exhorting us from the rostrum. This formula of facelessness governs our behavior: everyone gets a turn to speak at the book club meeting, but I don't expect the crowd of marchers to "not interrupt me" when I say something to the person next to me.

The Paradox of the Public

We're generally fine with this social diminution. It's been the only way to live with others in a mass society: we all become members of this uniquely human group, the public. The public has no formal structure, no leaders, no rites or rules of membership, no objectives, no charter, no dues, but it is undeniably real. And facelessness is a requirement for admission; we think of ourselves as being part of the public precisely when we're appealing to that which we have in common with others. "As a member of the public I demand . . ." prefaces a claim made on the basis of our simply being social animals rather than because of any special standing. We are proud of being unique individuals, yet we understand that when you put us all together, we become something different. . . .

Both the positive and negative side of the paradox of the public are based on the simple formula that says there's an inverse relationship between the size of the group and our individuality as participants in it. Rewrite that formula and the rules of groups come unstuck: do we behave at the book club the way we behave at the mass rally or vice versa? How much individuality are we allowed to bring to the party? What would it mean for us to be a member of a group, even a mass group like the public, without giving up our individuality? What would it mean if we could replace the faceless masses with face-ful masses?

Thanks to the Web, we're in the process of finding out. . . .

Groups on the Web

The range of groups on the Web, as off the Web, is staggering. You could be a member of a mailing list for people interested in word origins; someone who regularly plays Quake on a particular server where players start to recognize one another's names; an active participant in a discussion board that's been up for over a year and is dedicated to thoughts about one particular book; a contributor to a travel site where members share experiences; someone who receives progressive filmmaker Michael Moore's email rants about politics; a friend of Tim Hiltabiddle's to whom he occasionally sends out humor he's found on the Web; a participant in a mailing list for the attendees of a small telecommunications conference; and one of the regular advisors to a guy whose site you like. Each of these groups is different in its constitution, behavior, rules, and longevity. Probably the only thing they have in common is that I am a member of each—and they are all Web-based.

Web groups are different than groups in the real world, and not just because, free of geography, they are often more purely interest-based. Just as important, Web groups are different in time. Consider the difference between the Emily Dickinson Society, which meets once a month in the real world, and Dickinson readers who have found one another on the Web—imaginary examples in both cases. The real-world society sets aside the first Tuesday night of every month to get together. Although individual members may, of course, chat about the Belle of Amherst whenever they run into one another, the group's talk about Dickinson is confined to that two-hour session. Miss it and you've missed it for the month. The Web-based Dickinson group, on the other hand, is held together by a mailing list that lets each member send a message to all the other members. Merry may wake up on Wednesday convinced that a line in one of Dickinson's letters proves that Susan Gilbert was the object of "Wild Nights." She skips breakfast, writes up her idea, and sends it off to the Dickinson list. By the time Merry arrives at work, her message has been received by all 150 participants and two replies already await her. Throughout the day, more messages arrive. The list members read them when they check their email. Perhaps they find the time to dash off a note, or perhaps they come back to it later. The conversational thread is always there, waiting for them.

Threads of discussion take on a life of their own. They may meander and the frequency of contributions may slow, but so long as new messages are coming in, the thread is alive and open. Sometimes threads are explicitly killed: "Take it offline!" someone writes; but more often they simply die of neglect. And on occasion they explode, filling mail boxes with urgent, impassioned messages that beg for replies.

What do we have like this in the real world? A book club meets for a few hours a month. Snail-mail letters going back and forth are slow and connect only two people at a time. A mailed newsletter arrives on the author's schedule and doesn't enable replies from recipients to all the other recipients. Classes on Emily Dickinson occur on a schedule and discuss the topics the professor finds interesting. Chance meetings in the street or the bookstore that lead to conversations about "Wild Nights" are lovely but accidental. Although elements of real-world conversations appear in threaded discussions, there is nothing quite like threaded discussions in the real world.

A Different Sort of Meeting

The differences go down to the details. Imagine the monthly meeting of Merry's book club is held in the dark, a spotlight shining on each person as she speaks. Imagine that the only sound you can hear is that of the person speaking. Imagine that you are unaware of the nodding and the uh huhs and the body language that says your listeners are uncomfortable with what you're saying or that encourages you to say more. This would be a very different sort of meeting. It might encourage you to speak more freely, or it might completely inhibit you; it depends on how you feel about literally being in the spotlight. It might, indeed, encourage you to say more and more outrageous things just to provoke an audible reaction. This would be especially true if you could wear a mask so that the people at the meeting only knew you by a name you chose for yourself—"The Anti-Emily" or "Sweetness and Spice" or "Sappho's Fire" or whatever. Step by step, our old-style meeting has become quite a different sort of beast. And, of course, this is exactly what happens on the Web. For example, if 90 percent of the people on the Dickinson mailing list agree with Merry's thesis about "Wild Nights," Merry may never know it, for it's generally considered bad form to send email that simply says "Uh huh" and "Me, too." These supportive comments, so important in real-world discussions, simply clog the pipes on the Web; no one wants to wake up to thirty-five messages in the "Wild Nights" thread only to discover that thirty-four are from people saying "I agree." So the discussion continues not until most people are nodding and agreeing but until the last remaining antagonist has said the last possible interesting thing. At that point, either the thread dies a natural death or someone says, "You're going down some trivial rabbit hole! Take it offline!"

Changing the Nature of Membership

Most important, because the threads are persistent, they create a new type of public space that enables a new type of participation. Real-world groups often have some process for applying for acceptance, whether it's as casual as asking your book club if your friend Pat can attend or as formal as filling out forms, supplying references, and waiting for the membership committee to vote. They do this because everyone has to fit into a room at the same time; and in the real world you have to filter out the bores because you can't just hit the delete key when they start talking. On the Web, the norm is for groups to be open to anyone who cares to join. What is the membership criterion? Interest. Membership and participation are identical for the most part with Web groups.

That changes the nature of membership. In a normal real-world group, you are either a member or you're not. On the Web, it's common for people to participate by "lurking," reading the postings without posting anything themselves. This is the ultimate in anonymity: not only don't people know who you are but they don't even know you're there. And lurking is considered very good form, for it lets "newbies" absorb the group's ethos and mores.

Expanded Interactions

Surveys and ethnographic studies show that rich, fertile, diverse, and expanded interactions are possible through the Internet. Impassioned members of many online groups provide emotional and other resources to each other, and users regularly rate communicating with others—family, friends, and new people they have met online—as their favorite and most important Internet activity. Some studies show that interactive Internet usage replaces passive television watching but that overall Internet users are greater media participants. Members of the Net generation may well be more literate, creative, and socially skilled than earlier generations because of their early familiarity with the Internet, including trying out various aspects of their developing identities online. Interacting with teachers and other students is easier when supported by the Internet, and both students and patients are more likely to talk about sensitive issues online, possibly because of the protection of anonymity. Users meet new people they come to call friends online, and some go on to meet these people in person. Several studies have specifically countered some prior research linking Internet use with isolation or depression, showing that experienced Internet users may find greater support online, become more satisfied with their interactions and communication, and generate new relationships through the ability to contact others more easily than they can offline. Indeed, some speculate that the Internet can also foster greater tolerance through exposure to a wider diversity of voices and even support spiritual growth. All these possibilities may lead to a major expansion of our concepts of identity, groups, and society.

James E. Katz and Ronald E. Rice, *Social Consequences of Internet Use: Access, Involvement, and Interaction.* Cambridge, MA: MIT Press, 2002.

The laxness of many Web groups about membership can make them as coherent and persistent as the passing lane of a highway. But it also allows these groups to grope towards somewhat persistent forms. For example, for $19.95 a year you can get access not only to each day's *New York Times* crossword puzzle but also to a bulletin board for subscribers. Many of the participants show up only when they're particularly vexed by a clue and may never show up again. Yet, even within this nonce group of random strangers helping one another with the day's crossword, voices emerge as particularly reliable or interesting. And social forms emerge that extend beyond a particular day's chatter; for example, you are asked not to reveal specific answers to that day's puzzle until after noon. If you reply to a request for the answer to a clue, the favored way is to change the font of the answer to white so that it's invisible to people perusing the discussion board for help with other clues. To make the answer visible, you have to use your mouse to "select" the text, causing its color to invert. If you don't know this, you will find the board frustrating, for messages promise answers and then go blank. These rules, forms, and personalities constitute an exoskeleton for the nonce group, another example of the ways small, loosely joined groups on the Web evolve into forms as unpredictable as humans.

So the Web version of a traditional real-world group is different in the nature of membership that makes it a group, how it acts as a group, and in the "when" of its existence. In short, the Web has kicked down most of the fencing that lets us recognize a group as a group.

Mutating Social Forms

In this new social clearing, types of associations are being created with a rapidity unequalled in our history. From www.k2bh.com that tries to layer virtual relations on top of real-world local communities, to www.jailbabes.com that lists incarcerated women eager for pen pals, the Web is a hotbed of experimental couplings. In fact, the Web sometimes seems to consist of 300 million monkeys chained to Web software development tools and randomly creating new ways for us to be together. The results are, at best, uneven. But we benefit from the Web's ability to evolve new forms so rapidly that if real-world evolution worked as fast, we could move from grapefruit to squid in a couple of months.

Amazon.com's review pages provide a convenient example of the rapid mutation of social forms. The site began with a simple idea: let people post reviews of books. But when bestsellers such as the first Harry Potter book prompted over 3 thousand reviews, the massness of the Web threatened to make the reviews' collected weight more daunting than useful. So Amazon now presents the average rating of the book—from 1 to 5 stars—as a way of harvesting intelligibility from the outpouring of evaluations. But while a 1–5 rating tells us something, it doesn't take advantage of the explicit and often helpful comments that thousands of people were willing to write. To enable readers to find the voices worth listening to in this mass, Amazon added another level of review: readers of the reviews can rate the reviews, indicating whether a particular review is helpful or not. Although there are still 3 thousand Harry Potter reviews to look at, at least you get some guidance about which ones other readers have found worthwhile. Then, with the massness of the Web threatening to outpace the efforts to harness it, Amazon began flagging the reviewers whose reviews were highly rated with a distinctive graphic so that their contributions stand out in the long list. This has the additional effect of making individual reviewers more recognizable. You might remember having liked "Rebecca's" review of *The Scream Museum* when you see her review of *The Viking Claw* because the "Top 50" reviewer graphic makes her comments conspicuous. If you want more context to better understand her reviews, you can click on her name and see a page about her maintained at the Amazon site. It contains a little autobiographical information—she turns out to be a sixteen-year-old who likes science fiction and fantasy, loves *Star Wars* movies, and hopes to write novels for young adults someday—and a collection of all 511 reviews she's written so far. If you find Rebecca's comments helpful, you can add her to your own page on Amazon so that you can keep up with her recommendations. You can also give your own friends access to your page at Amazon, and they can reciprocate; in this way, you can see what your buddies are saying about the books they read. Amazon also surfaces information about the various groupings that naturally occur. For example, Amazon lets you see which groups are buying which books—at this writing, people at Boeing are buying lots of copies of *Body for Life: 12 Weeks to Mental and Physical Strength*; the U.S. Marine Corps is buying *Dungeons & Dragons 3rd Edition Player's Handbook*; the consulting company KPMG is buying *The Beatles Anthology;* Brazil is buying Jerry Seinfeld's *SeinLanguage;* and everyone's buying Harry Potter.

This progression has an almost Hegelian logic to it, each step following from the other, each propelled by an internal contradiction: the Web consists of hundreds of millions of individuals. They are a mass, but each member is unique. Individuals write reviews. The massness of the individuals makes the aggregate of reviews useless. So Amazon captures summary information, 1–5 stars, from the mass of individual reviews. But because those numeric rankings slight the individual side of the Web, the site begins to star the individual reviewers—but by using the masses' review of the reviewers as its criterion. And so on. One can almost feel the breeze from the pendulum as it swings this way or that: massness, individuality, massness, individuality. And, most important, a new relationship between them: the Web consists of a mass that refuses to lose its individual faces. . . .

A Shared World

Ultimately, the world is *shared*. At every instant, our understanding and our behavior are shaped by the fact that there are other people. Even when we're alone, we understand our aloneness in relation to the world of others to which we are going to return. So, if I say that humans are social, I don't mean that we tend to like one another or even that it takes a village to raise a child. I mean simply that we live in a shared world. We are here with others. And that is the condition for there being a public.

Our shared world isn't the surface of the earth. What makes us social isn't shared space, for we share geography with nematodes and macaroons, but we are not *social* with them. What makes us social are shared interests. We care about one another and we care together about the world we've built out of the world we were born into. There should be no need to state such obvious truths. But our history has also brought us to an odd individualism—part of our default philosophy—that says that only individuals are real. Groups, according to this philosophy, are immaterial and thus unreal; a group is really nothing but a collection of

26

individuals. The moral conclusions this default philosophy sometimes draws are as repugnant as its ontological premises are faulty. Without groups, there would be no individual humans, only howling monkeys in human form. In fact, that's unfair to the monkeys. A human being raised in isolation would not be identifiably human in anything except DNA. Sociality grants a mute herd of brutes their souls and selves. The Web is a new social, public space. But because the Web has no geography, no surface, no container of space that preexists its habitation, we can't make the old mistake about what constitutes our sociality. The Web is a shared place that we choose to build, extend, and inhabit. We form groups there because our interests aren't unique. How could they be if we're truly social? But the ground rules are different from the real world precisely because there's no ground on the Web. In the real world, masses become more faceless the farther away they are. On the Web, each person is present only insofar as she has presented herself in an individual expression of her interests: many small faces, each distinct within the multitude. And since being on the Web is a voluntary activity, we are forced to face the excruciating fact that we spend so much real-world energy denying: *not only do we live in a shared world, but we like it that way.*

You could build a new destiny for your species on an idea as radical as that.

"The more time people spend using the Internet, the more they lose contact with their social environment."

Internet Use Decreases Social Interaction

Norman H. Nie and Lutz Erbring

Norman H. Nie is a professor of political science and the director of the Institute for the Quantitative Study of Society at Stanford University. Lutz Erbring is a professor of mass communications at the Free University of Berlin. In the following viewpoint, Nie and Erbring argue that Internet use has a negative effect on society because using the Internet is a solitary activity and therefore detracts from people's social lives. The authors came to this conclusion after designing an Internet survey and studying the responses of over four thousand participants. According to Nie and Erbring, the survey results show a clear correlation: The more people use the Internet, the less time they spend with family and friends, and the less time they spend outside the house.

As you read, consider the following questions:
1. What percentage of the U.S. population had access to the Internet at the time of the authors' study?
2. At what age does the use of Internet chat rooms substantially decrease, according to the authors?
3. In the authors' view, how is the Internet different from TV?

Norman H. Nie and Lutz Erbring, "Internet and Society: A Preliminary Report," *Stanford Institute for the Quantitative Study of Society*, February 16, 2000, pp. 275–80. Copyright © 2002 by Stanford University. Reproduced by permission of the publisher and the authors.

Over the last five years, the revolution in information technology (IT) has resulted in innovations that are having increasingly visible effects on the life of the average American. These developments affect not only how people work, but where they work, how much they work, or with whom they interact face-to-face or electronically. Will future workers continue to share physical proximity with their colleagues, or work largely alone wedded to digital devices with occasional electronic mail or voice communication? What will these changes mean for social trust and social life beyond the family? Will the growing trend of working at home with the aid of IT help strengthen the family or add to the intrusion of the workplace into the home? Will it reduce the hours people work, or increase them by infusing work into every sphere of life, devouring leisure time and family life? And how will the Internet affect the role and use of the traditional media?

These same IT innovations are revolutionizing information and entertainment delivery, affecting their production and consumption, transforming social life and behavior, even political institutions and the role of citizens within them. Some argue that the new technology of email, online discussions, on-demand information, and web-powered information diffusion and interest aggregation will lead to a more informed, engaged, and influential mass public. Will one live in a better informed and connected, more engaged and participatory society—or in a society of lonely ex-couch potatoes glued to computer screens, whose human contacts are largely impersonal and whose political beliefs are easily manipulated, relying on the icons of a wired or wireless society?

The human meaning of these changes remains unclear at present. Some greet these developments with euphoria, others warn of dire consequences. The truth is likely to be somewhere in the middle. Some of the social/political changes will be liberating, some will have little social effect, but others may be harmful or even socially and politically explosive; some may even be perverse, and the most critical ones may well be unanticipated by everyone. For answers to these questions, one must move from ideological claims to empirical evidence. This study is an attempt to do just that.

The Survey

The study is based on data collected using a revolutionary new methodology developed by Knowledge Networks to conduct surveys over the Internet. Unlike surveys of Internet users or households, which suffer obvious sample distortions and preclude generalizing results, this new survey methodology is based on a panel of households recruited as a genuine random telephone sample of the U.S. population. In order to use the Internet for the purpose of efficient multi-channel data collection, each household in the sample—with or without prior Internet connection—is equipped with a WebTV set-top box, with free Internet access and email accounts.

The data for the study were collected in December 1999, from a national random sample of 4113 individuals in 2689 panel households, as a baseline for a continuing research program. Questionnaires were completed independently by each member of a panel household using their television and their WebTV controls to answer the questions displayed on the screen. To avoid contamination of results due to the fact that the study was itself conducted over the Internet (all sample households have Internet access, as a result of having been equipped with WebTV), the results on Internet use presented in this study are based only on the responses of participants who had Internet access (at home or elsewhere) prior to and independent of the WebTV access installed by Knowledge Networks. The margin of sampling error is about 1.5 percent for results from the complete survey, and about 2.5 percent for the subset of Internet users.

Some 65 percent of American households have at least one computer (of that, 19 percent report a multi-computer household); 43 percent of American households are connected to the Internet.

In terms of individual Internet access, 38 percent of Americans over 18 access the Internet at home, 34 percent access the Internet elsewhere (17 percent exclusively, 17 percent in both places). Thus, 55 percent of the population currently have access to the Internet.

Four thousand respondents were asked to select among a list of 17 common Internet activities and say which they did or did not do. It was found that email is by far the most common Internet activity, with 90 percent of all Internet users claiming to be emailers. For the most part, the Internet today is a giant public library with a decidedly commercial tilt. The most widespread use of the Internet today is as an information search utility for products, travel, hobbies and general information. Virtually all users interviewed responded that they engaged in one or more of these information gathering activities. A little over a third of all Internet users report using the web to engage in entertainment such as computer games (such as online chess, role games, and the like). Thus, the current Internet is also emerging as an entertainment utility.

Figure 1: Social Isolation Increases with More Internet Use

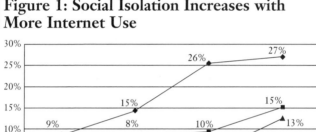

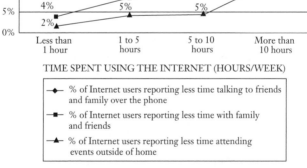

% of Internet users reporting less time talking to friends and family over the phone

% of Internet users reporting less time with family and friends

% of Internet users reporting less time attending events outside of home

Norman H. Nie and Lutz Erbring, "Internet and Society: A Preliminary Report," *IT & Society*, Summer 2002.

Chat rooms are for the young and the anonymous. Although a quarter of Internet users claim to have used chat rooms, this activity substantially decreases after age 25. And the chatters report that the overwhelming portion of their chat room interaction is with anonymous others whose identities remain unknown. Consumer-to-business transactional activity—purchasing, stock trading, online auctions, and e-banking—are engaged in by much smaller fractions of Internet users, with just more than a third reporting they make purchases online and under 15 percent doing any of the other transactional activities. Despite all of the sound and fury, business-to-consumer commercial online transactions are but in their earliest stages.

The average Internet user reports engaging in 7.2 different types of activities. While there is probably some double accounting due to an attempt to be comprehensive in the list of activities, the average user is engaging in at least 5 distinct types of activities on the Web: a combination of different types of information searches, entertainment and games, and for one quarter, some commercial transactional activity. The Internet has been around for about five years now, and the longer people have been web users the more hours and the more activities they report engaging in. Although self-selection may be playing a role with early adopters, the data strongly suggest a model of social change with not only a growing number of Internet users, but with web users doing more and more things on the Internet in the future.

Effects on Social Life

It was found that the more time people spend using the Internet, the more they lose contact with their social environment. Figure 1 shows that this effect is noticeable even with just 2–5 Internet hours per week; and it rises substantially for those spending more than 10 hours per week, of whom up to 15 percent report a decrease in social activities. Even more striking is the fact that Internet users spend much less time talking on the phone to friends and family: the percentage reporting a decrease exceeds 25 percent—although it is unclear to what extent this represents a shift to email even in communicating with friends and family or a technical bottleneck due to a single phone line being preempted by Internet use.

Moreover, the more time people spend using the Internet, the more they turn their back on traditional media. This effect increases proportionally with hours of Internet use: for every additional hour on the Net, people report further decreases in time spent with traditional media, reaching 65 percent for those spending more than 10 hours a week on the Net. Clearly the media are competing with the Internet for time, especially in the case of television where even with as little as two hours/week on the Net, a quarter of Internet users report decreases in TV viewing—one can't surf the web and watch TV at the same time. For newspapers, the same effect is less dramatic and may also reflect the fact that people could substitute reading the news on the web for reading the paper.

Besides, the amount of time spent using the Internet is found to be positively correlated with the amount of time spent working at home—and at the office. Even with less than 5 hours/week of Internet use, about 15 percent of full-time or part-time workers report an increase in time spent working at home. And as their amount of Internet use rises above 5 hours/week, a growing number—up to an additional 12 percent—even report spending more time working at the office, as well as at home. For heavy Internet users with regular jobs, a substantial portion of their total Internet use is likely to take place at the office to begin with—and it seems to be keeping them there for longer hours, in addition to invading their home. There are at present no indications suggesting the beginnings of telecommuting.

However, a negative correlation has been found between time spent using the Internet and time spent shopping in stores and commuting in traffic. This effect grows with the number of Internet hours/week, and as might be expected, stands out particularly clearly for people who use the web for researching product information or for actually making purchases online, thus saving trips to the store. But it does not affect time spent commuting in traffic, which decreases with the number of Internet hours for the nonworking population only, whether or not they shop on the web—working Internet users drive to work just as much as before.

Less Time with Real Human Beings

For the most part, the Internet is an individual activity. Unlike TV, which can be treated as background noise, it requires more engagement and attention. Although a number of commentators have speculated about how the Internet might change people's daily lives, and some studies have looked at the use patterns of nonrepresentative groups of Internet users, only a sample representative of households nationally allows analysts to make projections about future Internet usage and its likely consequences.

As Internet use grows, Americans report they spend less time with friends and family, shopping in stores or watching television, and more time working for their employers at home—without cutting back their hours in the office. A key finding of the study is that the more hours people use the Internet, the less time they spend with real human beings. It appears that time on the Internet is coming out of time spent viewing television, but it is also done at the expense of time on the phone with family and friends and time in conversations. A quarter of the respondents who use the Internet regularly (more than 5 hours a week) feel that it has reduced their time with friends and family, or attending events outside the home. This is an early trend that society really needs to monitor carefully. Email use is an additional medium now available for communicating with friends and family, but one can't share a coffee or a beer with somebody on email or give them a hug.

"The Internet provides citizens who are separated . . . by time and space a way to reconnect and become more concerned about . . . their society."

The Internet Helps Citizens Become More Active in Politics

Steve Davis, Larry Elin, and Grant Reeher

Steve Davis, Larry Elin, and Grant Reeher are the authors of *Click on Democracy: The Internet's Power to Change Political Apathy into Civic Action*, from which the following viewpoint is excerpted. In it, they argue that the Internet offers people new ways to become more engaged in politics. The authors maintain that since the mid-1960s, Americans have become less active in their communities, less interested in politics, and less aware of current events. In their opinion, the Internet has the potential to help reverse this decline in civic engagement. Davis, Elin, and Reeher maintain that the Internet benefits society by helping to create political communities where people can discuss issues and activists can organize.

As you read, consider the following questions:
1. In what ways has community involvement deteriorated, according to the authors?
2. What is the least active group of eligible voters, according to the authors?
3. What type of user dominated the Internet in its early days, according to the authors, as compared to the present?

Steve Davis, Larry Elin, and Grant Reeher, *Click on Democracy: The Internet's Power to Change Political Apathy into Civic Action.* Boulder, CO: Westview Press, 2002. Copyright © 2002 by Grant Reeher, Steve Davis, and Larry Elin. Reproduced by permission of Westview Press, a member of Perseus Books, LLC.

It was Thursday, August 24, when Drew McGarr, real estate agent, dropped the bomb on a tight circle of friends, political junkies all.

"If Al Gore wins, my wife and I have both pledged never to vote again. If Al Gore wins, we hang it up."

He said he meant it.

His friends were stunned. Indeed, they were alarmed to hear such a declaration from a sixty-year-old devotee of democracy who'd never missed a vote since he'd turned twenty-one. This was a man who loved voting, a man of such principle that he'd declared he questioned online balloting because he so believed in the process, in the public *act* of voting. "Over the years, my wife and I, we've always met and went to vote, and every time there's always that good feeling you have when you walk out of that school cafeteria, that lifted spirit," he'd once mused. He was proud that he'd brought up his three children—now thirty-six, thirty-seven, and thirty-eight—to feel the same way.

Yet in late summer 2000, he sounded depressed, punctuating his melancholy declaration by saying, "As I get older I seem to see the glass half empty."

A Percolating Conversation

His friends fired back. They tried to pump him up. One in particular, Alan Kardoff, voiced outrage. Alan could go on a bit, he could be hyperbolic, but he was genuinely passionate about politics. "Baloney. You're a fighter," he told Drew. "You believe in America. The day you stop voting is right after you, like the rest of us, go to Eternal Rest. I feel the same way, almost on the other side. I never figured you for a coward."

Kardoff believed he spoke for his friends. "If you bail out, we have to all adjust and readjust. So do you. That is, unless your participation so far has been a charade. I know this is not true. Are you the only one who may feel a bit disenchanted?"

Dave Kaplan chimed in: "Alan is exactly correct on this! We need debate on issues. We need each other. Americans of all ideologies join together to form and maintain our imperfect government and society, but it is still the best of any in the world. Why should one part leave voluntarily, and cause unforeseen adjustments in all parts of the system?

"Hang in there," he urged Drew. "No matter how empty the top half of the glass is, the bottom half of the glass is always half full." The conversation was percolating now; LuAnn Molloy threw her support to McGarr. "If Al Gore wins," she told the others, "I don't care anymore and renounce any interest in politics and will fit in with everyone else I know, too."

Now it was a debate in full flame. Mona Twocats weighed in. "No. No. A thousand times no. Even though I may disagree with your philosophy, it is imperative that we all continue to at least express our values at the polls. I try to tell people that not voting is only voting by omission. There is no such thing as not being involved in politics. When you refuse to support your value system, you are voting against it."

And finally, Kardoff (a Gore man) wrapped it up, emoting in one of his signature stem-winders. He advised the group that, rather than giving up on politics, "I am fed up so much that my commitment to trying to help our nation elect the better candidates will be intensified.". . .

An Online Community

Who are these Americans? And what neighborhood fence do they talk over? Drew McGarr is a real estate agent in Memphis, Tennessee. Alan Kardoff is a former business-school professor living in Melbourne, Florida. Dave Kaplan is a Des Moines, Washington, city councilman. A gay man, he came out not long ago. LuAnn Molloy is a mother of three teens in Minnesota who holds down two jobs. Mona Twocats, a Native American, is a Green party activist from Bakersfield, California.

How could such a disparate group come together, bond, and share such passion, empathy, and moral conviction?

On the Internet. All of them were part of an online community that they joined and nurtured during the 2000 election. Kaplan says the Internet connected him to the world of gay Republicans and emboldened him to come out. He realized he was not alone through online conversations with others, many of them members of the Log Cabin Republicans, a national political organization of gays and lesbians. Thousands of miles separate these friends, but they might as well have been sitting around the same kitchen table as cranking out their passions on Compaqs and Dells from desktops in dens or on laptops propped on bedroom pillows.

What makes this group's conversation politically meaningful? What is the Internet contributing here to the vitality of America's political life? At the very least, the fact that the conversation is taking place is significant. . . . These kinds of conversations have declined in recent years, a fact that should worry us. The Internet is the most efficient way for this diverse and scattered group to communicate at all. . . .

The Decline of Social Capital

The community that Drew McGarr, Dave Kaplan, Mona Twocats, LuAnn Molloy, and Alan Kardoff formed in cyberspace exemplifies a degree of connection that has become increasingly rare in physical space. As social scientist Robert Putnam hammers home in his book *Bowling Alone*, Americans gradually have withdrawn from almost every form of civic engagement over the past forty years. Regardless of the barometer, "the last several decades have witnessed a serious deterioration of community involvement among Americans from all walks of life," he says. By his calculations, we are 40 percent less likely to be involved in political or civic organizations of all kinds than we were in the mid-1960s. Membership has declined in organizations as wide-ranging as the PTA, labor unions, political parties, mainline Christian denominations, and even bowling leagues. Our own personal social connections have weakened, too. We are now less likely to visit friends, have dinner with our own families, or even have a drink in a bar with our coworkers. . . .

Although no one knows exactly what is causing the decline, it appears to have affected everyone, at every station in life. During the decades Putnam chronicles, we became a nation of suburbanites who spend about 25 percent more time in our cars than we did thirty years ago. Our roots are not simply shallow; they are hydroponic—veritably suspended in air. There are more two-income families, leaving many homes empty during the day and removing what had been a dependable supply of community volunteers. Our knowledge of and interest in current events, one of the most reliable indicators of civic engagement, is waning. . . .

We read newspapers less. This decline is more pronounced among eighteen-to-twenty-four-year-olds (down 57 percent) than those over sixty (down 10 percent). What is true for television news is also true for newspapers—there is a preponderance of soft, human-interest news. The news that is consumed is of little value. A generation of highly educated but less informed citizens looms as the entire population ages and the more informed die off.

Lost in the blizzard of disappointing survey results is the psychological toll inflicted on the individuals who collectively make up the statistics. We are a race of social beings who need healthy contact with each other but are spending less time even attempting to stay in touch. As individuals we seem to be inflicting on ourselves the most fearsome penalty we impose on our criminals: solitary confinement.

The Toll on Civic Engagement

This combination—disconnection from each other and uninterestedness in community affairs—has taken a measurable toll on every form of civic engagement. Even forms of civic engagement that usually become *more* evident during an important election year are suffering. According to Roper surveys taken between 1973 and 1994 we are 25 percent less likely to participate in any of the most common forms of political involvement, such as working for a political party, writing to an elected official, or signing a petition. Voting turnout in presidential elections has declined steadily to the point where in 1996, for the first time in the nation's recent history, fewer than half of all eligible voters went to the polls. In 2000, turnout was 51.2 percent, according to the Committee for the Study of the American Electorate—a slight increase perhaps attributable to the massive get-out-the-vote and registration efforts in battleground states, some of which took place over the Internet.

The decline in social capital is most acute among young adults. The most inactive generation of voters is between eighteen and twenty-four years old. In 1996 less than half the eligible voters in this age group registered and less than a third voted. These proportions rise steadily with age. Three-quarters of those over sixty-five are registered, and two-thirds voted. Each successive generation is better educated, more affluent, enjoys more leisure time, and is in almost every way more capable of participating in civic activities, yet younger Americans are withdrawing from the political process. Even the motor voter law, which made it possible to register to vote while getting a drivers license, and laws that made voting by mail the only method in Oregon and the preferred in Washington state, failed to significantly increase overall voter participation.

The Internet and Civic Engagement

Can the Internet help reverse the decline in voting and other forms of civic engagement? Will the news media, political parties, special interest groups, and grassroots political organizations effectively use it to reach citizens? Can the Internet increase our consumption of and interest in the news and make us better, more informed, and more active citizens? Will the Internet engage the young to fashion new forms of civic engagement? Will they become more interested in politics?

Our study of the people who used the Internet during the 2000 election offers strong evidence that the Internet *is* having an impact, though not in the manner we expected. We found that the Internet provides citizens who are separated from each other by time and space a way to reconnect and become more concerned about each other and their society. Most of our evidence shows that they are doing this without the assistance of the media and political institutions. . . .

In discussing the Internet's potential for regenerating social capital, Putnam observes that so far the social culture of the Internet is radically individualistic rather than communitarian and that the lower threshold offered by the Internet to expressing an opinion may in turn lower the quality of political discourse. He also argues that the Internet robs the participant of "social cues" and the depth and multiplicity of feedback necessary for "interpersonal collaboration and trust." There was a famous cartoon in the *New Yorker* magazine in which a dog, seated at a computer, tells another dog, "On the Internet, no one knows you're a dog." This illustrates Putnam's point perfectly.

Thus the Internet makes it easier to misrepresent and lie. Putnam further posits that the Internet makes it easier for ever-narrower interests to come together, to the exclusion of others. Diversity in social interactions could further suffer with the Internet, as "local heterogeneity may give way to more focused virtual homogeneity."

The Decline in Voter Turnout

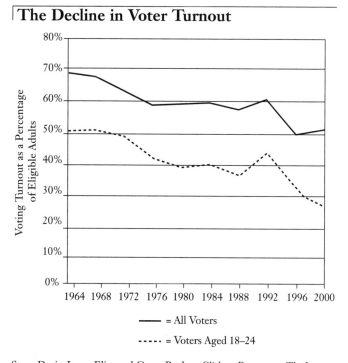

Steve Davis, Larry Elin, and Grant Reeher, *Click on Democracy: The Internet's Power to Change Political Apathy into Civic Action.* Boulder, CO: Westview Press, 2002.

Putnam notes that historically, most of the cybercommunities on the Internet have been discussion groups composed of individuals with narrowly defined common interests. This "cyberbalkanization," in which the inhabitants of online communities self-select into self-interest groups, is anathema to the offline communities we actually live in. In real-life communities, we have to deal with everybody we bump into, not just those with whom we are already in agreement. In addition, the Internet tends to be primarily a source for "passive, private entertainment," including the purchase of traditional retail goods, rather than a stimulant for active, real communication. Finally, Putnam also notes the presence of the digital divide that separates computer access between the haves and have-nots.

For all these reasons Putnam doubts whether the Internet can be another telephone, versus another television; that is, something that can facilitate our interpersonal connectedness versus something that further isolates us and makes us less socially engaged. Another way to frame the difference is that the Internet is creating virtual malls rather than virtual villages. Again, others have weighed in with similar concerns. [Renowned campaign manager] James Carville, for example, flatly states, "email's not a real connection to me. It's words on a screen." Can these supposed virtual communities hope to replenish the forms of social capital we are losing with something as apparently temporary and glib as a string of disconnected, sometimes invective-filled, and misspelled remarks by strangers? . . .

Generating Public Spiritedness

The Internet provides individuals . . . with the ability to participate in and influence the political system in ways heretofore reserved only for those with either great resources or institutional affiliations with large, established organizations. Furthermore, the political communities initiated on the Internet often progress into face-to-face experiences and other real exchanges. Prior identities are unveiled, thus thickening the selves that originally existed only as user IDs. In these ways, the Internet communities can generate the kind of public spiritedness that their critics perceive to be inherently absent. . . . We think that the future of the Internet in American political life may be considerably brighter, and its impact on social capital considerably more profound and positive, than do the skeptics we have just described.

During the latter half of our study, we found many instances in which enterprising Internet users employed its unique ability to create human networks. During Election 2000, some of these networks had specific purposes for short periods of time. They appeared, accomplished their stated goal, and evaporated. Others emerged and appear to be gaining momentum and growing; they are in it for the long haul. Either way, we began to see the use of the Internet for the creation of human networks as a hopeful and positive sign that it can have a positive net effect on civic engagement, social connections, and social capital. We found the Internet reached people who might otherwise never have become involved in the political process, and engaged them in activities that they never would have imagined possible with people they never would have met.

The Changing Face of Internet Users

During its earliest days, the Internet was populated by a homogeneous group of early adopters and technophiles mainly interested in the Internet itself. The chat-rooms, bulletin boards, and interest groups studied by social scientists during the dawn of the Internet were, perhaps not inappropriately, labeled as effete, self-absorbed, and exclusive. All those uninitiated in the ways of this select club were tabbed "newbies" and were often "flamed"—insulted for not knowing the correct etiquette. However, with the introduction of the World Wide Web, the Internet has exploded into 50 percent of American households in just the past few years. A *majority* of Americans now have access to the Internet at home or at work, the library, cybercafes, or other public locations. As more and more everyday people use the Internet, might they not use it for everyday things and behave in more socially acceptable, even normal ways? Is it possible that those aspects of their physical existence that make some forms of civic engagement difficult or impossible will become less relevant as people take their civic concerns and activities to cyberspace?

Alan Kardoff, a member of the online community that tried to "save" Drew McGarr, relies heavily on the Internet for a sense of connection to the larger society. "Personally, I'm a loner, I have no family," Kardoff said.

> Living alone, I developed a sense of community, some ties [on the Internet]. Some of the postings I didn't care to read, but it was virtually both sides. Doors opened to me that allowed me to have somewhat of a participatory life, a social life on the Internet that I wouldn't have otherwise. And I re-

fute those who say it kept me more isolated. I got to meet people who I would have never had the opportunity to meet, and I got to feel a part of something. It's like when I answered Harris Polls, but this is more personal because I got to know the people.

The Internet Fosters Attachment

... Kardoff and his online connections are good examples of the positive side of cybercommunities, described by social commentator Howard Rheingold as "social aggregations that emerge from the Net when enough people carry on public discussions long enough, with sufficient human feeling, to form webs of personal relationships." The difficulty of measuring "sufficient human feeling" notwithstanding, Kardoff derives important social pleasures online. Because the Internet is two-way and interactive, Kardoff gives back to the community by his active participation in it. He is to his online pals what they are to him—part of a reciprocal, honest, and trusting social network. As scholar Jan Fernback observed, "[Internet] users can assert victory in humanity's ancient struggle with nature by overcoming the constraints of geographical boundaries and form re-imagined social configurations." The new generation of Internet users is quite different than that studied by cybercommunity critics as recently as two years ago.

The Internet that fosters the kind of attachment that Drew McGarr's circle experienced is just off and under the social scientist's and media scholar's number-crunching radar. This Internet brought thoughtful people together in ways that had gone unnoticed. The Internet we observed may be supplementing the village square and traditional forms of face-to-face connections with virtual communities and coast-to-coast connections that appear to be relevant and actually pertinent, meaningful, and valuable. Communities formed, activists organized, petitions circulated. People volunteered, contributed money, registered to vote, and some even voted online. . . .

The Real Impact

The Internet's impact cannot be summed up in a sound bite. But it has changed everything it has touched and everyone who has touched it. The authors of this work tend to agree in principle and spirit with Doug Bailey, CEO of the Freedom Channel, organizer of Youth-e-Vote, and founder of the respected political newsletter *Hotline*. In an interview for this project, just a few weeks before the presidential vote, Bailey said:

> One view about the Internet and politics is that 2000 is supposed to be some kind of a gigantic breakthrough year, and because there's no candidate who has become the Internet candidate and has magically broken through, . . . the conclusion is that 2000 isn't a breakthrough year at all.
>
> The other school, of which I am a strong proponent, is that the notion that the Internet is not having a substantial impact on politics is just nuts. Of course it is. If you measure it by candidates who have invented themselves because of the Internet and have made a breakthrough, I can't name any, but that doesn't seem to me to be the point. The point is that more and more Americans are going to the Internet for their information—some to it exclusively for their information and some more to it as one of their sources for information, and every study that's done shows that that continues to rise.
>
> A major point that shouldn't be missed is that we are barely at the beginning of a gigantic transformation of how entertainment and information and communications happens in this country. . . . The capacity for sending and capacity for receiving become ubiquitous. That's a whole new world that is not only going to change our politics dramatically, it's going to change our culture and everything else. The world in which every one of us can become our own TV producers and pick what we want to see and when we want to see it, and what we don't want to see, that's just a whole new world, and that will change our world dramatically.

It is the way that the Internet behaved as a community builder, as a social-capital enhancer, that suggests the most promise for our nation's political life. This idea popped out at us as we puzzled over our data. . . .

By arguing that the Internet's positive impact was primarily interpersonal and community oriented, we do not mean to suggest that it was not *political*—quite the contrary. Part of the problem with civic engagement, especially among youth, is the assumption that *politics* can only mean narrow, partisan tactical battles and electioneering geared to the lowest common denominators of interest. Anything deemed political is thus tainted and to be avoided. But social connecting, talking, and doing is the very stuff of politics. Politics is the process by which we govern ourselves. It is the process of struggle, negotiation, and compromise. It is how we decide what we will do and who we will be. The story of Drew McGarr that opened this [viewpoint] illustrates this process as it occurred over the Internet. By enhancing those aspects of our lives, the Internet enhances politics, and by enhancing politics, it helps to reclaim the rightfully honorable place of politics in our lives.

"Unless current trends are reversed, Internet-mediated politics is more likely to accentuate than to cure [the proliferation of single-interest groups in politics]."

The Internet Fosters More Divisiveness in Politics

William A. Galston

William A. Galston is a professor at the Maryland School of Public Affairs. In the following viewpoint, he argues that the main problem in politics today is the proliferation of single-interest groups—political advocacy groups composed of very like-minded individuals who feel strongly about a single political issue and are generally unwilling to compromise on that issue. In Galston's opinion, such groups are a problem because they inhibit the debate and compromise that usually accompany legislative action. Galston contends that the Internet is likely to exacerbate the problem of single-interest groups in politics since the Internet makes it easier for individuals to associate only with people who share their specific views.

As you read, consider the following questions:
1. How do most people experience deep differences with others, according to Galston?
2. What two premises support Bruce Bimber's view of how the Internet will effect politics, as described by the author?
3. What view does Galston describe as a "cyberlibertarian fantasy"?

William A. Galston, *The Civic Web: Online Politics and Democratic Values*. Lanham, MD: Rowman & Littlefield, 2003. Copyright © 2003 by Rowman & Littlefield Publishers, Inc. Reproduced by permission.

The thesis of this [viewpoint] may be briefly stated: A central problem—perhaps *the* central problem—of contemporary American politics is the proliferation of single-interest groups and the simultaneous weakening of the institutions and processes needed to balance and integrate the interests these groups represent. And unless current trends are reversed, Internet-mediated politics is more likely to accentuate than to cure this problem.

The Choice Revolution

My argument for this thesis runs as follows:

> *During the past generation, unfettered individual choice has become an increasingly dominant norm in American culture.*

Scholars in a range of disciplines have traced the rise of choice as a core value. Daniel Yankelovich suggests that what he calls the "affluence effect"—the psychology of prosperity that emerged as memories of the Depression faded and as the middle class expanded—has weakend traditional restraint:

> People came to feel that questions of how to live and with whom to live were a matter of individual choice not to be governed by restrictive norms. As a nation, we came to experience the bonds of marriage, family, children, job, community, and country as constraints that were no longer necessary.

In Alan Ehrenhalt's account, the new centrality of individual choice is a key explanation for the transformation of Chicago's neighborhoods since the 1950s. Lawrence Friedman argues that individual choice is the central norm around which the modern American legal system has been restructured. And based on interviews with hundreds of families, Alan Wolfe finds individual choice to be at the heart of the nonjudgmental tolerance that defines middle-class morality in contemporary America.

> *As individual choice becomes more central, social bonds tend to weaken.*

Every student of the choice revolution has found evidence of diminishing bonds. A generation ago, [sociologist] Ralf Dahrendorf offered an influential account of this tension. Yankelovich summarizes the core argument as follows:

> Dahrendorf sees all historic shifts in Western culture as efforts to balance choices and bonds. Choices enhance individ-

ualism and personal freedom; bonds strengthen social cohesiveness and stability. In societies where the bonds that link people to one another and to institutions are rigid, the individual's freedom of choice is limited. As people struggle to enlarge their sphere of choice, the bonds that bind them together slacken.

Despite the attractions of individual choice, the desire for attachments is a permanent feature of the human condition.

Although individual human beings vary widely in their tolerance for solitude and desire for community, as a species we are not designed to live alone or in a series of transitory attachments. Much of modern literature (and popular culture, as limned in city-based television shows) traces the movement from the initial exhilaration of shedding strong bonds to the dissatisfactions of life lived without them.

To the extent that expanded choice leads to weaker attachments, therefore, it is bound to trigger an acute sense of loss, expressed in ways ranging from psychological disorders to an intense longing for community. Nonetheless, few Americans are willing to sacrifice the expansive liberty they now enjoy in the name of stronger marriages, neighborhoods, or citizenship. Many Americans regard with horror the prospect of being (as they see it) "trapped" in associations or relationships that no longer fulfill their desires or meet their needs.

Voluntary Communities

This tension between the longing for community and the fear of community constitutes what many Americans experience as the central dilemma of our age; as Wolfe puts it, "how to be an autonomous person and tied together with others at the same time." There is an obvious motivation for reducing this tension as far as possible—that is, for finding ways of living that combine a satisfactory measure of individual autonomy and satisfying social bonds.

The effort to reconcile individual choice and social bonds gives rise to a preference for a mode of association I will call "voluntary community."

This conception of autonomy-compatible community has three defining conditions: entry is by choice; barriers to exit are low; and intracommunity relations are shaped through mutual adjustment rather than authority or coercion. Part of the excitement surrounding the Internet is the possibility it offers for facilitating the formation of these voluntary communities.

Despite the attractions of voluntary community, its rise intensifies existing social and political problems.

In an earlier article of mine, I argue that, judged against the defining features of community, voluntary communities are thin rather than thick and weak rather than strong and are therefore unlikely to fulfill the needs and desires of those who enter them. I now want to focus on another feature of voluntary communities: namely, the tendency of each one to organize around a narrow range of interests in which the members are in broad agreement. I will argue that this feature exacerbates the growing problem of fragmentation (at least regarding domestic issues) in contemporary American politics.

To avoid misunderstanding, let me make it clear that I have no objection to many of the focused associations that the Internet facilitates; quite the reverse. For example, groups organized around specific diseases provide important emotional support and facilitate the rapid location and sharing of information about promising new therapies. Similarly, groups can form around shared hobbies, and the Internet makes possible interactivities that transcend previous barriers of space and time. My point is only that single-interest organizations are more deeply problematic in the contemporary political domain than in other aspects of our social and associational life.

Voluntary communities tend to be homogeneous.

When given a choice, most people tend to associate with others who are like themselves in the respects they regard as important. Above a relatively low threshold, most people experience deep differences as dissonant and unpleasant. Even when these differences need not be reconciled through explicit collective decisions, they suffuse the shared social space and reduce its appeal for many denizens. To be sure, many people experience differences in food, culture, and even opinion as stimulating . . . so long as they can sample the differences and leave when they choose. For most people, diversity is a nice place to visit, but they don't really want to live there.

Homogeneity on the Internet

Because Internet communities are voluntary, they are more likely to be homogeneous rather than heterogeneous, and group homogeneity can have negative consequences for society as a whole.

In an important theoretical paper, [researchers] Marshall Van Alstyne and Erik Brynjolfsson show how the Internet can translate even weak preferences for those like oneself into homogeneous subgroups whose internal interactions far exceed cross-group communications, a condition they term "cyberbalkanization." Left unchecked, cyberbalkanization can yield results that are economically efficient (in the sense that no individual can be made better off by switching from more focused to less focused association) but socially suboptimal. For example, the growth of hyperspecialized subcommunities can slow the growth of scientific knowledge, which depends on exchanging of information and theoretical perspectives across group boundaries.

[Political scientist] Bruce Bimber suggests that the Internet's probable effect will be the intensification of group-centered politics, which he terms "accelerated pluralism." His argument rests on two empirical premises: first, that the Internet will not alter the fact that most people are highly selective in their attention to issues and information; and second, that the Internet lowers the costs of locating, organizing, and mobilizing communities of like-minded individuals. On the one hand, this later development may be described as the "democratization" of group politics, as lowered transaction costs increase the organizational opportunities of resource-poor groups. On the other hand, accelerated pluralism decreases political coherence and stability and intensifies fragmentation as focused "issue publics" form for transitory purposes, exert single-issue pressure on the political system, and then dissolve. In the process, the power of more traditional public and voluntary sector institutions that currently enjoy some stability through time and work to integrate (or at least broker among) diverse preferences is likely to erode.

The rise of homogeneous communities tends not only to decrease intergroup community and increase political fragmentation, but it also tends to exacerbate the difficulty of reconciling diverse interests and worldviews. [Political scientist] Cass Sunstein summarizes a wide range of empirical studies, conducted in more than a dozen nations, that point toward a common conclusion: a group of like-minded people who engage in discussion with one another are likely to adopt more extreme rather than more moderate variants of the group's shared beliefs. And it turns out that particularly high levels of polarization occur when group members meet anonymously—which is precisely what the Internet permits. By contrast, face-to-face deliberation within heterogeneous groups is more likely to yield a moderation of views all around, or at least a willingness to listen to evidence and arguments and to alter one's considered judgments.

More of the Same

Rather than bring massive change, information technology is likely to further recent trends in political life. The Internet makes it easy to know more about whatever one is interested in, but by itself it does not change one's interests. Today, the people who actively participate in politics are those who are interested enough to do so. Information technologies will make it easier for these people to be involved, and will therefore likely make them even more so. For those people with little interest in politics, the Internet will make it easier for them to become more engaged in their own particular areas of interest, leaving them even less time for politics. The Internet does not simply offer us information, it offers us our choice of information. Most of us choose to become better informed about, and more active in, those areas that are already of interest to us. The Internet gives us the power to do more, but it does not of itself change what we want to do.

This suggests that for the political world, the age of the Internet means largely more of the same.

Yuval Levin, "Politics After the Internet," *Public Interest*, Fall 2002.

To be sure, anonymity can also foster heterogeneity by reducing the salience of the differences that hinder the formation of traditional groups. Online groups united by shared interests may be remarkably diverse in their ethnic, religious, class, and age composition, and the effects of differences (of gender, for example) that frequently skew active participation can be reduced.

Still, it is hard to see how this anonymous heterogeneity can yield stronger bonds across lines of division unless diverse individuals eventually reveal their identities to one another—that is, unless they are willing to forgo the comforts of homogeneity. It is a matter of utmost importance for citizens in a diverse society to understand that they can have something important in common, and can work, with others who are unlike them in important respects. For this lesson to be learned, group members must know one another in their differences as well as their commonalities. From this perspective, one might hypothesize that a socially optimal mix would be one of anonymous and identity-revealing political interactions. To the extent that virtual communities not only supplement but actually replace attachments to geographical communities, however, societies are less likely to reap the advantages of this optimal mix.

The Proliferation of Single-Interest Groups

The multiplication of single-interest groups is especially damaging at a time when the forces of fragmentation in American politics are more powerful than are the sources of integration across issues and interests.

During the past generation, single-interest groups have become a dominant feature of the American political landscape. [Journalist] Jonathan Rauch has documented the extraordinary growth of advocacy organizations, especially those created to push focused agendas through Washington-based lobbying.

At the same time as these single-interest groups have grown, long-standing sources of integration across issues and interests have weakened. Three developments are of particular importance:

1. As [sociologist] Theda Skocpol has shown, broad-based civil associations that assemble individuals across class lines and that link states and localities with the national political dialogue have weakened while narrower organizations with top-down structures have expanded in influence.

2. Network broadcasting has lost market share to the proliferation of smaller-audience niche alternatives ("nar-

rowcasting"). This is part of a larger trend in which what [legal scholar] Andrew Shapiro calls "general interest intermediaries" are losing ground to media that allow individuals to design their own mix of information and entertainment. This is the sociopolitical equivalent of the Internet-driven processes of disintermediation so clearly visible in financial markets.

3. As political parties have become more homogeneous internally, they have become less able to reach accommodations across partisan lines. And as a plebiscitary nomination process has displaced the prior system of brokered representative institutions, the capacity of political parties to conduct internal deliberations has diminished.

Inadequate Buffers

It may seem paradoxical that my analysis focuses on the proliferation of single-interest groups as the principal problem of modern American politics. After all, it was James Madison who famously identified the multiplication of "factions" as a key guarantor of individual rights and liberties. But Madison was equally cognizant of the need to reach agreements across factional differences in order to promote the common good, and he pointed to two features of the new constitutional order that he hoped would serve that purpose. First, he argued that electoral processes would tend to select individuals whose "enlightened views and virtuous sentiments" would make them more likely and more able to identify the public good through reasoned deliberation than would the people themselves acting directly. Second, he argued that although every constitutional institution drew its legitimate authority directly or indirectly from the people, many of those institutions were designed to be buffered against popular pressure and thus against the baneful influence of factions on public decision making.

Historians debate whether these Madisonian processes of filtration and insulation were ever adequate to their task. Whatever may have been true two centuries ago, it is hard to maintain that these two processes can suffice in modern circumstances. One may wonder whether the traits of mind and character needed to wage and win today's elections are congruent with the wisdom and virtue Madison hoped electoral competition would single out. Post-Madisonian constitutional developments—the rise of political parties, the evisceration of the electoral college as a deliberative body, and direct election of senators, among others—have increased direct popular influence over key institutions and have lowered barriers to factional influences in the policy process.

The Internet and Political Integration

If fragmentation is a central problem of contemporary American politics, then thinkers and policy makers—including Internet architects—must think harder about how existing institutions can be reformed (or new ones created) to deliberate on, or at least strike a reasonable balance among, competing interests and values.

It is now fashionable to denigrate the institutions of our official politics, starting with the Congress. If my analysis is correct—if long-standing unofficial mechanisms of political integration have weakened—then this stance has it exactly backwards. In current circumstances, official institutions are more important than ever as the principal venues within which competing interests and values must somehow be brought together into a course of common action.

When the American people reach broad agreement on what needs to be done, as they did about the Welfare system in the 1990s and as they appear to be doing about prescription drugs today, then official institutions can usually find ways to respond. But when the people are divided or have not focused on an issue and decisions nonetheless must be made (e.g., on telecommunications legislation), we must look for new ways of reducing the impact of single-interest groups on legislation and regulation while ensuring that these groups continue to enjoy a fair chance of expressing their views.

For example, more intensive press scrutiny of important but virtually invisible steps in legislative and regulatory processes would be a good start. No doubt the leaders of media organizations would resist this on the grounds that the people are not very interested in most legislative and regulatory outcomes, let alone the tedious and unsightly battles that produce them. To this we must reply: Maybe not, but part of your responsibility is to remember the distinction between what the people say they want and what they need for the exercise of informed citizenship. What the people do with the information is up to them, but if market-driven considerations lead you to edit it out in advance, the people will never have the chance to decide for themselves. And it is not enough to say that the information is available on, say, cable channels with minute ratings. General-purpose intermediaries still send important signals about what matters, and they have some responsibility to exercise their power in the public interest. If they refuse to do even the basics—for example, televising, important debates during presidential primaries—then perhaps we must seek constitutionally appropriate ways of mandating such coverage.

Restrictions on Choice

As I indicated earlier, we must also use our imaginations to think of new ways to enlist the Internet on the side of political integration. Let me be clear about the central presupposition of this quest: If individual choice—on the Internet as well as elsewhere—leads to the formation of voluntary communities, if these communities are homogeneous in crucial respects, and if this homogeneity is part of the overall problem of social and political fragmentation, then effective responses are likely to require some restrictions on individual choice.

These limitations need not, and probably should not, be imposed directly on individual choosers; rather, they can be built into the background architecture of the information system. For example, Andrew Chin and Cass Sunstein propose that the current legislative "must carry" doctrine mandated for cable systems should be extended to the Internet. Under this proposal, especially popular web sites would be required to link to a selection of sites that draw the public's attention to public issues and to increase the information they possess. No one would be forced to visit these public interest sites, but at least the chances for average citizens to know about them would increase.

I am not an expert on Internet design. But those who are must set aside the cyberlibertarian fantasy that unfettered choice always is conducive to the long-term welfare of the community as a whole. Neoclassical economists have persuasively analyzed a range of "market failures." It is time for the framers of the constitution for our information future to take these insights seriously in their own revolutionary domain, to consider the peril as well as the promise of unrestricted choice on the Internet, and—consistent with our constitutional traditions—to find new ways of enlisting the Internet in the cause of informed citizenship and the common good.

Periodical Bibliography

The following articles have been selected to supplement the diverse views presented in this chapter.

John A. Bargh	"Beyond Simple Truths: The Human-Internet Interaction," *Journal of Social Issues*, Spring 2002.
Andrew Boyd	"The Web Rewires the Movement," *Nation*, August 4, 2003.
Jeffrey Cole	"Now Is the Time to Start Studying the Internet Age," *Chronicle of Higher Education*, April 2, 2004.
Economist	"Good Intentions, Bad Technology," January 24, 2004.
Barry S. Fagin	"Intellectual Freedom and Social Responsibility: As We Grow More Dependent on the Internet, We Grow More Vulnerable," *World & I*, March 2002.
Garance Franke-Ruta	"Virtual Politics: How the Internet Is Transforming Democracy," *American Prospect*, October 2003.
Brendan I. Koerner	"Welcome to the Machine," *Harper's*, April 2004.
Yuval Levin	"Politics After the Internet," *Public Interest*, Fall 2002.
Phillip J. Longman	"The Slowing Pace of Progress," *U.S. News & World Report*, December 25, 2000.
Viveca Novak et al.	"The Vexations of Voting Machines," *Time*, May 3, 2004.
Deborah C. Sawyer	"The Pied Piper Goes Electronic," *Futurist*, February 1999.
W. David Stephenson	"The Internet's Three Positive Principles," *Christian Science Monitor*, April 10, 2001.
Bill Thompson	"Community Spirit," *Internet Magazine*, January 2004.
Tom R. Tyler	"Is the Internet Changing Social Life?" *Journal of Social Issues*, Spring 2002.

How Serious Is the Problem of Illegal Activity on the Internet?

Chapter Preface

As communication and commerce continue to thrive on the Internet, so too does crime. For example, the research firm comScore Media Metrix estimates that U.S. consumers spent $39.3 billion in legitimate e-commerce in 2002—and an estimated $36.5 billion on black market goods and services. Terrorists, drug dealers, child pornographers, and illegal casinos are all part of what *Business Week* calls the "Underground Web": "The Underground Web . . . enables—even encourages ordinary citizens to break the law. People who wouldn't even jaywalk find themselves bombarded with offers to place bets at offshore casinos or order drugs online."

While some parts of the Underground Web offer illegal gambling, drugs, or illegal music and video downloads, others are more predatory. Some seemingly legitimate e-commerce sites are scams that target visitors for fraud and identity theft. The anonymity of the Internet has made it easier for terrorists to communicate and organize and for child pornographers to buy and sell their wares. Finally, the growth of the Internet has provided countless new targets for cyberattacks by hackers.

In trying to police the Internet, law enforcement authorities are faced with a variety of legal, ethical, and technical problems. The authors in the following viewpoints debate some of the most talked-about aspects of the Underground Web and offer suggestions on what should be done about them.

"The potential for fraud connected with casinos and bookmaking operations in the virtual world is far greater than in the physical realm."

Internet Gambling Is a Serious Problem

John G. Malcolm

John G. Malcolm is a deputy assistant attorney general for the U.S. Department of Justice. The following viewpoint is adapted from testimony that he gave before the U.S. Senate in March 2003. In it, Malcolm argues that Internet gambling is harmful to society. He maintains that Internet gambling is too easy for minors and for compulsive gamblers to access. And whereas brick-and-mortar casinos are legal and regulated by the government, virtual casinos are not. Malcolm believes that this lack of oversight makes them much more likely to engage in fraud, have ties to organized crime, and be used as a vehicle for money laundering. Finally, he discusses how the government is fighting Internet gambling by persuading banks and credit card companies not to deal with offshore casinos.

As you read, consider the following questions:

1. How many Internet gambling sites were there at the end of 2003, as estimated by the author?
2. How are Internet casinos similar to scam telemarketing operations, in Malcolm's view?
3. In what ways can Internet gambling businesses be used to launder money, according to the author?

John G. Malcolm, testimony before the Senate Committee on Banking, Housing, and Urban Affairs, Washington, DC, March 18, 2003.

Today I am pleased to offer the views of the Department of Justice about Internet gambling, including the potential for gambling by minors and compulsive gambling, the potential for fraud and money laundering, the potential for the organized crime, and recent state actions. The Department of Justice generally supports the efforts of the drafters of these bills to enable law enforcement to cut off the transfer of funds to and from illegal Internet gambling businesses.

As you all know, the number of Internet gambling sites has increased substantially in recent years. While there were approximately 700 Internet gambling sites in 1999, it is estimated that by the end of 2003, there will be approximately 1,800 such sites generating around $4.2 billion. In addition to on-line casino-style gambling sites, there are also numerous off-shore sports books operating telephone betting services. These developments are of great concern to the United States Department of Justice, particularly because many of these operations are currently accepting bets from United States citizens, when we believe that it is illegal to do so.

The Internet and other emerging technologies, such as interactive television, have made possible types of gambling that were not feasible a few years ago. For example, a United States citizen can now, from his home at any hour of the day or night, participate in an interactive Internet poker game operated by a computer located in the Caribbean. Indeed, a tech-savvy gambler can route his bets through computers located in other countries throughout the world, thereby obscuring the fact that he is placing his bet from the United States or from some other country where it is illegal to do so.

Protecting Citizens

On-line gambling also makes it far more difficult to prevent minors from gambling. Gambling websites cannot look at their customers to assess their age and request photo identification as is possible in traditional physical casinos and Off-Track-Betting parlors. Currently, Internet gambling businesses have no reliable way of confirming that the gamblers are not minors who have gained access to a credit card and are gambling on their web site. Although some companies are developing software to try to detect whether a player is old enough to gamble or whether that player is from a legal jurisdiction, such software has not been perfected and would, of course, be subject to the same types of flaws and vulnerabilities that could be exploited by hackers.

Unlike on-site gambling, on-line gambling is readily available to all at all hours and it permits the user to gamble, in many cases, anonymously. This presents a greater danger for compulsive gambling and can cause severe financial consequences for an unsuccessful player. As was recently pointed out by the American Psychiatric Society: "Internet gambling, unlike many other forms of gambling activity, is a solitary activity, which makes it even more dangerous; people can gamble uninterrupted and undetected for unlimited periods of time." Indeed, the problems associated with pathological and problem gamblers, a frighteningly-large percentage of which are young people, are well-established and can be measured in the ruined lives of both the gamblers themselves and their families.

Although there are certainly legitimate companies that are either operating or want to operate on-line casinos in an honest manner, the potential for fraud connected with casinos and bookmaking operations in the virtual world is far greater than in the physical realm. Start-up costs are relatively low and cheap servers and unsophisticated software are readily-available. On-line casinos and bookmaking establishments operate in many countries where effective regulation and law enforcement is minimal or non-existent. Like scam telemarketing operations, on-line gambling establishments appear and disappear with regularity, collecting from losers and not paying winners, and with little fear of being apprehended and prosecuted.

Through slight alterations of the software, unscrupulous gambling operations can manipulate the odds in their favor, make unauthorized credit card charges to the accounts of unsuspecting gamblers, or alter their own accounts to skim money. There is also a danger that hackers can manipulate the on-line games in their favor or can steal credit card or other information about other gamblers using the site.

Additionally, the Department of Justice has a concern about the potential for the involvement of organized crime in Internet gambling. Traditionally, gambling has been one of the staple activities in which organized crime has been involved. Indeed, many of the recent indictments brought against members of organized crime groups have included gambling charges. We have now seen evidence that organized crime is moving into Internet gambling.

Legal Casinos' Opposition to Online Gambling

I am Frank J. Fahrenkopf, Jr., president and CEO of the American Gaming Association (AGA). The AGA is the national trade association of commercial casino companies, gaming equipment manufacturers, and other vendor-suppliers to the gaming industry. . . .

Our major concern with illegal Internet gambling as it exists today is that it allows the approximately 2,000 offshore Web sites to circumvent state policies, including current restrictions on the availability of gambling within each state. . . .

Illegal Internet gambling also allows unlicensed, untaxed, unsupervised operators to conduct business alongside gaming operators who are subject to some of the most comprehensive federal and state controls of any industry in this country. . . .

These federal and state regulations exist to, among other things, guarantee the fairness of the games; ensure proper taxation of revenues; acknowledge problem gambling and offset any potential consequences; prevent underage gambling; and prevent theft, loss, embezzlement or any other illegal activity—all safeguards that are vital to maintaining public trust and confidence in our business.

Illegal Internet gambling threatens the integrity of all businesses involved in legalized gambling in the United States.

Frank J. Fahrenkopf Jr., testimony before the Senate Committee on Banking, Housing, and Urban Affairs, March 18, 2003.

Most of these gambling businesses are operating offshore in foreign jurisdictions. If these businesses are accepting bets or wagers from customers located in the United States, then these businesses are violating federal laws, including Sections 1084, 1952, and 1955 of Title 18, United States Code. While the United States can bring indictments against these companies or the individuals operating these companies, the federal government may not be able to bring such individuals or companies to trial in the United States.

Money Laundering and Internet Gambling

Another major concern that the Department of Justice has about on-line gambling is that Internet gambling businesses provide criminals with an easy and excellent vehicle for money laundering, due in large part to the volume, speed, and international reach of Internet transactions and the offshore locations of most Internet gambling sites, as well as the fact that the industry itself is already cash-intensive.

It is a fact that money launderers have to go to financial institutions either to conceal their illegal funds or recycle those funds back into the economy for their use. Because criminals are aware that banks have been subjected to greater scrutiny and regulation, they have—not surprisingly—turned to other non-bank financial institutions, such as casinos, to launder their money. On-line casinos are a particularly inviting target because, in addition to using the gambling that casinos offer as a way to hide or transfer money, casinos offer a broad array of financial services to their customers, such as providing credit accounts, fund transmittal services, check cashing services, and currency exchange services.

Individuals wanting to launder ill-gotten gains through an on-line casino can do so in a variety of ways. For example, a customer could establish an account with a casino using illegally-derived proceeds, conduct a minimal amount of betting or engage in offsetting bets with an overseas confederate, and then request repayment from the casino, thereby providing a new "source" of the funds. If a gambler wants to transfer money to an inside source in the casino, who may be located in another country, he can just play until he loses the requisite amount. Similarly, if an insider wants to transfer money to the gambler, perhaps as payment for some illicit activity, he can rig the game so the bettor wins.

The anonymous nature of the Internet and the use of encryption make it difficult to trace the transactions. The gambling business may also not maintain the transaction records, in which case tracing may be impossible. While regulators in the United States can visit physical casinos, observe their operations, and examine their books and records to ensure compliance with regulations, this is far more difficult, if not impossible, with virtual casinos.

Government Actions

In addition to the federal government, various state governments have also taken actions against on-line gambling. For instance, in New York State, where unauthorized gambling is illegal, the New York State Attorney General reached an agreement with Citibank to block credit card payments of on-line gambling transactions by its customers. The same Attorney General recently reached an agreement with Pay-Pal, which agreed to stop processing payments from New York State customers to on-line gambling merchants.

Some companies have taken steps themselves against on-line gambling businesses. For instance, in 2002 PayPal was acquired by E-Bay, the on-line auction service, which announced that it would phase out PayPal's on-line gambling. Both Discover and American Express have company policies that restrict the use of their credit cards for Internet gambling and prevent Internet gambling sites from being issued credit card merchant accounts.

On behalf of the Department of Justice, I want to thank you again for inviting me to testify today. We thank you for your support over the years and reaffirm our commitment to work with Congress to address the significant issue of Internet gambling.

"A legalized regime is a better way to mitigate the potential dangers of Internet betting."

Internet Gambling Should Be Legalized

Koleman Strumpf

In the following viewpoint, Koleman Strumpf argues that the government's attempts to prohibit Internet gambling are both futile and counterproductive. Strumpf compares Internet gambling to sports betting. He contends that although sports betting is illegal in every state but Nevada, Americans spend billions of dollars wagering with illegal bookmakers. He believes that a policy of prohibition will be similarly ineffective for Internet gambling. In Strumpf's opinion, legal, government-regulated Internet gambling would benefit society more than the current policy of prohibition. Koleman Strumpf is a professor of economics at the University of North Carolina at Chapel Hill.

As you read, consider the following questions:

1. How much money do Americans wager with illegal bookmakers outside Nevada, according to Strumpf?
2. What two harmful policies do illegal bookmakers engage in, as described by the author?
3. Why has the United Kingdom moved to legalize online sports betting, in Strumpf's view?

Koleman Strumpf, "Why Prohibitions on Internet Gambling Won't Work," *TechKnowledge*, January 23, 2004. Copyright © 2004 by the Cato Institute. All rights reserved. Reproduced by permission.

With the steady rise of commercial activity on the Internet, Washington has been steadily moving toward a formal prohibition of online gambling. Recently, a series of bills sponsored by Senator Jon Kyl (R-AZ) and Representative James Leach (R-IA) have sought to achieve this goal by restricting the flow of funds into Internet gambling operations. [As of February 2005, the bills sponsored by Kyl and Leach have not been passed into law.] While such policies might spring from a certain moral viewpoint, they are unlikely to succeed in limiting online betting. Because Internet gaming operations are often located outside of the U.S., there is little Washington can do to restrict their actions.

Moreover, a prohibition policy has perverse effects and encourages the very behavior it seeks to curtail. This is illustrated by a close examination of one of the most popular forms of gambling: sports betting. There is a large demand for sports betting, and a large illegal sector has arisen to provide this activity despite a long-standing policy of prohibition. A similar ban on all Internet-based sports betting also is likely to fail. A legalized regime is a better way to mitigate the potential dangers of Internet betting. This argument is straightforward and it applies whether one regards gambling as a moral evil or a fundamental expression of individual freedom. Even if one takes the principled stand that gambling is fundamentally wrong, a policy of prohibition is unlikely to advance the goal of eliminating gambling altogether.

Gambling Is Already Widespread

To begin, let's take a closer look at betting on major sports, which is currently illegal in all states besides Nevada regardless of whether it involves the Internet. While these bans are primarily enforced by states, the federal government does get involved if wagers cross state lines or there is an alleged involvement of organized crime. So how successful has this regime of prohibition been at eliminating sports betting? By almost any measure it is a failure. A recently completed report from the National Gambling Impact Study Commission estimates that individuals wager between $80 and $380 billion dollars with illegal bookmakers. This is nearly one hundred times the amount bet on professional sports with legal bookmakers in Nevada.

The sheer size of the illegal sports betting markets only tells part of the story. I recently completed an analysis of illegal bookmakers in New York City using actual records seized in series of arrests by the Kings County (Brooklyn) District Attorney office. I found that illegal bookmakers utilize policies which exacerbate the potential harm of gambling. First, they offer short-term credit, and allow bettors to wager for a week or longer without fronting any money. Credit might allow individuals to gamble beyond their financial means and leads some bettors to wager intensively in an attempt to "catch-up" before their debt is due. In fact most of the bettors in my records would be considered compulsive gamblers, wagering almost every day and laying hundreds of dollars at a time.

The Threat to Privacy from Internet Gambling Legislation

In this privacy-sensitive era, the obvious question arises: Assuming you were gambling on the Internet, how would the government ever know about it? For the government to know about such personal, consensual behavior requires spying. And that's what anti-gambling legislation would require. Banks and Internet Service Providers would be drafted into the role of snooper, sifting all financial transactions. The notion of government mandating surveillance of private computers is repugnant. . . .

The bottom line is that even if one were gambling, government has no right in principle to know about it, or to force disclosure of that information. Lawmakers need to be questioned intently on the privacy implications of this crusade.

Clyde Wayne Crews Jr., "Should Washington Ban Internet Gambling?" *Cato Daily Commentary*, June 13, 2002.

Second, illegal bookmakers take advantage of people's mistakes. They know that many bettors are fans of certain teams. In the case of the bookmakers I have records for, about a quarter of the bettors appear to be New York Yankees fans who wager consistently on their team. The bookmakers understand this tendency and "price discriminate" against such bettors: they charge them a significantly higher price for their Yankees bets. While price discrimination does have an important role to play in free markets, it is likely that consistent use of it would be precluded if sports betting was legalized and above-board, much as they are in Nevada sports books or with off-track horse betting parlors.

There is little evidence from the U.S. experience with sports betting to believe a prohibition policy limits the activity or prevents individual excesses. When an activity is widely demanded and socially accepted (at least in some circles), markets will find a way to deliver it whatever the legality. Our initial experiences with Internet gambling bear this out. Despite the current attempts at prohibition and even the arrest of one Internet bookmaker, the sector is proliferating. Internet operations catering to U.S. citizens operate from bases in countries as diverse as Antigua, Costa Rica and Australia. Given that such countries view Internet gaming as a legitimate activity, there is little possibility these companies will disappear anytime soon.

Prohibition Exacerbates the Problem

Presuming the current attempts at prohibiting Internet sports betting persist, what might we expect to see? First, there will be a growing alliance between Internet bookmakers and the more traditional illegal bookmaker. The on-street bookmakers have experience in providing and servicing financial credit, which would be difficult for the Internet books to provide given the difficulty of enforcing a debt contract from afar. There is already evidence that Internet operations have started to pay their illegal onshore cousins to run their credit business. Such interaction will help reinforce the influence of the illegal sector and will exacerbate the perceived problems of sports betting, such as facilitating money laundering.

Second, prohibition will drive the Internet operators further from the U.S. An important feature of the Internet is that it makes physical distance largely irrelevant, and from a bettor's perspective it is just as convenient to wager on-line with an Antigua bookmaker as with one down the street. As bookmakers move further from U.S. soil to escape its influence, it will become harder and harder to legalize Internet gaming in the future as the bookmakers get ensconced in their offshore locations. This possibility was an important rationale behind the recent move in the U.K. to encourage the repatriation of online betting operations. And finally a prohibition policy will fail in its most fundamental goal, limiting the availability of gambling to vulnerable populations. Internet bookmakers have little incentive to keep out underage or addicted gamblers.

A far more sensible policy would be to legalize Internet bookmakers. This would allow policies to be put in place which could limit the potential excesses of gambling and minimize the role of the criminal element. As side benefits, a legalized regime would likely displace the widespread illegal operations. It is perhaps understandable that such an option is rarely considered. Gambling is a subject which many feel passionately about. But the argument for legalization and regulation should have appeal for opponents and supporters of gambling alike.

"Peer-to-peer technologies have decimated the music business."

Internet Piracy Is a Serious Problem

Steve Marks

Steve Marks is general counsel for the Recording Industry Association of America (RIAA), a trade organization that represents the music industry. In the following viewpoint, he argues that the sharing of digital music files via peer-to-peer (P2P) networks such as Kazaa has drastically reduced music sales and threatens the survival of the music industry. Marks contends that P2P networks could introduce technology to limit the illegal copying of copyrighted works, but have chosen not to. Marks describes the RIAA's strategy to combat piracy—which includes lawsuits against P2P companies and individual file sharers—but also notes that the music industry is working to develop new ways of using digital music technology to benefit consumers.

As you read, consider the following questions:

1. By what percent have CD sales declined since 1999, according to Marks?
2. How many songs were downloaded legally in the last six months of 2003, according to Marks?
3. What company controls the technology known as HD Radio?

Karl Kraus, an Austrian writer during the early twentieth century, wrote: "Technology is a servant who makes so much noise cleaning up in the next room that his master cannot make music." While poetic, and seemingly prescient given these turbulent times in the music business, the proclamation is, in fact, untrue.

For nearly a century, the music industry has been defined by advances in technology. From wax cylinders, to vinyl, to cassette tapes, 8-track tapes (which many of you probably have never had the pleasure of experiencing), and compact discs, the industry has developed new—and better—ways to offer music for the listening enjoyment of consumers.

With the digital revolution, the pace of technological advancement has exploded, leading to numerous new business models such as authorized download and subscription services, and Internet and satellite radio. A vision of the future is limited only by one's imagination. While not moving as fast as some may have wanted, the record industry has eagerly embraced new technologies and many of the opportunities that flow from them.

Unfortunately, there are those who have hijacked some technologies—such as peer-to-peer—for the purpose of short-term financial gain, offloading their legal liability to America's kids and unsuspecting parents while they rake in millions in advertising dollars.

What Is at Stake

Let me state this as clearly as I can: we believe that peer-to-peer technologies have enormous potential. However, the unauthorized use of peer-to-peer technologies have decimated the music business and left in its wake innumerable lost jobs, slashed royalties for songwriters and artists, and thousands of shuttered record stores. The toll—a 22 percent decline in CD sales since 1999—has been unparalleled in the history of the music business. Millions and millions of people now download billions of songs for free that they used to buy. Simply stated, an industry cannot survive when its content can be acquired for free with no more effort than the click of a mouse.

Technology itself is not the issue; it is the use of that technology. The debate is no longer old versus new or digital versus plastic. It's legitimate versus illegitimate. Will the awesome power of new technologies be harnessed for good—to serve music fans as well as those who create music—or will it be used to undermine and potentially destroy a vital sector of our economy?

As Hewlett-Packard's Carly Fiorina pointed out, "Just because we can do wrong doesn't mean we should. Just because we can steal music doesn't mean we should."

Nonetheless, as Ms. Fiorina so eloquently added, there is "Kazaa's law": "[the] sense of right and wrong does not evolve as quickly as technology." There will always be those who seek to view their illegal and harmful activity as justified in the name of technological advancement. And, unfortunately, there are those who provide support for such views. An academic study recently released by two professors concluded that file sharing has no impact on CD sales. In addition to the flawed methodology of the study, the conclusions fly in the face of countless other studies and plain-old common sense. If someone is interested in a product and can get it for free, he or she is certainly less likely to pay for that product.

Additionally, I would challenge these professors to run this theory by virtually any record store owner—those who know the evolving patterns of the music-purchasing customers best—and see what kind of reaction they get.

As Mike Negra, owner of Pennsylvania's Movies and Music, recently put it: "I wonder how the two professors can account for the simultaneous, worldwide revelation by college aged music buyers to suddenly *stop* buying music in August of 1999. Sure, Napster and the subsequent P2P sites have had *nothing* to do with it. I'm sure the ability of millions of people to procure entertainment at no cost could not *possibly* reflect on sales figures worldwide. How could it? Climb out of your ivory towers professors. Talk to the manager at a local record store if you can still find one in your college town. Their numbers will tell you the real story, just like mine do."

So, what is at stake? Quite a bit. The American music business has been the most vibrant music industry in the world—a multi-billion dollar sector delivering tens of thousands of albums to music fans. The motion picture and software industries report similar global success stories—in fact, the copyright industries of the U.S. collectively account for 5 percent of GDP and their copyrighted products are this country's number one export—exceeding Boeing's planes or General Motors' cars.

P2P and Filtering Technologies

File sharing businesses could do three simple things that would help immeasurably in protecting this country's valuable intellectual property: proactively warn their users about the illegality of file sharing, change the default setting on P2P software so that users are not unwittingly offering the contents of their entire hard drive to the world, and, most importantly, filter out copyrighted works.

The P2P businesses have said to date that a filtering capability is "not possible" and that they "can't prevent the rampant infringement occurring using [their] software." But filtering technology is completely viable. Companies like California-based Audible Magic show how it can be done. We have hosted a series of demonstrations of Audible Magic's filtering product for key Congressional staff, higher education leaders and other policymakers. If the file sharing businesses actually mean it when they say they want to become legitimate corporate citizens, solutions are out there. The irony is that the P2P businesses, who have wrapped themselves in the cloak of "technology innovators," are now behaving like digital Luddites, choosing to ignore—or worse, attack—technological solutions, so that they can continue making money off of illegal file sharing.

Any refusal to voluntarily adopt filtering software also affirms the stark qualitative contrast between legitimate businesses and illegitimate ones. The legitimate services create jobs, pay taxes, respect property law, compensate artists, protect consumers from viruses, spyware and unwanted pornography, and offer high-quality downloads. On the other side, the unauthorized P2P business model demands lawbreaking, is void of real consumer protections, contributes virtually nothing to the taxes and jobs ledger, punishes creators, is filled with bogus, junk files, and deluges users with pornography, spyware and viruses.

While technology is part of the solution to virtually any copyright piracy challenge, so is enforcement. Communicating a message of deterrence is essential. No matter how great a legitimate technology may be, there will always be some who, absent any threat of consequences, will flout the law and pursue the illegal avenue for personal gain.

Legal Actions

As many of you know, the record companies initially attempted to fight piracy by holding accountable these multi-million dollar enterprises that have abused a legitimate technology to facilitate and control the illegal uploading and downloading of songs.

Our objective and legal demands were never to shutter the technology. It was simply to ask that its operators respect copyright law and work to screen out those copyrighted works not authorized for download and distribution.

We have had some important successes—Napster, Aimster, Audiogalaxy—that have helped affirm important legal principles. Nevertheless, in one key case . . . against the P2P services Grokster and Morpheus, a court ruled against the interest of copyright owners, including our co-plaintiffs, the music publishers and motion picture studios. We have appealed that decision.

For several years, despite repeated efforts to educate the public about the law—through full page advertisements, public service announcements, outreach to the business and the university community—and the availability of legal online alternatives, the problem of illegal file sharing only grew worse. We learned that educational efforts helped people understand the impact of music piracy, but only the threat of consequences, removing the risk-free factor from the equation, truly got people to change behavior.

The record labels, and their partners throughout the music community, were left with little choice: hold accountable individual file sharers—especially those who were taking entire CD collections of hundreds or thousands of songs and distributing them to the world to copy for free—or watch the business disappear.

The immediate impact of our efforts has been profound,

but the larger effects will truly be felt only over the long term. Americans' awareness that it is illegal to share or download copyrighted songs through a file sharing network has doubled—from 35 percent in November of 2002 to 65 percent [as of April 2004]. The industry's efforts have ignited kitchen table conversations across the country. Parents are talking to kids, teachers talking to their students about illegal and immoral behavior.

Online Music Sharing Is Wrong

The unauthorized reproduction and distribution of copyrighted music is *just as illegal as shoplifting a CD*. Burning CD's from peer-to-peer networks like KaZaA, Morpheus or Gnutella is against the law. The rules are very simple. Unless you own the copyright, it's not yours to distribute. . . .

Most of us would never even consider stealing something of value from a neighbor's house. Our conscience, our sense of right and wrong, keep us from doing it. Sure, we know there are criminal penalties, but the main reason we don't steal is because we know it's wrong. . . .

[One] rationalization for stealing music is that illegal copying is a victimless crime that really doesn't hurt anyone.

Tell that to the struggling young musicians in a garage band who can't get signed because record sales are down.

Or tell it to the young singer-songwriter whose career dead-ends because people would rather download her music for free.

Music United Web site, www.musicunited.org.

Interest in legal online services is skyrocketing—Soundscan reported . . . 25 million legal downloads in the first quarter of 2004. There were 19.2 million legal downloads in the last six months [2003]. And various studies show that P2P use, at least in the United States, is on the decline.

Obviously, millions continue to engage in the illegal activity, including many students and kids, an especially difficult audience to reach. This is obviously an issue of particular relevance and interest to college administrators.

[In March 2004] we brought lawsuits against an additional 532 illegal file sharers, including 89 individuals who were using a university network to connect to a file sharing service and distribute copyrighted songs. We want everyone, including students, to recognize that downloading or 'sharing' a song without permission is illegal and that there are consequences. . . .

The Music Industry Must Adapt

Is enforcement the solution? Of course not. It is part of the larger equation—aggressive licensing of music online and elsewhere, coupled with education and the exploration of new business opportunities.

Record labels are actively and eagerly embracing technology and the digital revolution. It is really the only way to stay competitive. There is enormous demand from today's music fans to consume music in new and novel ways. While it is encouraging that CD sales are on the rise [as of early 2004], the long-term future of this industry is not solely in the sale of physical product. It is in maximizing revenue brought about by new consumptive trends, including the proliferation of digital alternatives.

For much of its history, the record industry has relied upon the sale of physical product for survival. As each new format—from wax cylinders, to vinyl, to cassettes, to CDs—was introduced and gained widespread acceptance, sales of the predecessor format dropped dramatically. But each new delivery format resulted in increased sales. On its own, the single stream of revenues enabled the industry to thrive and develop and promote new talent. Today, however, the sale of physical product is declining. And consumers no longer demand owning physical product in order to consume music.

Twenty years ago, music fans were limited to consuming music by either tuning into the radio or by listening to a purchased album. Now, not only are there download and subscription services like iTunes, Napster 2.0, Wal-Mart, Musicmatch, Rhapsody, buymusic.com, but satellite radio services like XM and Sirius; Internet radio webcasters like Yahoo! and MusicMatch; cellular phone "ring tones"; value-added physical products with special access to concert tickets, extra DVD footage and the like. We will soon even see the rollout of digital radio, commonly known as HD [high definition] Radio. With all of these new opportunities for consuming music, music fans no longer have to buy music in order to enjoy it.

Consumers now have the ability to personalize their own music channels through Internet music services, having a service play for them only the type of music they like. Music fans can also now listen to 60–70 channels of highly themed, CD-quality music on satellite services across the United States. And on-demand music services now permit consumers to listen to entire albums or individual tracks for immediate enjoyment.

Record labels are embracing technology to improve every aspect of digital commerce to improve the consumer experience. They are licensing all kinds of services to meet consumer demand—whether based on purchasing or listening. Last year, for example, the industry worked cooperatively with XM and Sirius on a mutually beneficial licensing arrangement as those services rollout.

Record labels are also working proactively in other ways to ensure that fans get music the way they want. For example, the Music Industry Integrated Identifiers Project (MI3P) is an initiative to develop a global infrastructure that will support digital music commerce on the Internet. The future world of music e-commerce is one where record companies, music rights societies, retailers and other business partners communicate and exchange key business information across networks through standardized message transactions.

The music industry is actively encouraging the early and widespread adoption of the MI3P standards by record companies and their representatives, music rights societies, music publishers and the business partners of all these—including distributors, retailers and intermediaries. Such adoption will facilitate the emergence of new business models by ensuring a seamless system from the consumer to the distributor to the creators. . . .

New Threats from Digital Radio

The rollout of HD Radio also presents new issues for the record industry. The technology behind HD Radio transmissions is controlled by a private company named iBiquity, which is in the enviable position of having had the FCC [Federal Communications Commission] adopt its proprietary standard as the sole standard for HD Radio in the US. HD Radio will provide consumers with CD-quality music, which we in the industry believe is an exciting development.

But it also poses threats. Device manufacturers are already planning to introduce radio receivers that will enable consumers to become worldwide distributors of recordings by making recordings available on the Internet. Such devices could also permit users to become owners of a personalized music collection through record functionality that transforms a passive listening experience into an on-demand service. Why would anyone spend 99 cents on a download if they could get the same quality recording for free?

Again, it comes down to using technology productively. Imagine if you could listen to an HD Radio broadcast and with the press of a button, purchase the song you are listening to and have it sent to an on-line jukebox or even a cell phone.

Broadcasters, technology companies, record companies, artists and music publishers would all benefit from such retail sales. The lost business opportunities would affect many companies that should otherwise receive—and in fact are entitled to receive—compensation for their creative efforts.

To be clear, the record industry supports HD Radio as a great technological advancement for consumers—but we support the adoption of appropriate content protection measures that will limit the significant threats posed by HD Radio.

A Comprehensive Strategy

I have spoken about the various strategies the record companies are employing to combat piracy and encourage fans to return to the legitimate marketplace. We are doing our part and encourage others who have a role to do so as well.

- ISPs can educate their users as to what's legal and illegal and cooperate with copyright owners to pursue long-term business models rather than short-term obstructionism.
- Congress should highlight the importance of copyright law, and help educate consumers and protect them.
- All artists need to embrace the opportunities of new

technology and allow their works to be distributed digitally through legitimate sources.

- Technology companies should manage inter-operability issues and enable seamless consumer experiences.
- Parents can talk to their children about what constitutes legal activity online and be aware of how their kids are making use of their online resources.
- Educators should teach the importance of copyright, setting out the basics of the law and the difference between right and wrong.
- And, as stated earlier, file sharing networks should provide three things: real, meaningful warnings; a change in the default setting so that uploading is not automatic; and installing filters for illegal material.

These are not easy times for any of us who create, make or care about music—from the label executive, to the artist, to the store clerk, to the fan in college. Reconnecting fans to the legitimate marketplace won't happen overnight, but it is happening.

*"File-sharing is not the end of the world,
and the existence of music and movies are
not being threatened."*

The Problem of Internet Piracy Is Exaggerated

Orson Scott Card

Orson Scott Card is the author of more than 30 novels and a regular contributor to the *Ornery American*, an online political newspaper. In the following viewpoint, he argues that the music industry has greatly exaggerated the threat posed by peer-to-peer Internet networks that allow users to swap music files. He believes that CD sales are not down because of Internet piracy, but rather because today's music offerings are poor and because most people have now upgraded their music collections from tape to CD. Furthermore, Card maintains that sharing music via the Internet generally helps artists get more exposure. Card concludes that the online music sharing controversy proves the need to update copyright laws to better benefit both artists and consumers.

As you read, consider the following questions:
1. Who are the "real pirates," in Card's opinion?
2. What solution has Senator Orrin Hatch suggested for dealing with online file sharing, according to Card?
3. How does Card feel that record companies should approach the problem of file sharing?

Since every penny I earn depends on copyright protection, I'm all in favor of reasonable laws to do the job.

But there's something kind of sad about the recording industry's indecent passion to punish the "criminals" who are violating their rights.

Copyright is a temporary monopoly granted by the government—it creates the legal fiction that a piece of writing or composing (or, as technologies were created, a recorded performance) is property and can only be sold by those who have been licensed to do so by the copyright holder.

Without copyright, once a work was performed or printed, other people who saw or heard or read it could simply do their own performance or print their own editions, and keep all the money without paying a dime to the creator of the work.

At the same time, a book or song isn't land or even corporate stock. In exchange for the private monopoly of copyright, when it expires the work is then free for anyone to perform or print or record. . . .

Who Are the Thieves in This House?

It's pretty hilarious to hear record company executives and movie studio executives get all righteous about copyright. They've been manipulating copyright laws for years, and all the manipulations were designed to steal everything they could from the actual creators of the work.

Do you think these companies care about the money that the actual creators of the work are being deprived of when people copy CDs and DVDs?

Here's a clue: Movie studios have, for decades, used "creative accounting" to make it so that even hit movies never manage to break even, thus depriving the creative people of their "percentage of profits." A few have dared to sue, but most figure that it isn't worth the ill will. (The sentence "You'll never work in this town again" runs through their minds. They remember what happened to [actor] Cliff Robertson after he blew the whistle on an executive who was flat-out embezzling!)

And record companies manage to skim enormous amounts of money from every CD sold. As you can easily calculate by going to the computer store and figuring out the price of an individual recordable blank CD. Figure that the record companies have been paying a fraction of *that* price for years. Then subtract that from the price of a CD. Figure the songwriters and performers are getting some ludicrously small percentage—less than twenty percent, I'd bet—and all the rest flows to the record company.

In other words, the people complaining about all the internet "thieves" are, by any reasonable measure, rapacious profiteers who have been parasitically sucking the blood out of copyrights on other people's work.

And I say this with the best will in the world. In fact, these companies have expenses. There are salaries to pay. Some of the salaries are earned.

But remember that huge fortunes like, say, [entertainment mogul] David Geffen's were made by getting ownership of record publishing companies. Count on it—Geffen got a lot richer than any but a handful of the actual performers. And when their careers are over, the record company owner keeps right on earning.

Not only that, but the digital technologies that allow perfect-quality copying came as a huge windfall to the studios and record companies.

I basically replaced all my vinyl records and cassette tapes with CDs, and then replaced all our VHS tapes and laserdiscs with DVDs. The record companies and studios would have laughed if somebody said, "This is just an upgrade. I should be able to turn in my vinyl and cassettes for CDs and my videotapes for DVDs, for no more than the actual cost of production." Ha ha ha ha ha.

In all the ridiculously overblown "estimates" of how much the studios and record companies are "losing" from "piracy," nobody bothers to calculate just how much extra money they made from consumers paying full price for music and movies they had already paid full price for only a few years before.

That's all right, you see, because that helps the companies' bottom line, whereas piracy hurts it.

But how much?

The real pirates—people who make knock-off copies of CDs and DVDs and sell them in direct competition (or in foreign markets)—make a lot of money in some markets, but most of those are overseas. It's a problem, but some reasonable combination of private investigation and police work and international treaties should deal with that.

Internet "pirates," though, usually are more like a long-distance group that trades CDs around.

If you got together with a few of your neighbors and each of you bought different CDs and then lent them to each other, that wouldn't even violate copyright.

In fact, the entire music business absolutely depends on the social interaction of kids to make hits. You stop kids from sharing music, and you've shut down the hit-making machine.

Farrington. © 2003 by Cagle Cartoons, Inc. Reproduced by permission.

Copyright violation comes from the fact that digital copies—even the compressed MP3 format—are nearly perfect. And when you "lend" your copy to someone over the internet, you still have your original. And he can lend to ten more or a hundred more or a thousand more, and the record company is only paid for that first copy.

Well, that's not a good thing—if that became the primary way music was published.

The record companies swear that it's making a serious inroad on sales, and they can prove it. How? By showing that their sales are way down in the past few years.

It couldn't possibly be because (a) most of us have already replaced all our old vinyl and cassettes, so all that windfall money is no longer flowing in, or (b) because the record companies have made some really lousy decisions as they tried to guess what we consumers would want to buy.

It couldn't possibly be that they've targeted all their marketing at precisely the market segment—high school and college students—who are most likely to be sharing MP3s over the internet.

Maybe if they started marketing more music that people my age would enjoy, they'd find that, lo and behold, there *are* customers who prefer to buy music the legal way!

It's All Happened Before

The irony is that we've played out this whole scenario before, more than once. When radio first started broadcasting records instead of live performances, the music publishing industry became livid. This was going to hurt sales! A compromise was reached whereby radio stations paid small fees to the publishers for each playing of a record.

But the truth is that it's a lot of bother for nothing. Radio didn't hurt record sales. Radio *made* record sales, because people wanted to own the records they heard on the radio. Radio let people hear musicians they might never have found otherwise.

Same thing with TV and movies. Yes, TV wiped out the B-movie market segment and it killed newsreels—but it opened up a lucrative aftermarket that kept movies alive long after they would have stopped earning money. That's how *Wizard of Oz* and *It's a Wonderful Life* and many other movies became American icons.

And again, with the VCR, studios were terrified that people would tape things off the air and stop paying money for movies. (And the TV networks were terrified that people would tape shows and skip over the ads; they didn't realize that most of us are too lazy to skip over commercials.)

And rental videotapes! That was the end of the world!

When the studios finally stopped charging ninety bucks for a videotape, they discovered that the videotape (and now DVD) aftermarket was often bigger than the original theatrical release.

The internet is similar, but not identical, to these situations.

First, most of the people who are getting those free MP3s would not be buying the CDs anyway. They're doing this in order to get far more music than they can actually afford. That means that if they weren't sharing MP3s online, they would simply have less music—or share CDs hand to hand. It does *not* mean that they would have bought CDs to get the tunes they're downloading from Napster-like sharing schemes.

That's why I laugh at their estimates of "lost sales."

How to Teach Your Customers to Hate You

It only gets stupider the more you think about it. The kids they're trying to prosecute and punish are in exactly the demographic that advertisers are most eager to target, not because they have the most money—far from it, people *my* age have all the money—but because they're "brandable." They haven't yet committed themselves to brand loyalty. They're open to all kinds of possibilities. And advertisers want to get to them and imprint their brands so that they'll own these consumers as they get older and start earning money.

So just how smart is it to indelibly imprint on their young minds a link between your corporate brand and outrageous punishments for music sharing?

Let's keep this in perspective. We're not talking about murder here, or child molestation, or even speeding on the highway. No one's life is put at risk. In all likelihood, nobody is really losing any money they would have had anyway. So just what kind of punishment is really deserved?

There is such a thing as defeating your own purpose. Like Queen Mary I of England, who tried to restore Catholic fidelity by burning a couple of hundred Protestants whose sins were as trivial as buying a Bible and having people read it to you. Every burning made it more certain that Catholicism would become loathsome to more and more of the population.

I was especially amused at Utah Senator Orrin Hatch's

support for seeding the MP3-sharing sites with computer-destroying viruses.

I mean, this is one of the leading figures on the Senate Judiciary Committee, and he actually wanted to punish people without any kind of due process—and all for an offense against copyright.

Open sharing of music files doesn't actually hurt the creators of music. It helps them. When friends can say, "Have you heard Eva Cassidy's music? Here, I'll send you a couple of songs, you won't believe how good she is," that's called "word of mouth," and what you'll get is more and more people who attend her live performances and buy her CDs.

More sales for musicians that might otherwise never have been heard of.

You should hear singers like Janis Ian go on about how much *good* file-sharing does for the careers of musicians who aren't the pets of the record companies. The record companies pretend they're protecting the rights of the musicians, but you have to be deeply dumb to believe that. What they mean is that they want to protect the rights of the musicians they have under contract—even if their "protection" hurts everybody else.

The real gripe for the record companies is not these fictional "lost sales." What's keeping them up at night is the realization that musicians don't need record companies any more.

Musicians can go into a studio, record their own music exactly as they want it, and not as some executive says they have to record it because "that's what the kids want."

Then they can sell CDs at their live performances and set up online, with a bunch of MP3s that people can share around. They also can sell CDs, and without a lot of expensive record company overhead.

Of course, fulfilment and website management can be an expensive pain, so what will emerge is a new kind of recording company—full-service online stores that make only as many copies of a CD as are ordered, so there's no inventory to maintain. They'll take a much smaller share of the money than the existing companies do, so the CDs can sell for much less—while the artist still makes more money per sale than the big record companies ever allowed. . . .

How to Stop the File-Sharing

Truth to tell, I don't have much patience with the websites and systems that allow indiscriminate sharing of MP3s among strangers. I'd like to see them shut down. But they can't be, not without changing international agreements, because how can the U.S. government stop a file-sharing scheme that works on a server in Singapore? And Orrin Hatch's killer-virus scheme would be a form of international terrorism.

The same thing that keeps us from blocking the scourge of internet porn also keeps us from being able to take any practical measures to block MP3-sharing websites. And frankly, I think the porn sites cause far more harm to Americans than MP3-sharing. If the government goes after teenagers sharing songs but does nothing about family-wrecking, soul-numbing porn, then something is deeply, deeply wrong.

Do you know how to stop file-sharing on anything other than a friend-to-friend, word-of-mouth basis?

Instead of turning the file-sharers into martyred heroes, the way the short-sighted executives want to do, just educate people that it's OK to let people hear a sample, but don't give away whole albums of work you didn't create. This is not a hard concept; people would get it.

Scorn works far better than lawsuits and punitive damages at changing society. I already react that way when somebody says, "Let me copy the CD for you." I affix them with a steely glare and say, "Do you own the copyright for that?" They usually say something face-saving, and I let them, because I'm not a puritan about it. But they not only never offer to copy songs for *me*, most of them also get more nervous to offer it to other people.

That will stamp out the "sharing" of whole CDs pretty quickly, if it catches on. . . .

Strip away all the pretension, and what you really have is this: Rapacious companies that have become bloated on windfall profits and ruthless exploitation of other people's talents are now terrified that the gravy train will go away.

Because in the brave new world of online distribution of cheap CDs, do you know who the *only* losers would be? Big-salary executives and owners of big record companies.

The movie studio executives are safer—it takes big money to make big movies, and nobody can distribute on the net the experience of going into a theater to see a first-run movie.

Clean Up Your Own Act First

Americans are generally good people. If you explain to them *why* a rule is necessary, they'll generally go along with it.

But you have to get rid of the hypocrisy first. File-sharing is not the end of the world, and the existence of music and movies are not being threatened, any more than they were with the advent of radio, television, and VCRs.

And let's just laugh at the self-righteousness of the "injured" studios and record companies. We can't take them seriously until they've tried the obvious *market* responses:

Drop those CD prices to a reasonable level—even if it means firing some of those big-salary execs and gutting out some of the percs. (It won't take the record companies long to figure out how to take a percentage of concert performances to make up for lost income, anyway—or are they already doing it?)

Start treating the artists better, and let copyright be awarded to the creators, not the backers. When the audience sees that copyright law is protecting the musicians from the corporate exploiters, then they'll be more likely to obey the copyright law. The emotional connection is between musician and audience.

Which is why the companies should stop threatening us and our children with ludicrous prosecution, or with software designed to sabotage our right to make backup copies and transfer files from one player to another for our legitimate personal use.

The more visible you make yourselves, all you executives, the more everybody will hate you. Disappear from the public eye and revise your business model to fit the current technology.

Meanwhile, any copy-protection scheme you come up with that would make it harder for me to copy songs onto the player I use when I'm running, and I'll simply stop buying any music from your company. I already have a lot of music. I can listen to it for years before I need to buy another CD, if you've made it so I can't use it in the lawful ways that I want to.

Then let's get back to the real world, instead of wasting any more time on the petty and mostly self-inflicted problems of rich but badly-managed corporations.

"The current generation of al-Qaeda terrorists understand the usefulness of attacking the U.S. cyber infrastructure."

Cyberterrorism Is a Serious Threat

Dan Verton

Dan Verton is the author of *Black Ice: The Invisible Threat of Cyber-Terrorism.* The following viewpoint is excerpted from his February 2004 testimony before the Senate Judiciary Committee. Verton argues that cyberterrorism—terrorism that is directed at or conducted via computer networks—is a real and growing threat. He maintains that the critical infrastructures in the physical world, such as electricity grids and financial institutions, are increasingly reliant on computer control programs. These programs, in turn, are often run via large computer networks that malicious outsiders may be able to gain access to. Verton believes that the al Qaeda terrorist organization is capable of cyberterrorist tactics, and he warns that a cyberterrorist attack would be most devastating in conjunction with traditional terrorist attacks.

As you read, consider the following questions:

1. What is a SCADA system?
2. What evidence of al Qaeda's cyberterrorist ambitions did U.S. forces in Kabul uncover in January 2002, according to the author?
3. What was the goal of the Black Ice exercise conducted in November 2000 that Verton describes?

Dan Verton, testimony before the Senate Judiciary Committee, Washington, DC, February 24, 2004.

Although I do not consider myself a technical expert, I have a professional background in intelligence and information security, and I'm the author of a recently published book by McGraw-Hill titled *Black Ice: The Invisible Threat of Cyber-Terrorism* that goes into detail regarding the subject of today's hearing and has been endorsed by some of the nation's leading authorities in critical infrastructure protection, terrorism and information security, including the president's two former chief cyber security advisors, Richard Clarke and Howard Schmidt. My statement for the record, which I will summarize for you now, is based primarily on my research for *Black Ice* and some of my more recent work in this area.

I would like to address the following three questions:

1. What is the nation's current level of vulnerability to cyber-terrorism?
2. What is al-Qaeda's capability to conduct cyber-terrorism?
3. What are the potential implications of a combined physical and cyber-terrorist attack against U.S. critical infrastructures?

Interdependency Between the Real World and the Cyber-World

1. What is the nation's current level of vulnerability to cyber-terrorism?

Before any meaningful discussion can be conducted about the nation's vulnerability to cyber-terrorism, it is important to understand that there is no longer any separation between the physical, real world, and the cyber-world. Computers and computer networks control real things in the real world. And many of those "things" are critical infrastructures, such as electricity, drinking water and real-time financial transactions that have implications for both public safety and the national economy.

And this understanding must lead us to a new, more flexible definition of the term *cyber-terrorism*. We can no longer view cyber-terrorism with blinders on, choosing only to consider the acts of somebody sitting behind a computer and hacking or disrupting the operation of other computers or networks as cyber-terrorism. If we learned anything from

9/11 it was that traditional physical forms of terrorism can have massive cyber ramifications that can severely impair the functioning of the nation's economy—an economy that is almost wholly dependent on the uninterrupted operation of a fragile, privately owned and operated digital infrastructure.

Likewise, it is just as important for us to recognize that there is no longer such a thing as an insignificant vulnerability. When vulnerabilities exist, regardless of how minor we may think they are, they open the door to the unexpected and the unanticipated. This is particularly true in the realm of information technologies, where hidden interdependencies exist throughout the nation's critical infrastructures.

And it is an unprecedented level of interdependency that accounts for the nation's current level of vulnerability to cyber-terrorism, in both its physical and its electronic forms. Today every infrastructure or sector of the economy is potentially the Achilles heel of other infrastructures and economic sectors. For example, there is little question about the critical role of electric power in the operation of all sectors of the economy, the dependence of the electric industry on natural gas, the dependence of reliable telecommunications on electric power, the dependence of financial, government, and emergency services operations on both electric power and telecommunications, and the potential impact from prolonged failures of these infrastructures on drinking water and transportation systems. And the interdependence and potential for the type of cascading failure I am describing here stems from the confluence of the physical world and the cyber world.

Vulnerable Critical Control Systems

Perhaps one of the most important areas where an unprecedented level of vulnerability has existed for years and still exists today is in the widespread adoption of wireless technologies. Although there are proven methods and security systems available for protecting wireless networks, they are not always understood and deployed properly, if at all. In my research I have found evidence of unprotected wireless networks in use at the following infrastructure settings: hospitals; airline baggage checking systems at some of the largest

U.S. air carriers; railroad track heating switches; uranium mining operations; water and wastewater treatment facilities; security cameras; and oil wells and water flood operations. Supervisory Control and Data Acquisition systems, or SCADA systems, are in many ways the crown jewels of some of the nation's most important industrial control settings, such as the electric power grid. But they are not—as their name might imply—built upon secret, proprietary technology. To the contrary, modern design specifications for SCADA systems, which I have documented through both personal interviews with experts and through open-source research on the Internet, presents us with the frightening reality that the SCADA systems being used in our nation's critical infrastructures are nothing more than high-end commercial PCs and Servers running Microsoft Corp. operating systems. In other words, the genie is out of the bottle and has been for years in terms of understanding how to disrupt or corrupt the operations of SCADA systems. Today, it's simply a matter of gaining access.

And as I have also documented in my research, gaining access to SCADA systems for the purpose of causing widespread chaos, confusion and economic damage is increasingly becoming a mere formality for professional hackers, virus and worm writers, and terrorist-sponsored saboteurs. . . .

Examples of Vulnerability

Consider the following . . . examples, which I document in my book, *Black Ice: The Invisible Threat of Cyber-Terrorism:*

The U.S. railroad system's increasing use of wireless technologies may present one of the most immediate dangers to both national security and local safety. Given the system's long, winding network of radio, telephone, and computer assets, voice and data communications networks provide vital links between train crews, trackside monitoring and repair staff, and rail control centers. Total control of the massive network is accomplished through a communication system that integrates trackside maintenance telephones, trackside transponders, security cameras and monitors, passenger information displays, public announcements, the public telephone network, radio bases, and control center consoles. However, wireless SCADA systems are increasingly providing the management glue that keeps all of these systems running together. In the colder regions of the country, underground heaters keep the rails from freezing in winter. These operations are also being controlled and monitored by wireless SCADA computers. The use of modern technology in this case means that in the case of a failure, railroads no longer have to dispatch technicians in the dead of winter to remote locations where heating switches are usually located. However, it also means that the security of these switching operations may now have a new series of security challenges to deal with. This is of particular concern given the dangerous nature of some train cargo. . . .

A Nation Dependent on Information Technology

For the United States, the information technology revolution quietly changed the way business and government operate. Without a great deal of thought about security, the Nation shifted the control of essential processes in manufacturing, utilities, banking, and communications to networked computers. As a result, the cost of doing business dropped and productivity skyrocketed. The trend toward greater use of networked systems continues.

By 2003, our economy and national security became fully dependent upon information technology and the information infrastructure. A network of networks directly supports the operation of all sectors of our economy—energy (electric power, oil and gas), transportation (rail, air, merchant marine), finance and banking, information and telecommunications, public health, emergency services, water, chemical, defense industrial base, food, agriculture, and postal and shipping. The reach of these computer networks exceeds the bounds of cyberspace. They also control physical objects such as electrical transformers, trains, pipeline pumps, chemical vats, and radars.

George W. Bush, *The National Strategy to Secure Cyberspace*, February 2003.

Uranium mining operations in Wyoming extract uranium from the soil through a process by which water is injected into the ground. Because of the contamination, remote terminals are necessary to control and manage the pumps that move the water and extract the uranium. Commercial PC-based remote workstations now support critical monitoring functions, such as pump failure, pump status, temperature, speed, and even the pump's on/off condition. But the security implications are enormous. When pumps lose power, water pressure starts building up in the plant. Software has been programmed to automatically reset certain pumps to get the pressure out as fast as possible. And it's all being done in the name of cost-effectiveness. . . .

For the most part, these dire warnings have gone unheeded by the private-sector companies that own and operate these infrastructure systems. Senior executives view such scenarios as something akin to a Hollywood movie script. However, throughout the entire post–September 11 security review process, a process that continues to this day, administration experts and other senior members of the U.S. intelligence community were quietly coming to the conclusion that they were witnessing the birth of a new era of terrorism. Cyberspace, with its vast invisible linkages and critical role in keeping America's vital infrastructures and economy functioning, was fast becoming a primary target and a weapon of terror.

My fear is that the next time we have a massive power failure, such as we experienced on August 14, 2003, it will not be a self-inflicted wound, but potentially a terrorist-induced failure that is quickly exploited by suicide bombings, rampaging gunmen or chemical and biological attacks against those stranded in the subway systems.

Al-Qaeda's Technological Sophistication

2. What is al-Qaeda's capability to conduct cyber-terrorism?

My goal in answering this question is to convince you and others in government to think differently about the future, and particularly, about the future of international terrorism. The high-tech future of terrorism is inevitable. And like the events leading up to the September 11, 2001, terrorist attacks (events that dated back 8 years), we are beginning now to see the indications and warnings that international terrorism is evolving its tactics to meet the new operational realities it faces around the world and to better achieve its strategic goals. . . .

Al-Qaeda's view of cyber-terrorism and its history in using information technologies is a case in point. But here, again, we face a significant perception problem. The picture that most Americans form in their minds when they think of al-Qaeda or of terrorists in general is a picture of a mindless horde of thugs living a hand-to-mouth existence in caves in Afghanistan. But this picture says nothing of the educated elite that forms the inner circle of the group's command and control, it says nothing of the technical support available on the open market in the form of out of work intelligence experts from a host of nations, and it says nothing of the threat posed by the continued radicalization of young people all over the world—young people who are studying computer science and mathematics and who may find it more advantageous to strike out directly at the U.S. economy than to strap explosives around their waste and walk into a crowded café.

That said, there is already ample evidence to suggest that the current generation of al-Qaeda terrorists understand the usefulness of attacking the U.S. cyber infrastructure. . . .

Since the start of the U.S. War on Terrorism, a significant amount of evidence has been unearthed throughout Afghanistan and various other al-Qaeda hideouts around the world that indicates terrorism may be evolving toward a more high-tech future at a faster rate than previously believed.

In January 2002, for example, U.S. forces in Kabul discovered a computer at an al-Qaeda office that contained models of a dam, made with structural architecture and engineering software. The software would have enabled al-Qaeda to study the best way to attack the dam and to simulate the dam's catastrophic failure. In addition, al-Qaeda operatives apprehended around the world acknowledged receiving training in how to attack key infrastructures. Among the data terrorists were studying was information on SCADA systems.

Despite all of the mounting evidence that suggests al-Qaeda is evolving toward the use of cyber-weapons, the terrorist group that started us down this path and that has posed the greatest threat of all terrorist groups to U.S. national security remains somewhat of a mystery. But the War on Terrorism has helped uncover some of the hidden trends.

Al-Qaeda cells now operate with the assistance of large databases containing details of potential targets in the U.S. They use the Internet to collect intelligence on those targets, especially critical economic nodes, and modern software enables them to study structural weaknesses in facilities as well as predict the cascading failure effect of attacking certain systems. But the future may hold something quite different.

Intent, Resources, and Opportunity

The three driving factors behind al-Qaeda's operations—intent, resources, and opportunity—all point to the future use of cyber-tactics.

First, the intent of Osama bin Laden is clear. He wants to cripple the economy of the U.S. as a means to force the withdrawal of U.S. military personnel from Saudi Arabia and curtail economic and military support for Israel. The targeting of corporate America and the digital economy is clear in this regard.

Second, the growing number of technologically sophisticated sympathizers, especially among Muslim youth, is providing al-Qaeda with a steady stream of new talent in the use of offensive cyber-weapons. In addition to the younger generations of hackers and virus writers, al-Qaeda and other radical Islamist movements can count on the intelligence services of various rogue nations who now and in the future will find themselves in the crosshairs of the U.S. military.

Finally, America continues to present al-Qaeda and other radical Islamist groups with ample economic targets in cyberspace, thus driving these groups toward the increased use of cyber-tactics. Unless current trends are reversed and America's digital economy is no longer a target of opportunity, terrorist groups around the world will continue to dedicate time and resources to studying ways to integrate cyber-weapons into their operations.

The Threat of Combined Attacks

3. What are the potential implications of a combined physical and cyber-terrorist attack against U.S. critical infrastructures?

The blackout of August 14, 2003, notwithstanding, the danger stemming from this unprecedented level of infrastructure interdependency was proven during the first major infrastructure interdependency exercise, which took place in November 2000 in preparation for the 2002 Winter Olympics in Utah. Known by its code name, Black Ice, the simulation was sponsored by the U.S. Department of Energy and the Utah Olympic Public Safety Command. The goal was to prepare federal, state, local, and private-sector officials for the unexpected consequences of a major terrorist attack or a series of attacks throughout the region, where tens of thousands of athletes and spectators from around the world would gather. When it was over, Black Ice demonstrated in frightening detail how the effects of a major terrorist attack or natural disaster could be made significantly worse by a simultaneous cyber-attack against the computers that manage the region's critical infrastructures.

Without going into the details of the exercise, the conclusions drawn by the exercise participants are startling. Estimates showed the loss of electric power throughout a five-state region and three provinces in Canada for at least one month. Other estimates went as far as several months.

The important lesson is that *Black Ice* showed the growing number of critical interdependencies that exist throughout the various infrastructure systems and how devastating combined cyber-attacks and physical attacks can be. It proved for the first time that the terrorist's mode of attack is irrelevant when it comes to cyber-terrorism. Terrorist groups that want to amplify the chaos and confusion of physical attacks or directly target the economy can succeed by launching traditional-style terrorist assaults against the nation's cyber-infrastructure.

> *"Cyber terror or cyber attacks on infrastructure are an unlikely threat to the security of the United States."*

The Threat of Cyberterrorism Is Exaggerated

James Lewis

James Lewis is a senior fellow at the Center for Strategic and International Studies' Technology and Public Policy Program. In the following viewpoint, he points out that despite growing concern over the idea that terrorists might harm the United States via computer- or Internet-mediated attacks, there have in fact been no instances of cyberterrorism, before or after September 11, 2001. Lewis argues that terrorists prefer the high-profile impact of explosives to the more subtle threat of cyberterror. Moreover, he believes that America's critical infrastructures—such as electricity grids and water systems—are not nearly as vulnerable to computer-based attacks as some critics have claimed.

As you read, consider the following questions:
1. How many terrorist incidents were there between the start of 1996 and the end of 2001, according to Lewis?
2. Why are explosives the preferred weapons of terrorists, according to the source quoted by Lewis?
3. Rather than infrastructure attacks, what does the author believe is the threat that cybersecurity should emphasize?

James Lewis, "Cyber Terror: Missing in Action," *Knowledge, Technology, and Policy: The International Journal of Knowledge Transfer and Utilization*, vol. 16, Summer 2003, pp. 34–41. Copyright © 2003 by Transaction Publishers. Reproduced by permission.

The first warnings that America faced an "electronic Pearl Harbor" appeared in 1995. They have appeared regularly . . . since then. The threat entails [according to journalist J.M. Waller] "a surprise attack on the country's fragile information systems . . . crippling raids on public- and private-sector information systems on which the entire economy—and the American way of life—depend." Most recently, before the March 2003 conflict with Iraq, there was another round of speculation that the United States would experience cyber attacks in retaliation. However, since the end of major military operations in April, there have been no reported cyber attacks that damaged U.S. infrastructure or affected U.S. military operations in Iraq. This should not surprise us, as since 1995 there have been no reports of cyber attacks that created panic or terror, damaged U.S. infrastructure, caused casualties, or affected U.S. military operations.

This is not the result of inactivity by terrorist groups. The State Department reports there were 1,813 international terrorist attacks between the start of 1996 and end of 2001. While many of these attacks did not involve U.S. citizens or targets, they include some of the most damaging terrorist attacks in American history. They include the Khobar Tower bombings (June 1996), the U.S. Embassy Bombings in East Africa (August 1998), the attack on USS *Cole* (October 2000). Three hundred and twenty-seven people died in these attacks, which were followed by the horrific attacks on the World Trade Center and the Pentagon in 2001, which cost more than three thousand lives and caused billions of dollars in damage. In a period of major terrorist activity directed against the United States, cyber attacks are noticeably absent.

No Evidence of Cyber Plots

Since September 11, the United States discovered a number of terrorist cells operating within its borders and in other countries. The security services of other nations (the United Kingdom, Germany, Spain, and others) also discovered active terrorist cells. These terrorist cells reportedly were planning attacks against civilian and military targets in the United States and elsewhere, employing a wide range of weapons, including bio-toxins, chemical weapons, and radiological weapons, in addition to attacks using conventional explosives and firearms. None of these cells, however, are reported to have planned attacks using cyber weapons.

One fundamentalist cleric who lives in London and who frequently acts as a spokesperson for al Qaeda, threatened in November 2002 attacks against the U.S. economic infrastructure using all types of technologies, including the Internet. While al Qaeda has launched attacks in Morocco and Saudi Arabia, there have still been no cyber events.

The absence of cyber terror also does not reflect inactivity on the part of hackers. Carnegie Mellon's Computer Emergency Response Team has collected statistics showing that since 1996, there have been 217,394 computer security incidents reported. This number is probably an underestimate, given the reluctance of companies and organizations to report embarrassing hacks. None of these 217,394 security incidents created panic or terror, damaged U.S. infrastructure, caused casualties, or affected U.S. military operations.

Cyber Events During the Iraq War

A large number of cyber events did occur during the conflict in Iraq. Arab news sites reported hundreds of hacking incidents and a leading Arab news site found its English-language website replaced with a large American flag. Large numbers of anti-war or pro-Saddam hackers also defaced a number of U.S. and British websites. Some unclassified U.S. military networks reported "slower download times" because of the attacks. A small number of computer viruses were released as anti-war gestures, but there have not been any reports of significant disruption as a result (one security firm noted that the virus "Ganda," thought to be Iraq-related, "seems to be a protest against the Swedish school system rather than an anti-war protest").

U.S. military doctrine has been amended to include attacks on opponents' computer networks, but there are no reports of cyber attacks by U.S. forces against Iraq. This could simply be an absence of reporting on the use of secret cyber weapons or it may reflect the fact that Iraq had practically no computer network infrastructure. Iraq was an uninviting target for cyber attack, but it is not alone in this regard. One dilemma for the United States is that the countries where it has deployed military forces in the last few years—Iraq, Serbia, Somalia, Haiti—are not advanced economies and do not use computer networks for critical functions, making U.S. cyber weapons of limited utility. Another dilemma for future conflicts with more advanced opponents is that the United States might gain more from penetrating hostile computer networks and unobtrusively observing them while they continue to operate than it would get from disrupting them.

Cyber vs. Physical Terrorist Attacks
1996–2003
Computer Security Incidents 217,394
Terrorist Attacks 1,813
Cyber Terror Incidents 0
James Lewis, *Knowledge, Technology, and Policy*, Summer 2003.

The contrast between the thousands of terrorist attacks, tens of thousands of computer hacking incidents, and an absence of cyber terror or cyber attacks on infrastructure, is striking and suggestive. It suggests that, as so many commentators have noted, that cyber terror or cyber attacks on infrastructure are an unlikely threat to the security of the United States.

The Goals of Terrorists

Part of the explanation of this disparity lies with the goals and motives of terrorists. Terrorists seek to make a political statement and to inflict psychological and physical damage on their targets. If terrorism is an act of violence to achieve political objects, how useful will terrorists find a weapon whose effects may not even be noticed, or, in the case of economic attacks, where damage might be gradual and cumulative? One of al Qaeda's training manuals, "Military Studies in the Jihad against the Tyrants," notes that explosives are the preferred weapon of terrorists because "explosives strike the enemy with sheer terror and fright." Explosions are dramatic, create fear, and do lasting damage. They meet certain psychological needs of those who are attracted to terrorism. Cyber attacks would not have the same dramatic and political effect that terrorists seek. A cyber attack, which might not even be noticed by its victims, or attributed to routine delays or outages, will not be the preferred weapon of terrorist groups.

While the press has reported that government officials are concerned over al Qaeda's plans to use the Internet to wage cyber terrorism, these stories often recycle the same hypothetical scenarios previously attributed to China's cyber warfare efforts. The risk remains hypothetical but the antagonist has changed from hostile states to terrorist groups like al Qaeda.

When unclassified U.S. Department of Defense computer networks came under cyber attack in the late 1990s, the United States was quick to suspect Iraq or China as the culprit. U.S. officials debated whether this was an act of war that merited a cyber counter attack by the U.S. military. However, as tensions reached their peak, the United States discovered that far from being a hostile power, the source of the attack was two high school students in California. It is difficult, especially in the early stages of an incident, to determine if the attacker is a terrorist, group, foreign state, criminals, or teenager in California. However, a quick survey of incidents [from 1999 to 2003] suggests that criminals and bored teenagers are the most likely sources of attack. To this day, the vast majority of hacking incidents result from the actions of recreational hackers.

How Terrorists Use the Internet

Terrorist groups—al Qaeda, Hamas, and others—do make significant use of the Internet, but as a tool for intra-group communications, fundraising, and public relations. Terrorists, who in the past have often resorted to bank robbery to fund their operations, could also take advantage of the Internet to steal credit card numbers or valuable data to finance their operations. Cyber terrorism has attracted considerable attention, but to date, it has meant little more than propaganda, intelligence collection, or the digital equivalent of graffiti, with groups defacing each other's websites. Some experts go so far as to say that terrorists may avoid cyber weapons because of the potential risk they could pose to their own operations and communications.

The only new element attributed to al Qaeda is that the group might use cyber attacks to disrupt emergency services in order to reinforce and multiply the effect of a physical attack. If cyber attacks were feasible, the greatest risk they might pose to national security is as corollaries to more traditional modes of attacks. However, even this scenario is questionable in light of the experience of terrorist operations, which involve using vehicles containing large amounts of explosives to destroy individual buildings. In many cases after these explosions, traffic is snarled and water and electric power cut off as a result of the attack.

Vulnerabilities Are Exaggerated

In general, analyses of cyber terrorism or cyber warfare greatly exaggerate the vulnerability of infrastructure and nations to the effects of computer network attacks. The hypothetical vulnerability of various infrastructures—water systems, air traffic control, electrical grids—is routinely overstated in cyber attack scenarios. Very few, if any, of these infrastructures are dependent on computer networks (and the Internet) for their operation. Cyber attack scenarios also seem to assume a high degree of passivity or incompetence in their victims. The history of both terror and conventional military attacks shows that people in the United States and elsewhere are resilient and inventive in response to attacks and show a surprising, even heroic, capability to resist and restore.

A closer examination of infrastructure vulnerabilities points to three factors that greatly reduce any risk from cyber attack. First, while computer networks are vulnerable, critical infrastructures are not equally vulnerable. Gaining access to an infrastructure's computer network does not translate into control of the infrastructure or an ability to damage it. The infrastructures usually identified as cyber attack targets still require human intervention for most vital control mechanisms. Second, nations are robust and resilient in responding to attacks of all kinds, thus limiting the potential for damage from attack. Third, critical infrastructures in the United States are redundant, are accustomed to system failure, and know how to repair these failures. All of these factors make it difficult for remote computer attacks to disrupt critical functions. If there were cyber attacks, the effect on national security would be very limited. This may change over time as the Internet is incorporated into a wider range of routine operations and activities, but it is not the case now. . . .

Cyber Crimes, Not Terrorism

While there have been many instances of cyber crime (involving extortion or theft of valuable information or financial data), only two minor computer attacks against infrastructure have been confirmed. In 2000, an ex-employee of the company that installed a waste-management system for the Maroochy Shire Council in Australia was able to use his insider knowledge to pump sewage into a stream. After numerous attempts that went unnoticed by council authorities, the ex-employee was able to hack into the system. The Australian environmental protection agency reported that "the creek water turned black and the stench was unbearable for residents." The ex-employee was sentenced to two years in jail and fined $13,000 (Australian) for his action. There were no injuries or permanent damage as a result.

A teenage boy inadvertently hacked into a telephone company computer switch in 1998 and disabled it for six hours, preventing the air traffic control tower at a regional airport in Massachusetts from using its main radio transmitter or from remotely activating runway lights. The air traffic tower had a backup radio system, and there was no disruption to air traffic (which is very light at this regional airport). The teenager was put on probation and was required to perform 250 hours of community service.

Without making light of either of these incidents, they do not qualify as terrorism. Both were against low-level targets. It is unclear whether larger water systems would be as vulnerable and unlikely that major airports, which have many redundant systems and which do not rely to the same degree on telephone circuits, could be successfully attacked. Neither attack produced fatalities, injury, or permanent damage. There was little press attention and none of the political or psychological effects desired by terrorists. Terrorism requires overt, public acts of violence that create widespread shock and horror in the minds of opponents. Neither of these incidents (along with any of the thousands of other computer security incidents) had this effect and they cannot be regarded as terrorist acts or threats to national security.

The federal government, usually criticized for exaggeration, took a measured tone in its public pronouncements about the risks of cyber attack during the conflict with Iraq. A February advisory from the National Infrastructure Protection Center issued as tensions over Iraq increased offers a good model for thinking about cyber security. Instead of warning of catastrophic surprise attacks, infrastructure failures, or terrorism, it offered a risk scenario that emphasized "spamming, web defacements, denial of service attacks" and, potentially, computer viruses, and called on network operators to monitor their systems and use "best practices." The absence of cyber attacks [from 1995 to 2003] suggests that it makes sense to call for reasonable measures to safeguard information rather than to warn of potential calamity. It is worth noting that Richard Clarke, the former advisor to the president on cyber security, even went so far as to say in the fall of 2002, "I don't like the word 'cyber terrorism'. . . . We have not seen the traditional terrorist groups using cyberspace for malicious offensive activity.". . .

No Electronic Pearl Harbor Likely

Cyber security analyses would improve if they remembered that the most valuable part of Information Technology is information. Many of the existing analyses that predict "electronic Pearl Harbors" assume that there is a close connection between the physical and the cyber. In most instances, however, this connection seldom exists. Hackers, for example, cannot cause aircraft to fly into each other because there are still pilots and air traffic controllers who do not depend on computers. The real risk of cyber attack lies in the potential to manipulate or gain access to valuable information, e.g., espionage, theft of intellectual property or financial data, and vandalism. This is the area of greatest risk for users of computer networks, not infrastructure attacks, and it is the area cyber security should emphasize.

The dot.com era saw a profusion of concepts and ideas

(remember "give away your content") that, in retrospect, have proven to be unsound and reflective of the larger tech bubble and our enchantment with the wonderful new Internet. In business, most of the gravity defying theorems of the dot.com era have been shelved. Perhaps it is time for security to go through the same process and shelve the concepts of cyber terrorism and electronic Pearl Harbor.

Periodical Bibliography

The following articles have been selected to supplement the diverse views presented in this chapter.

Alex Adrianson	"Stopping Music Piracy Without Breaking the Internet," *Consumer's Research Magazine*, October 2003.
Economist	"Fighting the Worms of Mass Destruction," November 29, 2003.
Mike France	"Striking Back; How the Music Industry Charted Its Crusade Against Web Pirates," *Business Week*, September 29, 2003.
Joshua Green	"The Myth of Cyberterrorism," *Washington Monthly*, November 2002.
Lev Grossman	"It's All Free! Music! Movies! TV Shows! Millions of People Download Them Every Day. Is Digital Piracy Killing the Entertainment Industry?" *Time*, May 5, 2003.
John Horn	"Point and Bet," *Newsweek*, October 28, 2002.
Richard Johnston	"The Battle Against White-Collar Crime," *USA Today*, January 2002.
John W. Kennedy	"Addiction a Click Away," *Christianity Today*, April 2003.
Charles C. Mann	"Heavenly Jukebox," *Atlantic Monthly*, September 2000.
Newsweek	"Now, Weapons of Mass Disruption?" October 29, 2001.
Newsweek	"The Web's Dark Secret," March 19, 2001.
Ira Sager et al.	"The Underground Web," *Business Week*, September 2, 2002.
Christopher H. Schmitt and Joellen Perry	"World Wide Weapon," *U.S. News & World Report*, November 5, 2001.
Jacob Sullum	"Abetting Betting," *Reason*, April 9, 2004.

CHAPTER 3

How Should the Internet Be Regulated?

Chapter Preface

In May 2004 the Supreme Court agreed to resolve conflicting rulings by courts in New York and Michigan over whether states can ban out-of-state companies from shipping wine, beer, and liquor directly to customers. The New York court had ruled that states can ban interstate alcohol shipments, citing the Twenty-first Amendment, which both repealed Prohibition and gave states the right to regulate alcohol within their borders. The Michigan court, on the other hand, ruled that such laws violate the Commerce Clause of the Constitution, which bars states from stifling interstate commerce.

Confusion has reigned in the realm of state-to-state alcohol regulations for decades. But the issue has only now reached the Supreme Court, in large part because of the Internet and online alcohol sales.

Out-of-state vineyard owners had challenged the New York ban on alcohol shipments, arguing that laws requiring alcohol sales to be done through state-regulated distributors were designed for a time when there were far fewer products competing for shelf space. Today there are more than one hundred thousand wine labels in the United States, and vineyard owners argue that only e-commerce can provide consumers with access to so many small wineries.

Defenders of state alcohol regulation, on the other hand, argue that bans on interstate shipping are needed more than ever because of the Internet. They point to the possibility that minors, using an adult's credit card, could order alcohol online. In their view, state laws against direct shipping of alcohol are a legitimate means to prevent underage drinking.

Underage drinking, consumer choice, states' rights, and constitutional law—the issue of how to regulate online alcohol sales is a complex one, and it is just one of many topics that is forcing governments to reevaluate and revise pre-Internet laws. The authors in the following chapters examine several such issues, including online privacy and Internet pornography.

"Consumer participation in cyberspace should not be conditioned on a willingness to relinquish control over one's personal information."

Stronger Internet Privacy Laws Are Necessary

Ernest Hollings

Ernest Hollings is a Democratic senator from South Carolina. The following viewpoint is excerpted from his April 2002 remarks before the Senate, in which he urges his fellow legislators to pass the Online Personal Privacy Act into law. Hollings argues that the act is necessary to ensure that unscrupulous companies will not share the personal information that individuals must provide to Web sites in order to make business transactions online. Hollings argues that companies should be required to adopt security measures regarding personal information and to post clear notices about their information-sharing practices. In addition, much stronger protections for sensitive information such as health records, ethnicity, religious affiliation, sexual orientation, and political affiliation are needed. Hollings believes that providing these privacy protections is not just morally right, but would also ease consumers' fears about the Internet and boost e-commerce.

As you read, consider the following questions:

1. What proportion of the public provides false information on the Internet, according to the author?
2. What are the five core principles of privacy protection, as listed by Hollings?
3. How does Hollings describe the approach to privacy protection taken by the European Union?

Ernest Hollings, address before the U.S. Senate, Washington, DC, April 18, 2002.

Today I rise to introduce bipartisan legislation that will establish baseline requirements for the protection of personal information collected from individuals over the Internet. This bill, the Online Privacy Protection Act, represents the work of many months and important input from consumer groups, affected individuals, and most importantly, many Senators on the Commerce Committee. The origin of this emerging consensus position began to take shape at a Commerce committee hearing last summer [2001] that focused generally on whether there was a need for online privacy legislation. At that time, members of the committee began to articulate the notion that not all personal information is created equal. I agree. Some, highly sensitive personal information, such as personal financial or medical information or a person's religious beliefs are clearly more sensitive than other garden-variety types of information, such as a pair of slacks that an individual may purchase. Since that hearing, and in numerous meetings with members of the Committee, we have worked hard to develop a balanced approach to Internet privacy regulation that recognizes and builds upon best practices in the online community while establishing a federal baseline standard for the protection of individuals' privacy on the Internet. . . .

Consumers' Concerns

Some have argued that Americans' concerns about privacy no longer exist in the aftermath of September 11th. But poll after poll consistently demonstrates that the American people want companies they patronize to seek their permission prior to using their personal information for commercial profit. These concerns are heightened with respect to the Internet, which, in a digital age, enables the seamless compilation of highly detailed personal profiles of Internet users. Accordingly, fears about privacy have had palpable effects on the willingness of consumers to embrace the full potential of the Internet and e-commerce.

Distrust of false privacy promises has sparked a rage of online self-defense, especially the providing of false information by individuals. Industry analysts estimate that between one-fifth to one-third of all individuals provide false personal information on the Internet. This response is understandable given that consumers have few tools to discover whether their personal information is being disclosed, sold, or otherwise misused—and they have virtually no recourse.

Privacy fears are stifling the development and expansion of the Internet as an engine of economic growth. Because of consumer distrust, online companies and services are losing potential business and collecting bad data, blocking the Internet and its wide range of services from reaching its full potential. The lack of enforceable privacy protections is a significant barrier to the full embrace by consumers of the Internet marketplace. According to a recent Harris/Business Week poll, almost two-thirds of non-Internet users would be more likely to use the Net if the privacy of their "personal information and communications were protected." Moreover, according to a recent Forrester study, online businesses lost nearly $15 billion—or 27 percent of e-commerce revenues—due to consumer privacy concerns. Those numbers are significant in light of the economic downturn and its disproportionate impact on the high tech Internet sectors. Good privacy means good business and the Internet economy could use a healthy dose of that right now.

Accordingly, our legislation offers a win-win proposition for consumers and business: it will protect the privacy of individuals online and provide online businesses with a new market of willing customers, while protecting the necessary business certainty of a single federal standard.

The Shortcomings of Industry Self-Regulation

Online companies have long argued that privacy regulations would hamper their ability to efficiently conduct business online and give consumers the tailored buying experience they now expect from the Internet. Online merchants also touted self-regulation as sufficient privacy protection. We know otherwise.

Privacy violations continue to make headlines: a major outcry erupted last year [in 2001] after Eli Lilly disclosed a list of hundreds of customers suffering from depression, bulimia, and obsessive compulsive disorder over the Internet. Moreover, just last week [April 2002] *New York Times* article ("Seek-

The Surveillance Society

A society capable of constant and pervasive surveillance is being rapidly built around us, sometimes with our co-operation, more often without our knowledge. Opinion polls consistently show that the public would prefer more privacy, and is concerned about its erosion. Occasionally there is a burst of publicity about some particularly intrusive new method of data collection. But once the fuss is over, the public acquiesces in the surrender of more information—until the next revelation.

This is what has happened since the terrorist attacks of September 11th 2001. Governments everywhere, not just in the United States, have rushed to expand their powers of surveillance. Even the European Union, which has long been at loggerheads with America about data protection, performed a sharp U-turn, relaxing legal restraints on the collection and use of information by governments. Last June [2002] the EU adopted a new directive to allow member states to require firms to retain data on everyone using mobile phones, landlines, e-mails, chatrooms, the internet or any other electronic device. In America, the USA Patriot Act, passed in the wake of September 11th, made it much easier for the authorities to obtain court permission to monitor internet traffic and obtain wiretaps. The technology to do this is being built into the internet's infrastructure. Campaigners for privacy protection sometimes give the impression that the battle is already lost.

That may be the wrong conclusion. Instead, privacy is likely to become one of the most contentious and troublesome issues in western politics. There will be constant arguments about what trade-offs to make between privacy on the one hand and security, economic efficiency and convenience on the other.

Economist, "No Hiding Place," January 25, 2003.

---

ing Profits, Internet Companies Alter Privacy Policy") recounted how Internet companies such as Yahoo had changed their privacy policies in order to require consumers to restate their privacy preferences even if they had previously withheld consent for the use and commercialization of their personal information. Accordingly, these companies expanded their ability to use an individual's personal information for online and offline marketing purposes notwithstanding that individual's prior policy preferences. Still other businesses confound consumers with opaque privacy policies that begin with, "Your privacy is important to us"—but in the subsequent legalese, outline a series of exceptions crafted with double-negative verbs that allow virtually any use of a consumer's information. Still other commercial web sites fail to post any privacy policy at all, safe in the knowledge that they face virtually no legal jeopardy for selling personal information.

To be fair, some companies have taken consumer privacy seriously. Earthlink launched a national television advertising campaign touting its policy of not selling customer information. U-Haul's web site simply says: "We will never sell or share your information with anyone, or send you junk mail—we hate that stuff, too." Companies like Hewlett Packard, Intel and Microsoft, giants of the high tech industry, already provide individuals opt-in protection with respect to their personal information. But, in the final analysis, despite the best of intentions and some successful efforts, reliance on self-regulation alone has not proven to provide sufficient protection. In its May 2000 Report to Congress, the Federal Trade Commission clearly recognized this shortcoming having studied this issue diligently for five years:

> Because self-regulatory initiatives to date fall short of broad-based implementation of effective self-regulatory programs, the Commission has concluded that such efforts alone cannot ensure that the online marketplace as a whole will emulate the standards adopted by industry leaders . . . The Commission recommends that Congress enact legislation that, in conjunction with continuing self-regulatory programs, will ensure adequate protection of consumer privacy online.

The Online Personal Privacy Act

Our legislation aims to do just that.

Fundamentally, our legislation is built upon the five core principles of privacy protection identified by the Federal Trade Commission in its 1995 report to Congress regarding online privacy—(1) Notice, (2) Consent, (3) Access, (4) Security and (5) Enforcement. Those principles are tried and true and formed the framework for the bipartisan Children's Online Privacy Protection Act of 1998, which was hailed by industry far and wide as a template for protecting children's personal information that is collected on the Internet.

The bill we introduce today takes a singular approach. It divides online personal information into two categories: sensitive information and non-sensitive information. Sensitive information is narrowly tailored to include actual information about specific financial data, health information, ethnicity, religious affiliation, sexual orientation, and political affiliation, or someone's social security number. Non-sensitive information is all other personally identifiable information collected online.

In this respect, the legislation is also similar to the two-tiered approach taken by the European Union in which companies are required to provide baseline protections governing the use of non-sensitive information—and stronger consent protections governing the use of sensitive data. More than 180 American companies—including Staples, Marriott, Microsoft, Intel, Hewlett Packard, DoubleClick, Kodak and Acxiom—doing business in Europe have agreed to provide such protections with respect to the personal data of European citizens. They have signed up for the EU Safe Harbor and their names are listed on the Department of Commerce's web site. Our bill simply asks these and other companies to provide similar protections for U.S. citizens.

Notice and Consent

First, with respect to notice and consent, the bill would require web sites and online services to post clear and conspicuous notice of its information practices. In other words—plainly state to individuals what you plan to do with their personal information. To the extent that a web site collects sensitive information, it would also be required to obtain a consumer's affirmative consent—so-called "opt-in" consent—prior to the collection of such data. To the extent that a web site collects only non-sensitive personal data, it would be able to collect such data for other uses as long as it provides individuals with an ability to "opt out" of such uses and provides the consumer with actual notice at the point of collection—so-called "robust notice"—which briefly and succinctly describes how the information may be used or disclosed.

Many Internet companies are doing this already. For example, on the same page where an individual provides his or her personal information, the web site for 1-800-Flowers states: "You will be receiving promotional offers and materials from

118

us and sites and companies we own. Please check the box below if you DO NOT want to receive such materials in the future and do not wish us to provide personal information collected from you to third parties." Similarly, NBC's web site says the following on the webpage where individuals register their personal information: "As our customer, you will occasionally receive email from shopnbc.com about new services, features, and special offers we believe would interest you. If you'd rather not receive these updates, please uncheck this box." It's as simple as that. And it provides the individual the ability to make an informed choice at the critical point at which he or she is providing a company with personally identifiable information.

Access, Security, and Enforcement

Next, our legislation requires companies to provide individuals with the ability to find out what personal information a web site has collected about them. While important, this right of reasonable access is not unqualified. Rather, it considers a variety of factors including the sensitivity of the information sought by the consumer and the burden and expense on the provider in giving consumers access to their personal information. In addition, the bill would permit online companies to charge individuals a reasonable fee to access their personal data—as is similarly provided under the Fair Credit Reporting Act.

In addition, our bill requires that web sites adopt reasonable security procedures to protect the security, confidentiality, and integrity of personally identifiable information, just as Congress required in the children's privacy legislation.

Moreover, the bill grants consumers important rights of redress. First, the Federal Trade Commission and state attorneys general are empowered to take action. If the FTC collects civil penalties, the bill creates a mechanism whereby those injured can petition to receive up to $200 of the award. For more serious violations involving sensitive information, the bill would additionally permit individuals on their own to pursue redress for damages in federal court.

Finally, in addition to following these fair information principles, the legislation also takes the critical step of establishing a uniform federal standard for online privacy protection by preempting State Internet laws. Inconsistent state regulation of privacy is already causing problems for online businesses. Vermont has adopted "opt-in laws" governing financial and medical privacy. In Minnesota, the state Senate has adopted "opt-in" online privacy legislation by a vote of 96-0. In California, state privacy legislation is again moving through the state legislature, offering the very real possibility that online businesses will sooner rather than later face the prospect of trying to bring their online operation into compliance with inconsistent state laws.

Because new technologies make privacy protection a constantly evolving issue, the bill requires the FTC not only to implement the requirements of the law, but further, to issue periodic reports about how the law is working; whether similar privacy protections should apply offline or to pre-existing data; whether standardized online privacy notices should be developed; if a meaningful safe harbor should be constructed; and whether privacy protection technologies in the marketplace such as P3P can help facilitate the administration of the Act.

Consumer participation in cyberspace should not be conditioned on a willingness to relinquish control over one's personal information. Rather, for the medium to truly flourish, we must establish baseline consumer protections that will eliminate the tyranny of convenience in which consumers are forced to choose between disclosing private, personal information—or not using the Internet at all. Congress has a moral obligation to protect American individual liberties, including the right to better control the commercialization of one's own personal, private information.

This bill is an important first step. The privacy protections in this legislation will instill more confidence in people to use the Internet and create a consistent legal framework for online businesses. It will provide better online privacy protections for consumers, better commercial opportunities for businesses who respond to consumer privacy concerns, and a better future for Americans who will embrace the Internet rather than fear it.

[Editor's note: As of February 2005, the Online Personal Privacy Act has not been passed into law.]

> *"Legislation will never be an adequate or timely deterrent to privacy problems."*

Stronger Internet Privacy Laws Are Unnecessary

Jeremy D. Mishkin

Jeremy D. Mishkin is a lawyer specializing in technology-, Internet-, and First Amendment–related issues. In the following viewpoint, he discusses several significant court cases involving Internet privacy. In each of them, consumers sued because they believed a company had misused personal information that it had collected through its Web site. Mishkin also discusses several of the laws that have been passed to protect online privacy and how they applied to each case. Mishkin predicts that online privacy concerns will only grow as new technologies such as "spyware" are developed to extract individuals' personal information from their computers. However, he does not believe that further legislation is the best solution, since in his view, overly strong laws against information-sharing may actually violate the First Amendment's guarantee of free speech.

As you read, consider the following questions:

1. What company was sued because its Web site's advertisement placed cookies on the computers of people visiting the site?
2. In what European country was a privacy-protection law used to curtail free speech, according to Mishkin?

Jeremy D. Mishkin, "Privacy Online 2.0." Reproduced by permission of Jeremy D. Mishkin, jmishkin@mmwr.com, Partner, Montgomery, McCracken, Walker & Rhoads, LLP.

The "right to privacy" has been around since the early part of the last century. It has evolved to apply—more or less—to a disparate array of social and economic issues, ranging from the desire to avoid publicity (*Time v. Hill*) to abortion (*Roe v. Wade*). The recent explosive growth of Internet use has created its own set of privacy concerns arising from this new medium. By mid-2001, the Federal government already had these major privacy laws on the books:

- Fair Credit Reporting Act
- Privacy Act
- Family Educational Rights and Privacy Act
- Right to Financial Privacy Act
- Privacy Protection Act
- Electronic Communications Privacy Act
- Video Privacy Protection Act
- Employee Polygraph Protection Act
- Telephone Consumer Protection Act
- Health Insurance Portability and Accountability Act
- Driver's Privacy Protection Act
- Identity Theft and Assumption Deterrence Act
- Gramm-Leach-Bliley Act (Title V)
- Children's Online Privacy Protection Act

This laundry list of legislation was in place before the terrorist attacks of September 11, 2001. Until then, debate had centered around what new measures could protect individuals' private information and communications while online. Now, public opinion regarding the primacy of privacy is dramatically different. The principal developments in the law of online privacy in the past twelve months [2002] have involved the government's response to the reality and ongoing threat of terrorism, and the American public's altered attitudes about the proper "balance" between privacy and self-preservation.

How Privacy and Cyberspace Mix

The law of online privacy has focused primarily on users' unhappy experiences with web pages, and how those pages collect and handle information about those who visit them. To understand how these disputes arise, it is important to understand that a web page can, in fact, learn quite a lot about those who click to them, browse through them and interact with them. This can occur even without the knowledge or consent of the visitor to the page. . . .

In response to users' distaste for such surreptitious intelligence-gathering, many web sites now post "Privacy Policies" that are usually accessible on the front page of the site. . . .

Using Privacy Policies, honorable web pages disclose to their visitors when and how they collect private information, as well as what is done with the information thereafter. The concept is simple: say what you do, and do what you say. The execution of that concept, however, has been uneven. Most commonly, a web page asks for a user's name, address and e-mail information in exchange for providing something to the user. More than one naive user has signed up for a "free" goodie by providing his e-mail address to a web page, shortly to find his e-mail box flooded with unsolicited offers, come-ons and outright cons commonly known as "spam." How? The web page has shared his e-mail address with a direct-e-mail marketer. As a way of regaining users' trust, a number of pages go out of their way to promise their visitors that private information would never, ever be disclosed to anyone under any circumstances.

Cyberprivacy in the Courts

Not all web pages proved worthy of such trust. Still others faced unanticipated difficulty in keeping their confidentiality promises. Today's debate about online privacy is framed by some of the most well-known betrayals.

One of the earliest such incidents involved GeoCities, a web site devoted to creating online "communities." In signing up for the privilege of participating, users were asked for a great deal of information about themselves with the express assurance that they would not be used beyond the GeoCities space. Sadly, it turned out that GeoCities actually did use the information, but in a well-publicized Consent Decree with the Federal Trade Commission [FTC] they promised they would not do it again.

Others misbehaved as well. Liberty Financial operated the Young Investors web site, devoted to adolescents and teens. The site included a survey that gathered private information (social security numbers and telephone numbers, for instance), promised prizes for completing it and assured users that "all of your answers will be totally anonymous." In fact, the FTC found that Liberty did not keep the information anonymously and did not even award the prizes it had promised. Liberty entered into a Consent Decree in 1999, promising to (a) stop making false claims about anonymity; (b) post a Privacy Policy; and (c) obtain "verifiable parental consent" before gathering private information from children under 13 years old.

In the Liberty action, the FTC was foreshadowing the requirements of a law that went into effect the following year—the Children's Online Privacy Protection Act ("COPPA"). Under COPPA, a web site that is principally directed towards children under 13 years old must abide by some very strict rules before gathering personal information from users. COPPA requires a much more detailed Privacy Policy and goes further to require a direct notice to the parents, and that the web site operator has "verifiable parental consent" as was done in the Consent Decree with Liberty Mutual. According to the FTC, to be "verifiable" the site must get the parent to send a signed form by mail or fax, a valid credit card, a phone call to "a toll-free telephone number staffed by trained personnel" or an e-mail that contains a digital signature.

[Editor's note: COPPA should not be confused with the Child Online Protection Act (COPA), discussed elsewhere in this chapter.] . . .

"Users" or "Chopped Liver"?

Privacy litigation has also involved technology that is invisible to the user. One of the leading web advertising companies, Doubleclick, places banner ads onto a user's screen when the user browses a particular web site that has sold advertising space. While the user sees what appears to be a single screen, in reality that screen is composed of elements that come from a variety of origins. Doubleclick's service is to place the right ad at the right spot, but it does more than that—it keeps track of what ads a user has already been presented with and the user's responses to those ads by placing a software "cookie" on the user's computer. It therefore builds a database of user profiles and uses them to sell targeted ads. Doubleclick was sued by a purported class of individuals who claimed that Doubleclick invaded their privacy, violated the Electronic Communications Privacy Act ("ECPA"), and the Computer Fraud and Abuse Act ("CFAA") as well.

Asay. © 2000 by Creators Syndicate, Inc. Reproduced by permission.

In a very thorough analysis, Judge Naomi Reice Buchwald granted Doubleclick's Motion to Dismiss. The ECPA claims were dismissed because, the court found, it only protects "users," a word which the statute defines as "any person or entity who (A) uses an electronic communication service and (B) is duly authorized by the provider of such service to engage in such use." Under these facts, the plaintiffs were not the "users" of internet access—the web sites that hired Doubleclick were, and they of course consented. The court noted that "in every practical sense, the cookies identification numbers are internal Doubleclick communications—both 'of' and 'intended for' Doubleclick. In this sense, cookie identification numbers are much akin to computer bar-codes or identification numbers placed on 'business reply cards' found in magazines. These bar-codes and identification numbers are meaningless to consumers, but are valuable to companies in compiling data on consumer responses (e.g., from which magazine did the customer get the card?)." The court found that since the people who were online were not "users," Doubleclick did not violate the ECPA. In a memorable critique of this reasoning, Professor Paul Schwartz asked "so what are the individual consumers, chopped liver?"

Plaintiffs fared no better with their claims under the Computer Fraud and Abuse Act. As the court correctly observed, one of the essential elements for civil recovery under the CFAA is that plaintiffs suffer "damage or loss" in excess of $5,000, consistent with congressional intent to "limit the CFAA to major crimes." Plaintiffs' alleged "damage or loss" included "(1) their cost in remedying their computers after Doubleclick's access and (2) the economic value of their attention (to Doubleclick's advertisements) and demographic information." Neither, in the court's view, was sufficient to meet the statutory threshold. It is clear that the Court's analysis was influenced by the view that users could easily and completely protect themselves from the "cookie monster" (by changing the settings on the browser or e-mailing an opt-out request to Doubleclick). Moreover, the cookies only tracked the user's interaction with other Doubleclick content. The court found that there was no suggestion that Doubleclick had accessed any "files, programs or other information on users' hard drives." Common law privacy claims were therefore dismissed as well. . . .

Current Technology and New Laws

This past year [2002] has also seen the dramatic increase in the use of technology that obtains information directly from a user's computer. "Spyware" is the common name for an application that a user downloads without knowing it—frequently, it is packaged with something the user wants to download, such as a game—and proceeds to send information about the computer system it now inhabits back to whoever programmed it. You can think of Spyware as a cross between a stool pigeon and a homing pigeon. Just as Darwin would have predicted, this new form of computer activity has led to the development of defensive measures that users can employ to protect themselves.

More pervasive, and potentially much more insidious, has been the dramatic growth of "peer-to-peer" systems. So-called "P2P" is the ultimate form of computer networking and file-sharing among PC's, literally allowing one user to access the hard drive of another user's PC. The most quickly-adopted computer application in history—Napster—was nothing more than P2P. As employed by Napster, this technology allowed music files ("MP3"s) to be shared and copied worldwide on a huge scale until that service was shut down as a result of litigation by music publishers. . . . Since then, however, many P2P services have emerged and while music publishers have filed suit against them, the fate of those suits is far less certain due to critical differences in how those services operate. Regardless of who wins the battle over copyright income, the technology itself presents a serious privacy issue for uninformed users. One popular system, Kazaa, was the . . . subject of a recent study that confirmed how easy it is for unscrupulous users to extract private information from others' PCs. And Kazaa itself appears to have been loaded with spyware. . . .

In an increasingly-futile effort to keep up with technology, the U.S. Congress has dozens of new privacy bills pending. Which ones (if any) will become law is guesswork, but one that has attracted a lot of attention is the proposed "Online Personal Privacy Act," . . . sponsored by Senator Hollings. According to the Senator, the "bill mirrors the European Union privacy directive," sets a "uniform, federal standard for the protection of online personal information and codif[ies] the five core privacy protection principles outlined by the Federal Trade Commission: consent, notice, access, security and enforcement." The bill would give consumers the right to choose who may send them e-mail solicitations and would preempt State privacy standards. [As of February 2005, the Online Personal Privacy Act has not been passed into law.] . . .

Is Privacy a Trojan Horse for Violations of the First Amendment?

Paradoxically, the demand for privacy may be one of the most clear and present dangers to the First Amendment since the

Nixon administration. What may be an asserted privacy right to one person could, simultaneously, be a new legal weapon to restrict the free-flow of ideas and comment. This tension was explored in detail by Professor Eugene Volokh, in a review [*Stanford Law Review*] article entitled "Freedom of Speech and Information Privacy: The Troubling Implications of a Right to Stop People From Speaking About You:

> The difficulty is that the right to information privacy—my right to control your communication of personally identifiable information about me—is a right to have the government stop you from speaking about me. We already have a code of "fair information practices," and it is the First Amendment, which generally bars the government from controlling the communication of information (either by direct regulation or through the authorization of private lawsuits), whether the communication is "fair" or not. While privacy protection secured by contract is constitutionally sound, broader information privacy rules are not easily defensible under existing free speech law.

Similarly, scholars are now exploring the societal costs imposed in the name of "privacy." In their article "Putting People First: Consumer Benefits of Information-Sharing," Professors Fred H. Cate and Mich'l E. Staten posit that a reasonable balance between privacy interests and individual preferences is the best approach: "Information-sharing plays a significant role in reducing the prices that consumers pay for goods and services and in expanding the range and affordability of methods of paying for them. Widespread information-sharing provides consumers with unprecedented convenience, and greatly enhances the speed with which decisions can be made and services provided. We tend to take the information infrastructure for granted, until we are faced with the daunting prospect of learning to live without the many benefits that flow from it."

And history teaches that the cause of privacy can quickly be redirected into repression. Ominously, that lesson is being learned again under the banner of the European Union's 1995 Data Protection Directive, which declared privacy to be "a fundamental human right." As reported by Bruce Johnson in "The Battle over Internet Privacy and the First Amendment," [*The Computer & Internet Lawyer*, Volume 18,

No. 4 (April 2001)], the Spanish Ministry of Justice shut down the web site of the Association Against Torture in March 2000, on the grounds that it named the government agents who had been accused of torture or brutality. Spain had passed a broad privacy law, making it a crime to disclose information about someone without their consent. What public figure could resist using such leverage? While the First Amendment would undoubtedly prevent enforcement of such a law in the United States, it illustrates the potential for mischief that can be accomplished under the guise of protecting privacy.

The familiar parade of horribles about the need to protect privacy invariably includes identity theft, credit card fraud and receiving unwanted advertisements. Yet the first two are already illegal under Federal (and many states') laws, and the latter is an annoyance at worst. Proposed legislation will never be an adequate or timely deterrent to privacy problems, since bad actors (and malicious code-writers) are global and they move fast. There are ample laws protecting privacy on the books, and increasingly useful technologies so that users can protect themselves. Moreover, new laws can have unintended consequences that would dramatically limit the freedom of expression. Privacy is valuable, but not more valuable than the First Amendment. The Internet has made everyone a publisher; the right of privacy should not be permitted to make everyone a censor.

"Requiring an adult to present an adult ID or a valid credit card number in order to obtain access to [Internet pornography] is not an unreasonable burden."

The Government Should Regulate Internet Pornography

American Center for Law and Justice

The Child Online Protection Act (COPA) was first passed by Congress in 1998. The law sets criminal penalties for Web site operators who allow children to view pornography. In 1998 and again in 2003, the Supreme Court struck down the law, ruling that it was too vague and too broad. In June 2004 the Supreme Court again heard arguments about the constitutionality of COPA. In the following viewpoint, the American Center for Law and Justice, an advocacy group committed to the defense of Judeo-Christian values, sums up the pro-COPA position. The center argues that COPA is little different than state laws that require pornographic magazines to be kept out of the sight of children. The center also contends that filtering software designed to block access to Internet pornography—which the Court had previously recommended as an alternative to COPA—is ineffective.

As you read, consider the following questions:
1. How would adults be able to access online pornography under COPA, according to the ACLJ?
2. Why is COPA's screening requirement more effective than filtering software, in the authors' view?

American Center for Law and Justice, "Child Online Protection Act Position Paper," www.aclj.org. Reproduced by permission.

The American Center for Law and Justice is committed to the defense of federal statutes restricting online publication of obscenity and child pornography, and the online publication of indecent materials to minors. The Internet is a highly effective, open, unregulated medium of communication with no one agency or government body watching over the content of material made available on the World Wide Web. The Internet is becoming the fastest growing medium for pornography distribution, and some have characterized it as the best hunting ground for pedophiles. In enacting the Child Online Protection Act ("COPA"), Congress demonstrated its constitutionally reasonable judgment that those commercial vendors of indecent materials should bear the costs of insuring that children are not likely to access their wares.

The Child Online Protection Act requires commercial producers of indecent materials to take appropriate measures to insure that minors do not have access to such materials online. COPA authorizes the imposition of criminal and civil penalties on any person who "knowingly and with knowledge of the character of the material, in interstate or foreign commerce by means of the World Wide Web, makes any communication for commercial purposes that is available to any minor and that includes any material that is harmful to minors."

Weak Objections

COPA opponents argue that 1) its definition of "material that is harmful to minors" is not narrowly tailored; 2) its limitation to communications made "for commercial purposes," does not sufficiently narrow COPA's reach; 3) its methods of compliance unconstitutionally burden adult access to protected speech; and 4) filtering software is a less restrictive means to achieve COPA's objective of restricting minors' access to harmful material. Each of these arguments lacks merit.

COPA is narrowly tailored because it applies only to material displayed on the World Wide Web, covers only communications made "for commercial purposes," and restricts only "material that is harmful to minors." COPA's definition of "material that is harmful to minors" parallels the definition of obscenity upheld by the Supreme Court of the United States in *Miller v. California* (1973), and mirrors the statutory language examined and approved by the Court in *Ginsberg v. New York*; therefore, it is consistent with current First Amendment jurisprudence.

Internet Pornography Is Widespread and Troubling

The following charts provide the results of surveys of New Jersey residents conducted by the *Star Ledger* in conjunction with Rutgers University's Eagleton Institute of Politics.

Among weekly home Internet users: "Have you ever encountered pornography by chance when you were browsing the Internet?"

	Yes	No
February 2003 Weekly Internet Users	61%	39%
Gender:		
Male	68	32
Female	52	48
Age:		
18 to 29	80	20
30 to 49	66	34
50 and older	38	62

Star Ledger/Eagleton-Rutgers Poll, February 23, 2003, http://slerp.rutgers.edu.

In targeting communications made for "commercial purposes," COPA is modeled after state laws that require local stores to place pornographic material that is harmful to minors behind blinder racks, in sealed wrappers, or in opaque covers. Courts of appeals and state courts consistently have upheld those state display laws on the ground that they further the government's compelling interest in shielding minors from material that would impair their psychological and moral development, without imposing an unreasonable burden on adults who seek access to such material. COPA is constitutional for the same reasons.

No Threat to Free Speech

Furthermore, COPA provides "an affirmative defense to prosecution" for businesses that restrict access by minors to harmful material by requiring use of a credit card or an adult ID. That defense allows adults to obtain access to this speech, while protecting minors from material that is harmful to them. The claim that COPA's requirements, such as the age verification, are too burdensome to the right of adults to access pornography on the Internet is a weak one. Requiring an adult to present an adult ID or a valid credit card number in order to obtain access to harmful material is not an unreasonable burden. The alleged burden which COPA places on commercial websites and its patrons should be viewed no differently than those imposed at the state level, requiring a grocery store, for example, to shield indecent magazines from unsuspecting minor patrons. At worst, COPA's requirements create a slight inconvenience; requiring adults to verify their age to access indecent online materials does not rise to the level of an unconstitutional burden.

COPA opponents also portray as a constitutional crisis the possibility that some adults will be deterred or too embarrassed to pursue the material beyond these age verification screens. Given the known risks posed to children, it is altogether appropriate that the adult users and the Web site operators should bear the relatively minor burden associated with keeping harmful material away from minors.

Filters Are Inadequate

Finally, the use of filters and/or blocking software, although less restrictive, is not an effective method for achieving the government's compelling interest in protecting children from the dangers of pornography on the Internet. As applied to commercial Websites that display harmful material as a regular course of their businesses, COPA's screening requirement is far more effective because COPA *compels* persons who display material on the Web to take steps to prevent minors from obtaining access to material that is harmful to them. In addition, blocking software is not without its deficiencies. Filters can block inoffensive materials while failing to screen other, offensive materials. Computer-savvy minors can easily defeat such filtering programs. And filtering software is not cheap to buy, or cheap to maintain. Furthermore, because the content of the Internet is ever-changing, it is virtually impossible for blocking software and filtering technology to keep up.

Because of the care taken by Congress, COPA is, in fact, the least restrictive means to accomplish the compelling interest in protecting minors from the harm associated with exposure to indecent materials on the World Wide Web. The requirements imposed by COPA will not destroy the Internet. The measures prescribed by COPA do not trench upon the rights guaranteed by the First Amendment. COPA simply places a reasonable restriction on access to commercially marketed indecency to prevent access to such materials by minors.

"*[The Child Online Protection Act] is vague, overly broad and would subject thousands of legitimate Web operations to malicious or frivolous prosecution.*"

The Government Should Not Criminalize Internet Pornography

Mike Himowitz

Mike Himowitz is a columnist for the *Baltimore Sun*. In the following viewpoint, he discusses the Supreme Court's June 2004 ruling on the Child Online Protection Act (COPA), in which the Court decided that the law—which would impose criminal penalties on Web site operators that allow minors to access pornographic material—is a violation of the First Amendment right to free speech. The Court also suggested that filtering software that blocks access to certain Web sites is a better solution to the problem of Internet pornography. Himowitz supports the Court's ruling, arguing that filtering technology is providing parents with the means to control what their children see. This technology, Himowitz concludes, makes COPA-style government regulation unnecessary.

As you read, consider the following questions:
1. What does the V-chip do, as described by the author?
2. Why is filtering software preferable to COPA, according to Anthony M. Kennedy, as quoted by Himowitz?

Like most First Amendment watchers, I was relieved this week [in June 2004] when the Supreme Court once again blocked enforcement of a bad law with good intentions—the Child Online Protection Act [COPA].

The 1998 legislation, which has been challenged since its inception and never enforced, would impose harsh fines and jail terms on Web site operators who allow minors access to material deemed "harmful" under "contemporary community standards."

The law—Congress' second attempt to protect children from online porn via legislation—is vague, overly broad and would subject thousands of legitimate Web operations to malicious or frivolous prosecution, without diminishing the flow of porn from one of its major sources—overseas Web sites. So it not only threatens civil liberties—it's unlikely to work.

The challenge to COPA by the American Civil Liberties Union was joined by a broad coalition of publishers, online rights groups and Web site operators. A federal court in Philadelphia blocked enforcement of the act pending a trial on its merits. This week's decision didn't settle the issue—it doesn't declare COPA unconstitutional—but affirms the lower court's 1999 decision to keep the act in abeyance until the issue is ultimately decided.

Parents' Responsibility

But the court's narrow 5-4 majority opinion suggested strongly that commercial Web filtering software—available to all parents for a few dollars and greatly improved since the law was enacted—represents a far less restrictive solution to the problem than broad criminal legislation.

As a civil libertarian, I have to agree. The question is whether parents are willing to step up and take on that responsibility. Their track record isn't good.

Consider the V-chip. Under a 1997 Federal Communications Commission order, every television with a screen bigger than 13 inches made since January 1, 2000, has been equipped with one of these devices, which allows parents to block shows containing objectionable content—sex, bad language or violence—under a rating system established by the television industry.

The V-chip isn't that hard to use, and the ratings, if not perfect, are at least understandable. But the instructions for setting V-chip filters are usually buried deep in a manual that most buyers ignore. And how many parents want to dig into their TV set's setup screen to turn off the chip whenever they want to watch a show that's not suited for kids?

As a result, almost nobody uses it.

So the V-chip is the perfect example of a content filtering system that's universally available—at least in newer TVs—and only minimally intrusive. If you don't have kids, you can ignore it completely. But controlling youngsters' exposure to sex and violence obviously is not important enough for most parents to spend even the minimal time it takes to punch a few buttons on the remote control. And that's disturbing.

ClearPlay's DVD Filters

Of course, consider what's happening to parents who are interested—and want to clean up the movies their kids watch. Several years ago, a Utah-based company called ClearPlay (www.clearplay.com) began marketing a technology that applies electronic "filters" to commercial DVDs.

ClearPlay's employees have screened hundreds of movies for instances of objectionable material in 14 categories, including sex, nudity, profanity, extreme violence and blasphemy. The company's filters bleep out whatever mix of naughty audio and video Mom and Dad want to keep away from the kids.

The results range from barely noticeable to ridiculous, especially with raunchier titles. But parents get what they want, and the original DVD remains intact. ClearPlay makes its money by selling downloadable filters—$1.50 per title or $49 a year for its entire catalog.

As long as the filters' use was limited to DVD drives installed in computers, ClearPlay's appeal and impact were limited. But a few weeks ago the first standalone ClearPlay DVD player arrived on the shelves at Wal-Mart for $70, turning the system into a cheap, mass-market item.

Hollywood was aghast from the outset. The Directors Guild of America, eight major studios and a who's who of directors filed a federal lawsuit against the firm in Colorado two years ago [in 2002], claiming copyright infringement because ClearPlay alters the content of films without the creators' consent.

The filmmakers say they don't object in principle to releasing cleaned-up versions of films for audiences—they do it for airlines all the time. They just want control, or approval, of the process—instead of having it done by some guy they've never heard of (and who makes a few bucks that the studios can't touch).

Why COPA Is Unconstitutional

COPA raises major constitutional problems in the following ways:

• It imposes serious burdens on constitutionally-protected speech. . . .

• It fails to effectively serve the government's interest in protecting children, as it will not effectively prevent children from seeing inappropriate material originating from outside of the US available through other Internet resources besides the World Wide Web, such as chat rooms or email.

• It does not represent the least restrictive means of regulating speech, according to the Supreme Court's own findings that blocking and filtering software might give parents the ability to more effectively screen out undesirable content without burdening speech.

"Child Online Protection Act—Overview," Center for Democracy and Technology Web site, www.cdt.org/speech/copa.

After fruitless negotiations with Hollywood, the filter-makers got their allies in Congress to introduce the Family Movie Act, which would pre-empt the lawsuit and protect filtering technology from copyright infringement claims as long as the original work isn't altered and its use is limited to the home—as opposed to movie theaters.

"Parents should be able to mute or skip over anything they want if they feel it's in the interest of their children," Representative Lamar Smith, a Texas Republican and chief sponsor, said at a June 17 [2004] hearing on the bill. "And as a practical matter, parents cannot monitor their children's viewing habits all the time. They need an assist."

To which Representative Howard L. Berman, a California

Democrat who represents the Hollywood area, replied, "Technology should not become an excuse for avoiding the hard work of parenting."

Technology Can Empower Parents

It would be a good idea if the two sides settled out of court and out of Congress. But it seems to me that ClearPlay has the right idea. Even though you or I might disagree with their choices, parents deserve to control what their children see, and if technology can help without infringing on anyone else's right to see an uncut version of a film, that's fine.

Likewise, I have to agree with [Supreme Court] Justice Anthony M. Kennedy's argument . . . that Internet porn filtering is preferable because it imposes "selective restrictions on speech at the receiving end, not universal restrictions at the source."

Those "universal restrictions" are the easy way out for lawmakers, and that's why so many attempts to legislate restrictions on freedom of expression scare me. I believe that the authors of the Bill of Rights were being serious, if not literal, when they started the First Amendment with the words, "Congress shall make no law . . ."

On the other hand, as a parent, I understand the anger many feel when they see their kids bombarded with sexual messages and images.

The problem is that if parents don't take matters into their own hands, Congress will come up with a law that's almost as bad as COPA but that satisfies one more justice—and puts all our liberties in danger.

"[My e-mail] in-box, like so many others, is . . . bursting—most depressingly with porn, and with sick porn, and most alarmingly with enticements to child porn."

The Government Should Ban E-Mail Spam

Jay Nordlinger

Jay Nordlinger is managing editor of the *National Review*, a conservative political magazine. In the following viewpoint, he argues that unsolicited e-mail, or "spam," is a serious problem that warrants government intervention. He describes how many e-mail users receive dozens of unsolicited e-mails each day, many of them containing obscene subject lines and pornographic images. Most disturbingly, he writes, many of these e-mails advertise child pornography. Nordlinger contends that most people are embarrassed by these pornographic e-mails and prefer not to talk about the problem. However, he argues that a law against e-mail spam is needed, both because spam wastes computer resources and because much of it promotes child sexual abuse.

As you read, consider the following questions:

1. Approximately how many child pornography sites are on the Internet, according to the author?
2. What is the biggest anti-spam group, in Nordlinger's view?
3. Why should anti-spam legislation be "content-neutral," in the author's opinion?

It's a disgusting topic, and one that most people would rather turn away from—which is just how the pornographers like it, of course. They would rather we just shuddered and threw up our hands. This goes for all pornography, but I am concerned for the moment with the kind that arrives by e-mail, cluttering and blighting your in-box.

How's your e-mail been lately? Mine's been pretty foul. I get between five and ten porno e-mails a day. Others get upwards of 50—through no fault of their own, mind you. Let me provide some choice recent samples from my in-box. This isn't "nice" porn; it isn't pretty ladies and men posing on European beaches. It's sick stuff, with a very heavy emphasis on children, incest, and bestiality.

Child Pornography on the Internet

One e-mail has on the subject line, "Family." And inside: "Incest at Its Finest. Grandparents give grandkids sex lessons. Dad & Daughter. Young girl cannot control her urges." One e-mail address is "teeniesuckathon." Another e-mail has on its subject line, "Sorry about the late Christmas gift" (this came in early January). Inside: "Girls F***ing Animals After School" and "Teen Sluts Covered in Sperm." Another e-mail informs, "We have selected a list of the 25 best pay sites in the preteen industry."

Note "preteen": In all likelihood, this is no idle boast, as anyone in the anti-child-porn field will tell you. Preteen means preteen. And that is not only abhorrent, but illegal—a crime.

A great many people are embarrassed about being the mere recipient of these e-mails. They're apt to think they've done something wrong: that they perhaps were on a naughty site, and thus ensnared for all time. And if they squawk about the porn they're receiving, others might say, "Gee, why are you so interested? Turn you on a little, huh?" (Anti-porn activists get this frequently.) Some people are also afraid of being thought prudish or illiberal if they complain about porn: These things are part of the big, wicked world, and there's the Bill of Rights, of course.

But it bears repeating: Child porn is illegal, and so, for that matter, is "obscenity," whose definition is a lot less slippery than some people think, or than some interested parties pretend. Many people want to do more than "just hit delete" ("JHD," as Internetters put it). If the material is sufficiently bad—particularly when it involves children—they want to do something, not just sit there helpless. And they can.

What Citizens Can Do

For one thing, they can contact the National Center for Missing and Exploited Children in Washington. Four years ago, the center set up what they call the Cyber Tip Line, found at www.cybertipline.com. There a concerned citizen can make a report. He can say, "I found something fishy. Looks like it involves kids. Here it is—please check it out." People can also go directly to a Justice Department website, www.usdoj.gov/criminal/ceos/report.htm, where further information on reporting child porn is available. No one has to sit helpless, if he doesn't want to.

At the National Center, there are not only the outfit's own staff but federal agents from the Postal Service, Customs, and the FBI. All of these scour the Internet and deal with citizen tips. According to John Rabun, chief operating officer of the center, the more tips about one site—or one "spammed" e-mail—the better. "It's the old squeaky-wheel thing." Law enforcement is making plenty of arrests off the tips; the center has been receiving about 900 a week. But the arrests, says Rabun, constitute just a drop in the bucket—which is better than nothing at all, of course.

One citizen who is very definitely "on the case" is Julie Posey, a homemaker in Colorado. She's a heroine of the anti-child-exploitation movement, its archangel, or avenging angel, its Joan of Arc. When you read about her and talk with her, you think, "They should really make a movie about her." And they are: A company has just bought the rights to her story.

Julie Posey's role in life is to monitor the Internet looking for the abuse of children, sniffing out the pedophiles who lurk there. Her entire operation is detailed and resident at www.pedowatch.org. "My mission," she says on her site, "is to protect children online from the predators who abuse them. I do this by receiving tips from people on the Internet about suspicious activity that they have found and following up on the information. I then identify the suspects involved and pass the information along with all evidence to law enforcement for further investigation." Her work has led to more than 20 arrests and convictions. Nothing gives her more satisfaction than to see a pedophile hauled away. The average pedophile, she says, will rape or otherwise molest 200 children in his "career." Every time she busts someone, or leads to that bust, she thinks, "Well, that's X number of children saved from that particular pedophile." The drops in the bucket add up. . . .

Percentage of Spam in Personal and Workplace Inboxes on a Typical Day

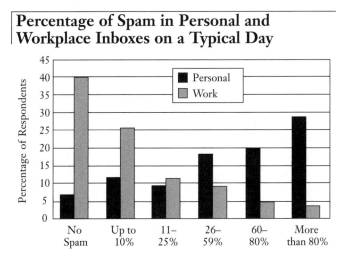

Percentage of Spam in Inbox

Deborah Fallows, *Spam: How It Is Hurting E-Mail and Degrading Life on the Internet*, Pew Internet and American Life Project, October 22, 2003.

Child porn has exploded in recent years. Never has there been so much of it; never has it been so widely disseminated. There are at least 100,000 child-porn sites—not just pornographic sites, mind you, but sites devoted entirely to child porn. The demand for the stuff seems insatiable. As you investigate these matters, it seems bad enough that there are countless producers and purveyors of child porn—but then it hits you that there are many more countless consumers of it. One's neighbors, presumably. The problem is far larger than the average person imagines; law enforcement and activists sometimes have to fight incredulity.

Pornographic E-Mail Spam

Much of the porn is circulated via "spam," which is the slang term for (the more formal) "unsolicited commercial e-mail," or UCE. Spam is a bear to combat. There are many "filter" systems, but they work imperfectly. Once you're on a list, it can be impossible to "unsubscribe"; they make you jump through hoops, and by the time you spend a couple of minutes on it, you may be no better off. It's rather futile to "block" offensive addresses too, because pornographers—and other spammers, of course—just switch to another address. Porn—and, again, spam generally—can get so bad, you quit your account and acquire a new one. But the new one, too, can quickly get spoiled and overrun with spam. Some people—including Julie Posey—report that, when they start a new account, the porn spam begins arriving within 24 hours. . . .

Then there's the question of spam at large: Ban it? Try to ban certain types of it? Many states have anti-spam laws, but these tend to be ineffective, and anti-spam activists claim that a strong, clear federal law is needed—similar to the one, now ten years old, that prohibits "spam" by fax. There have been many bills proposed in Congress, coming from both liberal Democrats and conservative Republicans, and from those in between. None has so far come to fruition. One of the bills, the project of Senator Conrad Burns of Montana, is called "The Can Spam Act."

Of the anti-spam groups, perhaps the biggest and best organized is the Coalition Against Unsolicited Commercial Email (found at www.cauce.org). They have branches in several countries, and sport the slogan, "Take back your mailbox!" Many libertarians, of course, are opposed to legislation against spam. The Cato Institute's Clyde Wayne Crews Jr., in a white paper, summarizes, "At bottom, spam legislation kicks open the door to further regulation of business communications." It would "create incentives for enforcers to go on 'spam hunts,' looking for evil embedded in every e-mail." And it "would have significant implications for anonymous speech—a cornerstone of our Republic."

A Conservative Argument for Government Regulation

Yet others counter that spam ought to be banned on precisely free-market principles, including property rights. Matthew Mitchell, an Internet investigator and anti-spammer in Philadelphia, says, "Spamming is theft of services, just as if someone came into your office and insisted on using your copier to print his advertisements." Though spammers "like to invoke the mantra of private enterprise and small businesses," he continues, "spam hurts many businesses," costing them time, money, and aggravation (the same things it costs an individual). In Mitchell's view, any anti-spam legislation should be "content-neutral," banning it altogether, pornography or no pornography. Otherwise, First Amendment issues may come into play. This, he says, is what makes the law against fax ads formidable.

A Hooters restaurant in Augusta, Georgia, knows this well. We at *National Review*, editorially, cited the Hooters case as an especially egregious example of American litigiousness. A man got together a class-action suit against the restaurant after receiving some faxes offering discounts off food. A jury awarded a $12 million judgment against the restaurant—which promptly filed for bankruptcy. Junk faxes are verboten. Send me a coupon for buffalo wings, and you could find yourself out millions. Yet you can apparently stuff my e-mail in-box to bursting with impunity.

And that in-box, like so many others, is, indeed, bursting—most depressingly with porn, and with sick porn, and most alarmingly with enticements to child porn. Inertia, confusion, and embarrassment, as always, are the pornographer's friends. It's encouraging to know that some brave and generous-hearted people—like Julie Posey and the staff of the National Center for Missing and Exploited Children—are on the case. But they could use some help.

[Editor's note: The CAN-SPAM Act, which includes criminal penalties for senders of unlawful marketing e-mail and requires special warnings for pornographic messages, was passed by Congress in 2003 and went into effect on January 1, 2004.]

"Regulating communications isn't something to be done lightly."

The Government Should Not Ban E-Mail Spam

Clyde Wayne Crews Jr.

Clyde Wayne Crews Jr. is vice president for regulatory policy and director of technology studies at the Competitive Enterprise Institute. In the following viewpoint, he argues that, in trying to address the problem of unsolicited commercial e-mail, or "spam," the government should not pass overly broad restrictions on commercial communications. Writing in May 2003, Crews discusses the federal CAN-SPAM Act, which went into effect on January 1, 2004, and argues that its provisions will do little to control spam but may have harmful effects on Internet speech. Rather than turning to government regulation, Crews believes that individuals should use e-mail filtering software and other technologies to combat the problem of unwanted spam.

As you read, consider the following questions:

1. Why does Crews feel that the ability to send anonymous e-mails should be protected?
2. What are some of the technological solutions to the problem of spam, according to Crews?

Unsolicited commercial junk e-mail, or "spam," is a huge problem. Especially the porn; I have to shoo my kids out of the room when I check my e-mail. But junk legislation offered up to presumably solve the problem can make things worse.

Last week [May 2003], Senator Charles Schumer, D-N.Y., proposed a law that would impose subject-line labeling requirements for commercial e-mail (it would have to say "ADV" [to indicate an advertisement]); forbid concealing one's identity; mandate an "unsubscribe" mechanism; ban the use of software capable of collecting e-mails from the Internet; set up stiff noncompliance fines; and establish an expensive (and likely hackable and thus worse-than-useless) Do-Not-Spam list at the Federal Trade Commission. [In June 2004 the FTC reported to Congress that creation of a Do-Not-Spam list would be unlikely to reduce the amount of spam consumers receive.] Of course, politicians exempt themselves as possible offenders under anti-spam legislation, remaining free to send us junk campaign material.

The downside to an Internet in which you can contact anyone is that anyone can contact you. Spammers pay no postage or long-distance charges. The solution is to shift those costs back to the spammer; the question is whether to do that legislatively or technologically.

Plainly, peddling fraudulent merchandise or impersonating somebody else (such as a person or organization like AOL) in the e-mail's header information should be punished, as should breaking an agreement made with an Internet service provider that prohibits bulk mailing.

The Threat to Legitimate Mass E-Mail

But in the debate over the outpouring of spam, it's important to avoid unintentionally stifling beneficial e-commerce. Regulating communications isn't something to be done lightly. If a law merely sends the most egregious spammers offshore to continue hammering us, that may simply create legal and regulatory hassles for small businesses trying to make a go of legitimate e-commerce or for mainstream companies that are not spammers. Commercial e-mail, even if unsolicited, may be welcome if the sender is a business selling legal and legitimate products in a non-abusive manner.

As the market works to shift costs of commercial e-mail back to the sender, we must guard against legislative confusion in approaches like Schumer's: How might the definition of "spam" expand beyond "unsolicited" and "commercial" e-mail?

The Problem of Enforcement

None of the anti-spam laws passed so far has been effective, and that's not likely to change. Lots of spam includes opt-out instructions that don't work; the key is getting businesses to honor them. A do-not-mail registry would double as a free address registry for spammers based offshore. And requiring a physical address for the sender would, like any mandated identification system, make anonymous speech on the Net illegal. Just about everyone is against spam, but most people are for anonymous speech and its ability to let whistleblowers and other vulnerable people speak their minds. Existing and proposed legislation seriously threatens anonymity, raising legitimate worries about censorship.

The ultimate problem with legislation is that spam is a global problem, not a state or federal one. A patchwork of conflicting laws will do nothing to improve the ease of use of e-mail communications. None of the laws so far passed have diminished the amount of spam flooding the Net. Lawrence Lessig, a Stanford law professor and the author of *Code and Other Laws of Cyberspace*, believes the problem is enforcement, and his proposal is for the government to pay a bounty to any geek who can track down and identify a spammer. He's even offered to quit his job if this scheme is tried for a year and fails.

Wendy M. Grossman, "The Spam Wars," *Reason*, November 2003.

What about unsolicited political or nonprofit bulk e-mailings, press releases, resume blasts and charitable solicitations? What about newsletters that contain embedded ads? Or what about one's personal e-mail signature line with a link back to one's employer? That's a subtle solicitation, whether we admit it or not. At the very least, unwise legislation would create serious headaches for noncommercial e-mailers like nonprofit groups. Would pop-up ads become suspect in the aftermath of spam legislation? They're not e-mail, but they are unsolicited and commercial.

The Threat to Anonymous Free Speech

Finally, legal bans on false e-mail return addresses, as well as bans on software capable of hiding such information, have worrisome implications for free speech and anonymity for individuals—and will be ignored by spammers anyway. Well-meaning individuals can use "spamware" to create the contemporary version of the anonymous flyers that have played such an important role in our history. Individuals should retain the ability to safeguard their anonymity even with (or perhaps especially with) a mass communications tool like e-mail. In an era in which so many people are concerned about online privacy, a law that impedes a technology that can protect such privacy would be curious indeed.

Smarter approaches to the spam epidemic include better e-mail filtering, such as setting the owner's screen to receive only from recognized and approved e-mail addresses. That's particularly appropriate for children's e-mail accounts. Emerging "handshake" or "challenge and response" systems capable of totally blocking spam show promise: Because the most offensive spam is sent by automatic bulk-mailing programs that aren't capable of receiving a reply, spam no longer appears in the inbox.

Identifiers or "seals" for trusted commercial e-mail could be another means of helping ISPs block unwanted e-mail. A new consortium—including AOL, Microsoft and Yahoo—to establish "certified" e-mail would bolster this approach.

Given the perfectly understandable desire to stop unsolicited e-mail, it is all too easy for Congress to undermine legitimate commerce, communications and free speech. And crippling Internet commerce would be especially pointless if spam continued pouring in from overseas. A better target is junk press conferences, like the one at which Schumer announced his bill. $25,000 fine, at least.

Periodical Bibliography

The following articles have been selected to supplement the diverse views presented in this chapter.

Stephen Baker   "The Taming of the Internet," *Business Week*, December 15, 2003.

William Beaver   "The Dilemma of Internet Pornography," *Business & Society Review*, Fall 2000.

Economist   "No Hiding Place," January 25, 2003.

Economist   "Stop Signs on the Web: The Battle Between Freedom and Regulation on the Internet," January 13, 2001.

James Fallows   "Can the Net Govern Itself?" *American Prospect*, March 27, 2000.

Simson Garfinkel   "Privacy and the New Technology," *Nation*, February 28, 2000.

David Gelernter   "Will We Have Any Privacy Left?" *Time*, February 21, 2000.

Wendy Kaminer   "Porn Again," *American Prospect*, July 1, 2002.

Lawrence Lessig   "Innovation, Regulation, and the Internet," *American Prospect*, March 27, 2000.

Toby Lester   "Reinvention of Privacy," *Atlantic Monthly*, March 2001.

Aaron Lukas   "Should Internet Sales Be Taxed?" *USA Today*, January 2001.

Pamela Paul   "The Porn Factor," *Time*, January 19, 2004.

Brad Stone   "Soaking in Spam," *Newsweek*, November 24, 2003.

Chris Taylor   "Spam's Big Bang!" *Time*, June 16, 2003.

Jonathan Wallace   "Preserving Anonymity on the Internet," *USA Today*, November 2000.

Shyla Welch   "Should the Internet Be Regulated?" *World & I*, February 1998.

CHAPTER 4

What Will Be the Future of the Internet?

Chapter Preface

Numerous, and often conflicting, predictions about the Internet fall in and out of vogue each year. But since the mid-1990s, one prediction has been repeated again and again, gaining near-universal acceptance: The Internet of the future will be wireless. "By 2010," writes *Futurist* editor David Pearce Snyder, "80% to 90% of all Internet access will be made from Web-enabled phones, PDAs [personal digital assistants], and wireless laptops."

Technical issues made wireless Internet technology relatively expensive until 1997, when a new wireless Internet standard called "Wi-Fi" (a twist on the term "hi-fi," which is short for "high fidelity") was published. As Steven Levy explains in *Newsweek*, "Apple Computer seized on the idea as a consumer solution, others followed and now Wi-Fi is as common as the modem once was." "Homes, offices, colleges and schools around the world have installed Wi-Fi equipment to blanket their campuses with wireless access to the Internet," write the editors of the *Economist*.

Wi-Fi is a short-range technology, however. Many wireless enthusiasts argue that truly mobile Internet access will be achieved through mobile-telephone networks, using a technology known simply as "third generation," or 3G. In their view, text messaging and camera phones are just the beginning of mobile phones' evolution.

Regardless of which specific technology prevails, writes the *Economist*'s David Manasian,

> The power of computing and communications looks set to continue to grow, and its price to fall, at a steady rate for the next few decades. . . . We are heading toward a networked society of ubiquitous, mobile communications. . . . Whether this arrives in 20, 30 or 40 years really does not matter. The point is that the destination seems not merely plausible, but probable, so it is not too soon to ask: What do we want this technology to do?

The authors in the following chapter explore how the wireless, ubiquitous Internet of the future will affect daily life and society.

"The earliest claims of cyber-dreamers—that the internet will produce a shift of power away from political elites to ordinary citizens—may well become reality."

The Internet Will Empower Individuals

Economist

The *Economist* is a weekly magazine of business and politics. The editors of the *Economist* argue in the following viewpoint that, for millions of people, the Internet serves as a powerful medium through which to express their views. The *Economist* argues that the Internet will hasten the shift from representative democracy—in which the public elects leaders (such as congressmen) to decide issues for them—to direct democracy—in which the public votes on policy issues themselves. The authors note that there are potential drawbacks to direct democracy but conclude that, for better or worse, the Internet will give individuals a stronger voice in government and society.

As you read, consider the following questions:

1. How many states have a provision for some form of direct ballot, according to the authors?
2. What is the biggest obstacle to director democracy, in the *Economist*'s view?
3. In the authors' view, what is the main criticism that opponents of direct democracy will face?

In the early, heady days of the internet, many of its most zealous proponents expected cyberspace to transform the political landscape. Autocratic governments, they thought, would be scuppered by their inability to control the free flow of information. That could yet happen. But cyber-optimists' hopes were even higher for established democracies, where they saw the internet restoring the electorate's civic engagement. Citizens would no longer have to rely on information spoon-fed by politicians, but be able to find out for themselves. Eventually, people would vote directly from the comfort of their own homes. The political apathy which has spread through western countries in recent decades would be reversed. Democracy would be rejuvenated, at last achieving its original meaning of "power of the people".

Judging by the most obvious political effects of the internet, so far this has not happened. Established democratic governments have published enormous amounts of information on the internet and moved towards the electronic delivery of some services, but this does not seem to have made much of a difference to the conduct of politics. The structures of democratic government remain intact. Political parties and candidates have set up websites and flooded voters with e-mails. But internet campaigns, according to most studies, have appealed to the same band of already committed voters who are also reached through letter boxes and by knocking on doors. Broadcast advertising still dominates campaign spending.

Governments in Britain and the United States have conducted experiments with electronic voting in real campaigns. A number of European countries are also planning trials. Some experiments have produced a rise in voter turnout, as hoped, but most have not. On the whole, the internet seems to have had remarkably little impact on mainstream politics.

That will not remain true for much longer. Communication is the lifeblood of politics, and every big change in communication technology, from the printing press to television, has eventually produced big, and often unexpected, changes in politics. As the internet becomes mobile and ubiquitous, it will bring about changes of its own. Precisely what these will be is not yet clear, but the earliest claims of cyber-dreamers—

that the internet will produce a shift of power away from political elites to ordinary citizens—may well become reality. One of the big political debates of the next three decades will be about the relative merits of direct versus representative democracy.

A Different Kind of Politics

Indeed, it has already got under way. In a recent book, "Democratic Phoenix: Reinventing Political Activism", Pippa Norris, a political scientist at the Kennedy School of Government at Harvard, rejects the conventional view that there has been a pervasive decline in political participation in western democracies. Voter turnout and membership of political parties may have declined in some countries, she concedes, but much more political activity is now being channelled through single-issue, grass-roots organisations and expressed by means of "protest politics", such as petitions, demonstrations and consumer boycotts. This trend was well established before the internet, but the web's arrival has accelerated it. The ability to organise, proselytise and communicate at low cost has been a huge boost to such groups, be it a locally based effort to block an airport expansion or a global environmental campaigner such as Greenpeace.

Joining in a protest or a web discussion is not the same as stuffing envelopes for a big political party, but it is political participation nevertheless. According to Ms Norris, survey evidence shows that this kind of protest politics is particularly strong among the well-educated managerial and professional classes in post-industrial societies, and that it is no longer confined to the young. In other words, the bulk of those who are organising themselves on the internet and engaging in "direct action" politics are not anarchists or anti-globalisation protesters, but the kind of people who join political parties and are most likely to vote.

The growth of "protest" politics is not the only evidence for a slowly mounting demand for direct democracy. Over the past few decades, the popularity of direct voting by electorates has sharply increased. Through a variety of mechanisms—local and national referendums, initiatives placed on the ballot by citizens, and advisory votes—governments are now consulting their electorates directly.

Not all such plebiscites are respectable. When Saddam Hussein pushed up the proportion of voters approving his rule from 99.96% to 100% in [2002] referendum, the rest of the world could only laugh at the sick joke. But such manipulation does not invalidate the device itself, properly used. Referendums have helped establish popular approval for new constitutions in eastern Europe, accompanied the periodic reforms of the European Union, sometimes with surprising and awkward results, and have been embraced even by Britain, a country with a strong tradition of parliamentary sovereignty.

Vote Often

In Switzerland, where various forms of direct democracy have long been an integral feature of government, the number of direct ballots has climbed sharply in recent decades. The same is true in the United States, where direct votes of one kind or another have been used since colonial times. Since 1980 there have been more than 600 state-wide direct votes, and thousands more at city and county level. Twenty-seven American states now have a provision for some form of direct ballot. In some states, such as California, Oregon and Colorado, voters face a slate of referendums every year.

Moreover, public-opinion polling has become endemic in most democracies, with politicians, political parties, the media and even governments continually conducting polls to gauge opinion. Instant, and blatantly unscientific, polls have become a regular feature of news shows and websites. Even that most passive of all media, broadcast television, has spawned scores of websites where couch potatoes passionately debate popular shows such as "The Sopranos" or "Buffy the Vampire Slayer". These sites are now monitored by television producers to see how audiences are reacting, episode by episode.

In modern societies, in other words, the public is now accustomed to being consulted regularly, and when most people get the chance, they like expressing their view on anything under the sun. Although representative democracy is the basic structure of all western governments, it is accompanied today by a penumbra of direct popular control.

Time for People to Make Decisions on Their Own

With the advent of the Internet, Direct Democracy's time has finally come. It is time for people to make decisions on their own. . . .

Ever since the dawn of the Internet, people have been making decisions on it. In fact, it's been those very decisions which caused the Internet to take the shape it did. The model of free decision making which the Internet follows is the precise model which brought freedom of communication and expression to the world. What's more, it didn't happen in the centuries that other methods of decision making take to produce political change—the web is only ten years old. That's right—by collaborating over the net, we can progress at a phenomenal rate. The very fact that local laws of countries have been unable to keep up with the internet's rate of change proves that it is a superior system—one that can adapt to new circumstances, situations, and social needs faster than any before.

There is only one thing to be done with this great new opportunity—take advantage of it. Build an organised system out of it, and start to take back control from the governments which are no longer needed.

Jel, "AMPU—Delivering Direct Technology Through the Internet," *Kuro5hin*, www.kuro5hin.org/story/2002/2/13/02930/1767.

Opinion polls in America and Europe suggest that large majorities are in favour of referendums.

Not everyone is happy about this. Politicians are regularly derided for being "poll driven", as if that were a synonym for public pandering. David Broder, a veteran political reporter and columnist on the *Washington Post*, entitled his recent book about America's initiative campaigns "Democracy Derailed". Mr Broder is appalled by the intrusion of direct ballots into the governance of American states, believing that such ballots are too vulnerable to control by powerful moneyed interests—a remarkable claim for someone who has been covering America's Congress for most of his career.

Widespread Support for Referendums

And yet despite his scathing criticism of such initiatives, Mr Broder is honest enough to report that his view is not widely shared by voters. "In every state I visited in my reporting, the initiative process was viewed as sacrosanct," he writes. "In most of them, the legislature (even though term-limited) was in disrepute." Moreover, he is convinced that it will not be long "before the converging forces of technology and public opinion coalesce in a political movement for a national initiative—to allow the public to substitute the simplicity of majority rule by referendum for what must seem to many frustrated Americans the arcane, ineffective, out-of-date model of the constitution."

Mr Broder is right, and not just about America. The growing expectations of an educated public for whom individual choice is an important value, combined with the technology of an increasingly pervasive internet, will challenge the structures of all western governments based on representative models of democracy. Once reliable methods for validating electronic votes have been found and internet penetration rates approach saturation, the internet will remove the biggest single obstacle to direct democracy—the physical difficulty of distributing information to a large population, engaging it in debate and collecting its votes. When this happens, probably during the next decade, many people will come to see national elections every few years as an extraordinarily blunt instrument for expressing the popular will, a remnant from the age of steam, when most representative institutions were invented.

Constitutional change is never easy, nor should it be; and moves towards direct democracy are likely to be fiercely resisted, by politicians and lobbyists out of self-interest, by many others out of a genuine fear of the unknown and by some, like Mr Broder, out of a principled belief that, even if technically possible, government by referendum would be a "tragic mistake".

The Many Faces of Democracy

Assuming that frequent mass polls will become a practical possibility, critics of direct democracy will argue that, without intermediary institutions such as political parties and legislatures, the kind of rational trade-offs necessary for good government will become impossible. The bargaining that takes place in legislatures may not be pretty, but without it successive referendums are likely to result in contradictory policymaking and instability. Critics will also say that most citizens simply do not have the expertise or the time to examine the complex issues that must constantly be decided in modern societies. Impatient or distracted by other demands on their attention, voters will be prone to snap judgments and vulnerable to manipulation. Professional politicians, for all their faults, do serve a useful purpose.

Those arguing for more direct democracy will reply that regular polls of the electorate should go a long way towards avoiding irrational policymaking. If voters find that they have made conflicting decisions, then another ballot can be held to resolve them. Moreover, even in a direct democracy not all intermediary institutions, such as political parties, government departments or even legislatures, will necessarily be abolished. Legislatures might survive to monitor elected governments, just as they do today, and to formulate and propose legislation. Voters might confine themselves to making the final decision about what legislation to enact. Evidence from the hundreds of initiatives held in Switzerland and in American states does not bear out fears that voters will take undue risks or oppress minorities. Electorates are generally risk-averse, upholding the status quo unless they are thoroughly convinced that change is needed.

Even in a direct democracy, most people do not want to live, eat and sleep politics, so new intermediate institutions may have to be found. James Fishkin, a political scientist at the University of Texas, has experimented with "deliberative polls", both national and local, in the United States, Britain, Denmark, Australia and Bulgaria. These polls are, in effect, large juries of ordinary voters (200–500 people at a time), selected to mirror the general population, who gather to interrogate experts on both sides of an issue over a couple of days and then debate among themselves in moderated groups. Participants are polled both before and after their discussions to see what difference these have made.

Mr Fishkin's results have been encouraging. Minds were opened and some attitudes changed. Judging by the evidence of lengthy questionnaires before and after each poll, it seems that all socio-economic groups (not just the rich or well-educated) are capable of considering complex issues; that participants are able to absorb information even if it clashes with their own views; and that such groups are able to weigh alternatives and set priorities even when difficult trade-offs are involved.

The Jury Is Out

In a direct democracy, voters might well trust such juries of fellow citizens more than they would groups of professional politicians. With a ubiquitous, video-enabled internet, such juries would not need to assemble physically, as did most of Mr Fishkin's. Voters could follow the deliberations of the group as it wrestled with a decision, review the evidence presented to the jurors, and consider the jury's decision when it was made. Juries could be used as advisers to the electorate before votes, or some decisions could be delegated directly to the juries themselves. A poll by the Center on Policy Attitudes, a Washington-based think-tank, found that two out of three Americans believed that such a jury would make better decisions than Congress, mainly because it would be less subject to lobbyists' attempts to influence it.

Such innovations may still seem a long way off. But in trying to hold back the demand for more direct democracy, the defenders of traditional representative institutions will have a fundamental problem: any criticism they make will sound as though it is aimed at democracy itself. If voters are not wise enough to make direct policy choices, how can they be wise enough to choose legislators, or governments, to do it for them?

The financial corruption and lobbying by special interests that plague all democracies today are much harder to stamp out in a representative system than they would be in a system with more direct voter involvement. Mr Broder is right that big-money interests have also tried to manipulate many American initiative ballots. But it is hard to bribe an entire electorate, or even to mislead it for very long, if there is a free flow of information and open discussion. In any case, most research by political scientists has found that, contrary to Mr Broder's view, state-wide initiative campaigns are, on the whole, remarkably difficult for big spenders to control.

To function effectively, of course, even direct democracies will need rules, procedures and an array of institutions. Most of these are likely to be adapted from existing ones. Others will have to be invented, and voters persuaded of their merits. One of democracy's greatest virtues is its flexibility, but the changes about to be wrought by new communication technologies will stretch the adaptive abilities of western democracies to their limit.

"There are extremely strong interests allied against the neutral platform of the original Internet."

The Internet Will Empower Corporations

Lawrence Lessig, interviewed by *Multinational Monitor*

Lawrence Lessig is a professor at Stanford Law School and the author of *The Future of Ideas: The Fate of the Commons in a Connected World* and *Code and Other Laws of Cyberspace*. The following viewpoint is adapted from an interview that Lessig gave the magazine *Multinational Monitor* in March 2002. In it, he argues that a variety of corporate interests are competing to control different aspects of the Internet. First, he warns that as more people access the Internet through cable rather than phone lines, cable companies will have the power to control what types of content users can access. Second, he argues that copyright law is stifling technological innovation on the Internet since current laws make it easy for copyright holders to sue the developers of any new technology that might threaten their interests. Lessig believes that in both cases the government should legislate to preserve the free and open nature of the Internet.

As you read, consider the following questions:

1. What is the problem with policy-based routing, in Lessig's opinion?
2. What system did Congress develop to balance the interests of broadcast and cable television companies?

M ultinational Monitor: *What do you mean in describing the Internet as free?*

Lawrence Lessig: Think of the Internet as broken into layers. There is the physical layer, which are the computers and wires that make the Internet run; the logic layer, which are the protocols that make it function; and the content layer, which includes the programs that run on it—MP3, for example. When I say the Internet is free, I'm referring to the middle layer, which is unowned and embraces an architecture that ensures that people can innovate for this network without the permission of anyone else. But obviously, the physical infrastructure—the bottom layer—is owned by people, and much of the content is owned and controlled, so those parts aren't free. But the core is free.

The Concept of the Commons

You suggest that things that are owned may in some cases also be understood to be free.

Right. One central idea in the book is the concept of the commons, which I define as a resource that is either completely unowned or whose access is granted to people equally. For example, if you charge people a dollar for admission to a park, it functions as a commons because you've charged a price equally to people regardless of what they want to do with the park.

Common carriage regulation in that sense takes what is otherwise owned property, like a telephone system, and makes it function like a commons, because there's no discrimination in access to the resource.

[Editor's note: Common carriage regulation requires telephone companies to make their services available to the general public at reasonable rates.]

At the physical layer, the original Internet was layered on top of a telephone system that was regulated to be free in that sense: under common carriage regulation the phone system was regulated to make resources—the telephone lines—available to others on an equal and neutral basis.

When you talk about the code layer of the Internet, one of the central ideas is end-to-end. What does that mean and why is it important?

The core architecture of the network is "end-to-end." That means that the network itself is designed to be as simple as possible. All the intelligence is placed at the end, or edge of the network.

Peer-to-peer is one implementation of this network. What it means is that computers at the edge of the network are communicating directly with each other, not through a server in the center of the network or some central computer which is allocating resources to the edge.

Napster was a kind of peer-to-peer system. You were essentially transferring files from one person on the edge of the network to another person on the edge of the network.

Instant messaging technologies are peer-to-peer, because one computer at the edge of the network is talking to another computer at the edge of the network.

These systems importantly are not controlled by anything built into the network.

Cable Companies Control the Net

The central theme of your recent book is that some of these core aspects of how the Internet has been free or decentralized are under threat. To what extent is the physical layer, including the existing telephone wires and DSL and cable, open, and what are the trends that seem to be dominating in that physical layer?

As the Internet moves from narrow band to broad band—from telephone lines to cable lines—cable companies have the power and the right legally to exercise much more control over what happens on the network, because they are building and deploying technologies that will enable discrimination in the content and applications that run on the network. That's the kind of discrimination that the original architecture of the network didn't allow. That's solely a function of moving from telephones to cable, and an accidental feature of regulation—which is that cable has no mandate to be neutral and open, whereas the telephone companies did.

What kind of discrimination might the cable companies be able to exercise?

There is a technology called policy-based routing, for example. Policy-based routing is implemented through a router that allows the cable owner to choose which content flows quickly, which content flows slowly, what applications are permitted and what applications are not. It's like a television set where channel 6 is clear and channel 12 has static on it, and it just so happens that the television manufacturer also owns channel 6.

What this means is the platform of the Internet, which is what you expect to get when you connect broadband, is no longer neutral among the different uses of broadband technology. Instead, it's tilted in favor of some content and some applications, and against others. It's that compromise of neutrality that is going to create a great burden for innovation and creativity.

Is there evidence that the cable companies would use these kinds of technologies?

First of all, they're deploying them now. Secondly, they've exercised this kind of control with respect to video across the network. Yair Landau, the head of Sony's broadband technology, described at a Stanford event how cable companies had told him that if Sony delivered pay-per-view movies across the Internet, then cable companies would shut down the Internet before they would ever allow that on their system.

So the answer is yes, they certainly have expressed the desire and are already deploying the technology to enable that kind of discrimination. . . .

The Evolution of Copyright

You talk about copyright in the pre-Internet era as embodying a kind of balance between competing interests. What competing interests did that balance serve and how did it play out as technologies evolved pre-Internet?

Copyright has always been understood to be a balance between incentives to create and access of the public to the things that are created. The notion was, once you've created the incentive to produce something new, as quickly as possible you want to pass it into the public domain so that other people can build on it in a free way. The framers' [of the U.S. Constitution] conception of copyright initiated that move into the public domain very well, because their conception of copyright had a very short term—basically 14 years, renewable once. And they applied it to a relatively narrow range of rights, basically protecting only maps, charts and books against re-publication. That was their striking of a balance to ensure there was an incentive to produce while guaranteeing that creative works would pass into the public domain after a short interval.

Now that balance has changed. Increasing copyright protections have occurred, and largely for good reasons. A lot more is protected. But at some point that protection becomes too strong. The balance is no longer a balance. That's where I think we are now, because it's not just that the term is extremely long—the life of the author plus 70 years—but the scope of the right is extremely broad. It covers copying, derivative works, using the works in different media. All of this control in the hands of the original copyright owner can inhibit follow-on innovation. This is particularly true of digital technologies, which enable that kind of innovation.

"The best thing about the Information Age is, we lawyers are still in charge!"

As new technologies evolved pre-Internet, how were conflicts between providing protections and facilitating new innovation resolved?

There's been a pattern where when a new technology comes along that changes the mix between protection and access, for Congress to deal with this through something like a compulsory licensing regime. Compulsory licensing is a regime that gives the new technology access to the copyrighted material, but makes sure that the new regime pays for that access.

The first example of that is the player piano. Before the player piano, copyright owners of music made their money by selling sheet music. The player piano made it possible for makers of player pianos to Napsterize the sheet music market by buying one copy of the sheet music, converting it into a piano roll, and then selling the piano rolls—thereby making it no longer necessary for people to buy sheet music. The U.S. Supreme Court held that that was not a copyright violation.

So Congress had to regulate through a change in the statute. When they changed the statute, they gave the sheet music manufacturer the right to make copies after an initial mechanical production has been made and pay a fixed rate for those copies, like two cents per copy. That was a way to make sure copyright owners got paid, but the sheet music industry couldn't leverage their power over sheet music into control over the next technology, which was player pianos.

The same thing happened with cable television. Cable TV is the most dramatic case of Napster before Napster. They set up technologies—television receivers—on top of hills, stole the content of broadcasters and sold it to their customers, delivering broadcast programming by cable. Twice the Supreme Court was asked to strike this down, and twice the Supreme Court said it was not a violation of copyright law. For 20 years, the cable television industry got to Napsterize broadcasting content without regulation of copyright law. When Congress got around to regulating this, they struck the same balance that they struck in the context of player piano rolls. They said that cable companies have the right to get access to broadcast television content, but they have to pay for the content. So Congress created a compulsory licensing right with respect to broadcasting content.

In both cases, the objective is to make sure that one industry doesn't leverage control into the next generation. That's what a compulsory license right does. The same opportunity could exist in the context of the Internet, if Congress would ever get around to protecting the Internet from overly strong copyright regulation.

Stifling Innovation

Except that the Napster case came out the other way, and the court ruled that Napster was violating copyright.

Partly because copyright law itself had been so broadly expanded, the court felt it could not conclude that this use of content could occur without the permission of the copyright owner. So the growth in copyright law meant that there was no doing-nothing option here. The copyright law would shut that down relatively quickly. And that's the problem, because essentially what this means is that any new technology doesn't just have to defend itself in the marketplace, but in the court room against copyright owners before it's allowed to exist in the marketplace. That seems to me a good way to stifle innovation.

The background law has evolved so that the presumption is to shut down the new technology. That changes the dynamic in the regulatory system and Congress altogether. Now Napster is the one who has to muster the political will to get a compulsory license, instead of the recording industry.

Yes, and I think that tipping of the dynamic is devastating for this type of innovation. If you look at the way copyright law has been considered historically in Congress, leaving new innovation the opportunity to develop and then prove itself before you attempt to regulate it was a critical part of the balance. So player piano got to exist and take off long before any court tried to shut it down. No court did shut it down. It was Congress who had to regulate it. The VCR was the same thing. After it took off, the movie industry tried to shut it down via legal regulation, which failed, so then Congress got to consider whether there was something they wanted to do to deal with the VCR. Cable TV was the same thing. These are cases where we've been allowed to innovate first and regulate later. But the law now forces us to regulate first, and innovate later. "Later" in the sense a teenager would mean, i.e., never. . . .

Solutions to Excessive Cable Company Control

MM: In the area of the physical layer of the Internet, what would be the alternatives to the control the cable companies are exerting?

One thing is to expand the competition. I think wireless

could be an important new competitor in this field. So we should support a much broader space for unlicensed spectrum and encourage innovators to develop that space by guaranteeing there will be unlicensed spectrum for internet transmission for the long term. That would create a real kick-start to the competitive process. The existing duopoly between telecom and cable companies (even there, only where the technology overlaps) creates weak competition. What you need is a new competitor, and I think wireless can do that.

To the extent that wireless can't do that or it would result in insufficient competition, another solution would be to impose a common carriage regulation at the code layer. Not at the physical layer—this regulation would say, "You can build whatever wires or technology you want, you don't have to open your wires up to competitors. But if you're delivering Internet content, here are the rules under which the content must be delivered." That would create a kind of neutral platform, imposed at the code layer.

Thirdly, you can impose open-access requirements at the physical layer, so that you induce competition to guarantee that strategic behavior by the cable or broadband companies could succeed.

In the content layer, I think there should be radical change in the regulation of copyright law—not abolition of copyright law, but a change in its scope and certainly duration to enable a lot more content to exist in the public domain. A certain amount of compulsory licensing rights would also free up lots of content for innovation.

MM: Linus Torvalds, who has been central to developing GNU/ Linux, has recently published a much more optimistic book than yours. He thinks open-source code—which puts new innovations, like the GNU/Linux operating system in the public domain—has secured a permanent place for itself and that open-source innovation is thriving and here to stay.

I hope he's right, but I think he's wrong. I think there are extremely strong interests allied against the neutral platform of the original Internet. I'm not sure that that's Microsoft, but I am sure that there are businesses that don't succeed in the world of open competition that the Internet produced and that they are acting to change that world.

It's a separate question whether that means the end of open source. I don't think it necessarily means the end of open source. But I also don't think the survival of open source is a sufficient condition for the survival of the kind of innovation and creativity that I was describing. I hope I am wrong. But if you look at where the politics lie, and what the interests are, the powers on the side of changing the Internet are much stronger than the powers on the side of preserving it, and that is why there is a reason to be skeptical.

> *"Current concepts of national loyalty and citizenship are likely to change dramatically . . . as virtual nations become prevalent."*

The Internet Will Give Rise to Virtual Nations

Mike Dillard and Janet Hennard

In the following viewpoint, Mike Dillard and Janet Hennard predict that virtual nations (v-nations), formed through the Internet, will emerge and become powerful enough to rival the world's current nations. V-nations will arise, the authors argue, as people join with others around the world who share their goals and interests. Members of v-nations will then pool their resources to make their v-nation powerful. The authors point to the terrorist group al Qaeda as an example of an emerging v-nation, but they are quick to add that v-nations can also have positive goals and ideals. Mike Dillard is a consultant for Tatum Partners and corporate vice president of SAIC, both technology consulting firms. Janet Hennard is the founder of Strategic Marketing Services, a business consulting firm.

As you read, consider the following questions:

1. What characteristic of a v-nation did the Lifecast company lack, in the authors' view?
2. What are the two conditions necessary for a v-nation to arise, according to Dillard and Hennard?
3. What types of benefits might a v-nation confer on its citizens, in the authors' view?

Mike Dillard and Janet Hennard, "The Approaching Age of Virtual Nations," *Futurist*, vol. 36, July/August 2002, pp. 24–28. Copyright © 2002 by World Future Society. Reproduced by permission.

One of the most significant sociopolitical evolutions since the formation of cities and states may begin soon: the emergence of virtual nations.

Individuals bound by a common, passionate cause or set of beliefs form virtual nations (v-nations). Bridging time and space, the Internet provides fertile ground for members across the globe to fine-tune their ideologies and develop plans for their community's future. Ultimately, they strive to achieve all the elements of a nation, including leadership, governance, power, security, control, action, and loyalty. V-nations may also claim ownership of landmasses to increase their presence.

Posing a direct challenge to the world's existing nations, v-nations will be both the cause and effect of a monumental shift in global economic, political, and social structures. These new nations will at once threaten and stimulate hope for worldwide cooperation, security, and use of resources.

Using the openness and relative freedom of online networks, v-nations will transcend simple online communities or user groups that typically band together for common needs and interests. They will be far more ambitious, coalescing individuals to create power and influence. A v-nation will seek to defend and protect its people, to provide for their health and well-being, and to implement a monetary system in support of its economic, social, political, and/or religious goals.

As v-nations emerge, interlinked societies will form in an overarching space above the current "real" nations. V-nation citizens will give their allegiance to a new kind of organization whose people are united by common ideals, goals, ambitions, or needs, and where one is as likely to share loyalty with acquaintances thousands of miles away as with a next-door neighbor. The potential outcomes range from noble to sinister, from order to chaos.

The hope is that the formation of v-nations will lead to a higher level of human understanding and cooperation. The risk is that this evolution will tumble out of control, forever changing ordered societies as we know them. Free and democratic nations will need to prepare now for ways to combat the potential threats and to embrace the potential benefits that v-nations will bring.

Virtual Nationhood of a Company

Lifecast, a small entrepreneurial company in Dallas, worked to assemble an enormous online community of wealthy and powerful individuals in 1999. During its 14-month existence, and with less than $10 million in seed money, Lifecast's online membership grew to a staggering 1.4 million affluent participants. Their combined annual incomes totaled more than $240 billion, and their documented personal net worth exceeded $1.28 trillion.

Lifecast members included some of the world's most powerful politicians, educators, and athletes, as well as leaders in businesses, governments, and militaries around the world. More than 40,000 doctors and 80,000 attorneys signed up. As a group, members flew more than 32 billion miles annually. Economically, Lifecast would have ranked twenty-third among the world's nations.

Had this group wanted to, it could easily have created its own stock trading exchange, research centers, universities, and security force for protection. It could have bought its own airline, insurance company, health-care centers, and financial institutions. It could have driven the politics of many countries, influenced laws, and even started its own barter currencies. In other words, it could have become the equivalent of a nation, with an ability to provide the three basic functions of a nation: to defend and protect its people, provide opportunities for the health and well-being of its members, and implement a monetary system.

Lifecast no longer functions as a corporation, and it was never the intent of Lifecast to become a virtual nation in the first place. However, that small company demonstrated the ease with which an online group could form very quickly and amass potentially tremendous power.

Members of the Lifecast community had ample communications access through the Internet and the technical infrastructure that supported the group. However, the group never sought to effect change; rather, members were content to use their community for social bonding and information gathering. With no cause to promote, there was no need for a leader to step forward. This conceivable v-nation was likely unaware of its potential power and certainly uninterested in using the community for a nation-building purpose.

The Necessary Conditions—and the Catalyst

A potential virtual nation needs two basic conditions to surface: reliable communications access and a significant cause. But the v-nation will need more than that—a catalyst—to truly take hold. Just as any nation or coalition requires inspirational leadership to survive, a compelling leader must either be present at the onset of the v-nation or emerge quickly to ensure its sustainability. A powerful and charismatic leader who captures the hearts and minds of the fledgling members becomes the catalytic agent with the authority to demand unquestioning loyalty, inspire action, get people to change direction, and shape the future of the v-nation. Only then will the v-nation truly come to life.

A disturbing example of a rudimentary but menacing virtual nation exists today—one with all the required conditions. On September 11, 2001, we witnessed the power and force of that virtual nation, borne out of the combination of easy access to sophisticated communications, a fervent cause (the overthrow of "heretic governments" in their respective countries and the establishment of Islamic governments), and a charismatic leader.

Al Qaeda, a worldwide network of fundamentalist Islamic organizations, was formed in 1988 with a handful of members, no homeland, no army, no ongoing revenues, and only a few leaders operating from remote areas of the world. The Internet enabled al Qaeda to become a formidable virtual nation, gaining strength as Internet access spread globally and especially as its primary leadercatalyst, Osama bin Laden, earned the unquestioning loyalty of its members. In Afghanistan, al Qaeda demonstrated how a v-nation can further its causes by taking an entire country hostage and even dictating the actions of that country's ruling army.

The al Qaeda v-nation now operates in some 40 countries and is organized into hundreds of cells. Its economic power is believed to come from worldwide business enterprises, charities, international stock manipulation, and, at least until the fall of Afghanistan's ruling Taliban, from large, indirect profits of Afghanistan's production of an estimated 70% of the world's heroin cash crop according to the U.S. Drug Enforcement Administration. With little physical structure, the al Qaeda v-nation has been able to wreak horrific havoc on the world. . . .

The Emergence of Virtual Nations

Nations and societies have always been somewhat insulated by distance, ideas, culture, resources, and time. Earlier in history, societies and nations were formed around the distance one could walk, then by geographical or natural boundaries. Today, geography, history, inertia, patriotism, resources, and economic structure define them. But increasingly, loyalty, needs, goals, and fears will define them.

Nations as we know them will continue to exist. But among new societies we will see new reasons for existing and a synergy among entities that is likely to transcend the relationships among traditional nations. As this happens, people will not tolerate the current boundaries that cause inefficiencies in the use of the world's assets. They will use the world's online network to optimize the allocation of those assets or to promote their own agendas. The result will be societies with new methods of protecting people, new monetary systems, and new hierarchies—virtual nations that capitalize on online connectedness.

As a virtual nation emerges, its citizens can be from anywhere, but they will have a common bond based on one or more principles or needs. It will be as easy to start in Bangalore as it is in Sunnyvale, as easy in rich countries as in those with less wealth. Just as with a traditional nation, a virtual nation runs the risk of being captured by those with sinister or misguided goals. It will also have the same foibles and challenges as any other government or organization. And it will have to struggle with such questions as, Who will lead it? What will be its laws? Who will be a member? Who will govern and how?

Challenges to Our Current Nations

As virtual nations arise—whether they have the best intent for their members, or are sinister in nature, or even act as rogue nations—they will begin to immediately challenge our current nations, their way of life, and the security that we perceive in those nations. Especially critical will be challenges in areas of citizenship, loyalty, security, and quality of life. Innovative monetary systems will likely emerge to address bartering among v-nations.

The Internet's Threat to Traditional Government Regulation

[The Internet] may help restore a degree of limited government and personal freedom perhaps unknown for over a century. It is largely a matter of simple economic incentives, as people increasingly rely on the Net. If government imposed excessive taxes, healthy profits await those who can help the overburdened avoid these levies (this recently transpired when several Indian reservation-based cigarette stores created Web sites). . . . One remarkable facilitating trend is the rise of "virtual" nations, that is, Web sites located on artificial islands or in tiny compliant countries handling transactions currently off-limits to Americans. It's not that government willingly restrains itself in the face of citizens fleeing its authority; it may be a bit too much to expect lawmakers to acknowledge futility. Rather, the flight from government regulation will be largely invisible, and for better or for worse, citizens will now have options once thought beyond the reach of all but the very wealthy or politically connected.

Robert Weissberg, "Technology Evolution and Citizen Activism: The Net and the Rebirth of Limited Government," *Policy Studies Journal*, August 2003.

Current concepts of national loyalty and citizenship are likely to change dramatically and will be severely challenged as virtual nations become prevalent. People will inherit a citizenship based on place of birth, but they may elect to participate in a virtual nation or nations where loyalty brings them more health, wealth, safety, support, or religious approval. At the most basic level, citizens will want to protect themselves and be able to make a living for their families. Their allegiance will be to those nations, virtual or physical, that can best guarantee the right to a better education, better medical care, better income, opportunity to own land and property, religious freedom, or better jobs.

Eventually, individuals will want citizenship in numerous

nations and organizations, moving in and out as particular benefits are needed or desired. The concept of citizenship is likely to evolve into one of dual or even multiple citizenships and loyalties, and individuals will be torn between their land of ancestry and the lure of the virtual nations. In the end, the tug of the virtual nations will become too powerful for many to resist, and loyalty will shift to this form of organizational control. . . .

Trade

Intrinsic to virtual nations is the need to trade. Although not mandatory, it is highly likely that an "Internet barter dollar" will emerge to overcome the inefficiencies that will arise as v-nations attempt to exchange goods across old boundaries. Processes to complete a transaction, which require many steps, several currency conversions, and multiple tax calculations, will be considered absurd and unrealistic.

To meet these challenges, a new currency will emerge that will have the same value no matter where it is used. It might initially be something as simple as airline miles. It is easy to imagine a person offering 2,000 frequent flyer miles for a carpet from the Andes. But whatever form it takes, this new currency will likely begin on the black markets before gaining acceptance as a legal tender.

A Time to Act

Virtual nations will occur. The basic infrastructure is in place to enable them to emerge. Already we are seeing the first stages and examples, some good and some bad. It is unfortunate that our most visible example of the approaching age of v-nations was one with such sinister goals and actions—the al Qaeda v-nation. But it clearly lays out the challenges that mankind faces. As virtual nations arise, they offer untold opportunities for the advancement of society. However, we must understand that they don't change the attitudes of people; they only mirror those attitudes. There will be those with positive ambitions, and there will be those with sinister intent. We must develop strategies that deal with both, just as we develop strategies to deal with our nations of today. We must begin to consider whether to include virtual nations into the family of nations. If we do not plan for the reality of v-nations, we will find ourselves in a period of sustained and continuous turmoil.

Perhaps the most we can do at this point is to acknowledge the emergence of v-nations and, as much as possible, guide them in a direction that benefits mankind or legitimate businesses. We do have the potential to make this the best societal evolution yet—one led by the human spirit of survival, kindness, and free markets. We can create v-nations for research, pulling together the world's best minds. We can create nations for distributing the world's resources to benefit all humanity. We can create nations that specialize in providing educational benefits for all those around the world. We can use these nations to break down religious bigotry and persecution. We can help the long-called-for world order, where everyone is treated equally and where all people have the best education, shelter, and respect for their common value.

The great nations of the current world must help shape the world to come—a world of coexistence between nations and virtual nations, where well-meaning virtual nations are fostered, encouraged, and guided for the true causes that benefit mankind and free economies. Virtual nations will challenge our world as we know it—a breathtaking change. Now is the time to build a world that embodies the best of both the natural and virtual nations.

> *"As technology becomes more familiar and commonplace, it will expand the range of people, organizations, and institutions that will be on the system."*

The Internet Will Become a More Pervasive Part of Daily Life

Joseph F. Coates

Joseph F. Coates is president of Consulting Futurist, Inc., in Washington, D.C. In the following viewpoint, he argues that in the future people will use the Internet far more than they do now. The most important technological innovation for the Internet will be wireless telecommuncations, he writes, which will help integrate technology into different gadgets and places more seamlessly. Coates discusses the future of e-commerce, online advocacy groups, Internet surveillance, transnational communications, and home entertainment. Overall, Coates concludes that the Internet will greatly enhance people's lives.

As you read, consider the following questions:
1. How will shopping for clothes online be different than it is now, according to Coates?
2. What is the Tokyo system, as described by the author?
3. What does lexicographer David Crystal claim is emerging as a third form of communication after speech and text, according to Coates?

Joseph F. Coates, "The Future of the Web," *The World & I*, vol. 17, April 2002, p. 38. Copyright © 2002 by News World Communications, Inc. Reproduced by permission.

Through a series of scientific, technological, and business coincidences, the evolution of information technology has led to a disjointed, competitive, and piecemeal communications system.

The telegraph, telephone, and radio resulted from separate inventions, each converted into businesses by people with different objectives. Television came about as a spin-off from radio to compete with film. About 30 years ago the latest technological marvel, the Internet, was dropped into the middle of this communications chaos.

Unlike anything that came before, the Internet was free, or nearly so, in the minds of the early user. It featured video screens, computer keyboards, and communication to anyone, anywhere in the world, who was part of the Internet network. It has become increasingly sophisticated in quality and reliability, more convenient to use, and immeasurably more popular and valuable with the creation of the World Wide Web. Its democratic feature—open to anyone, anonymously, if you choose—was most appealing.

Considering the Future

Looking ahead 15 to 20 years, the Internet will be unrecognizable. The rest of the telecommunications industry will also be unrecognizable as we approach the goal of universal, seamless communication from anyplace to anyplace, at any time.

Technological integration will be required through patchwork arrangements, either voluntarily or by government intervention. Businesses may evolve in an intelligent way to assume more and more of the total information package needed to serve all customers. AOL-Time Warner is taking a slow start in that direction.

On the technological side, the biggest thing affecting the future of the Internet, aside from the integration of media, is the emergence of wireless telecommunications. The new third-generation wireless service in the United States has enough broad-bandwidth capacity to service the Internet. Broadband means the capacity to speedily carry voice, text, photographs, graphics, movement, and interaction.

Wireless Internet will become as familiar as wireline Internet, with which it will be seamlessly integrated. Continual decreasing computer size, declining cost, and increasing numbers of users worldwide will define the total emerging system. Broad-bandwidth imaging and interacting capabilities will have consequences in two categories.

Some repercussions will develop truly new applications. One category is already existing applications that are substantially enhanced or expanded. Let's look at a number of these and see where they are going. Keep in mind that if costs drop as technology becomes more familiar and commonplace, it will expand the range of people, organizations, and institutions that will be on the system. As Internet pioneer Robert Metcalfe proposed years ago, the value of a network increases geometrically as the square of the number of people on the network.

Business Uses

Shopping by Internet is now widespread, in competition with catalog buying or visiting the mall. It is especially attractive where there is no shop, supplier, or boutique nearby. Despite exaggerated expectations, Internet shopping is enormously successful. As the quality of images and the capability of interaction grow, the Net will be the big challenge to catalogs, which derive their strength from small size, convenience, and use of color.

The Internet will allow you to see yourself, having sent a picture and your measurements to a vendor. If you are buying clothes, you will be able to examine a wide range of outfits, and place an order without ever leaving your chair, desk, or plane seat. You will be able to see yourself walking, sitting, or rotated at various angles in your outfits. (Some people will always want to shop traditionally because that is recreation for them.)

As with most new uses, it will not be either-or but will offer a widening of choices based on people's preferences and short-term pressures. Comparison shopping will be a cinch on the Internet and will drive down prices. Business-to-business network commerce is already flourishing and will expand tremendously. Auctions and various forms of bidding are already common and will become ubiquitous.

One consequence of Internet-based purchasing will be a

radical change in logistics regarding the shipping of goods. As more things in smaller or larger packages are delivered to homes, offices, and business facilities, trucks themselves will change. The big ones will still be necessary, but there will be a lot more midsize and smaller ones to wend their way through the neighborhoods.

Some communities may resort to the Tokyo system, in which people place and pick up their Internet orders at a local chain, like 7-Eleven. The reason is that in Tokyo the street naming is so complex that it would be too expensive to deliver to individual addresses.

Wireline and wireless will help business operate not only around the clock but around the world, in the sense that any element of the business personnel or unit can contact any other element, anytime and anywhere. Out of that capability will come enhanced efficiency and effectiveness, tighter management, or looser reins where that is appropriate.

There will be more interpersonal action between people who are now normally distant. Groupware, the ability of multiple locations to simultaneously communicate, exchange ideas, discuss matters, and work on projects, will be a cohesive factor in global business.

On the other hand, we will develop an etiquette that will be a constraint on who has the right to contact whom, when, for what purpose, and under what circumstances. After all, the system could easily drive everyone to a frazzle without proper protocol. Small businesses will benefit: the global Internet will allow any size enterprise to market worldwide and find (or be found by) members of niche markets.

Some markets will shrivel and even wither away when it is cheaper, faster, and more reliable to do a task yourself. Examples include travel agents, financial service advisers, and automobile dealers. Their individual survival will depend on innovations in customer service.

The Emergence of Cyberunions

Arthur Shostak, a longtime student of organized labor, foresees the emergence of cyberunions. The Internet will not just improve the old tools of unionism but will open up new levels of excellence, making strategic planning more feasible,

The Growth of Daily Online Pursuits

Estimated growth in users who do these activities on a typical day (2000–2002)

Activity	First time we asked this **Do on a typical day (millions)**	Most recent time **Do on a typical day (millions)**	Growth %
Bank online	4 (March 2000)	8 (October 2002)	100%
Buy a product	3 (March 2000)	6 (December 2002)	100%
Download music files to your computer	3 (June–July 2000)	6 (October 2002)	100%
Look for info from a government site	6 (March 2000)	12 (November 2002)	100%
Check sports scores or info	7 (March 2000)	14 (September 2002)	100%
Research a product or service	12 (March 2000)	21 (December 2002)	75%
Look for political news or info	9 (March 2000)	15 (November 2002)	67%
Look for religious or spiritual info	3 (March 2000)	5 (November 2002)	67%
Play a game	5 (March 2000)	8 (June–July 2002)	60%
Research for your job	14 (March 200)	22 (November 2002)	57%
Get news	19 (March 2000)	29 (December 2002)	53%
Look for info on a hobby or interest	15 (March 2000)	22 (January 2002)	47%
Surf the Web for fun	18 (March 2000)	26 (January 2002)	44%
Search to answer a question	16 (Sept.–Dec. 2000)	22 (September 2002)	38%
Participate in an online auction	3 (March 2000)	4 (December 2002)	33%
Research for school or training	9 (March 2000)	12 (September 2002)	33%
Send an instant message	10 (March 2000)	13 (June–July 2002)	30%

Mary Madden, *America's Online Pursuits: The Changing Picture of Who's Online and What They Do*, Pew Internet and American Life Project, December 22, 2003.

flexible, and practical. As unions gain international breadth, their actions will become more sophisticated.

In negotiations, if unions are able to call up the same in-depth information about the firm available to the employer, this will make solutions more mutually significant. The Internet will also allow unions to become more collegial, restoring the socialization and important interpersonal linkages that are so important to group cohesion and action.

Paralleling the new business-union relations will be public interest groups and nongovernmental organizations dealing with national or international governing bodies. The ability to gather, collect, process, and deliver information in depth and on demand during a negotiation or discussion will change relationships. The ability to confront solid information with solid information will reduce hostile confrontations. In almost all interorganizational negotiations, the best route is establishing cooperation on as much common ground as possible.

Surveys and panel voting will be common. Most promising will be real-time voting during TV programs on individual characters, acts, sequences, and outcomes. The questionable judgments of those who manage the media may be replaced by the more practical and down-to-earth judgments of viewers.

Always Connected

A surprisingly high percentage of people require supervision, whether as a condition of parole or for medical reasons. The availability of wireless-bandwidth capabilities will make it practical to have two-way audio, video, and data communication with them, ensuring that they remain law-abiding, safe, and healthy. The Internet will be able to identify where people are, remind them of what they must do— take a pill, exercise—and where they must go, and verify the safety of those who are at risk.

There will be a great deal more interaction through wireless Internet as the devices shrink in size and capacity grows. We might have wrist TVs, from the size of a wristwatch face up to anything that will be comfortable on your forearm.

The events of September 11 have reminded all of us that

oral communication is invaluable in an emergency. We will add to that the capability of imagery, which will be a primary improvement in dealing with physical, medical, social, occupational, or traffic emergencies. In a disaster, a picture will be invaluable in allocating resources, mobilizing, setting priorities, and managing rescue workers.

Sports and Driving

When you take part in sports and recreation using the Internet, you will be able to have outstanding coaches watch you swing the club, toss the caber, or race the horse. The ability to have expert knowledge brought to a sports activity without the tremendous burden of cost and time will open up new capabilities to enhance individual performance. A related benefit will be the correction of potentially dangerous patterns or maneuvers that occur in every sport.

The Internet will lead to public voting on sports in real time to conjecture on the next move, as the rugby or football team moves into action. Fox TV used this technology during the recent Super Bowl, when it asked fans to submit answers to upcoming plays by the Patriots and Rams. Instant display of results will add an exciting element to watching sports. Other kinds of recreation will be opened up by wireless devices: tiny cameras will allow us to see what a snorkeler sees, or to view the face of a person bungee jumping or driving a race car.

The Internet can be a factor in automobile safety. Some 42,000 people die each year in traffic accidents in the United States. The most dangerous drivers are the young and the elderly. Technology will provide real-time monitoring of their performance, reporting to the driver vocally while driving ("You took that turn too fast," "You are closing too quickly," or "You are delaying too long in applying the brakes").

Real-time reporting can become a combination of training and monitoring for young drivers and a refresher course and safety device for older drivers, who have slower responses. The feedback could be sent to your parents by Internet, or it could be replayed in the evening when you return home. For those with questionable driving records, monitoring could be mandated as a condition for maintaining one's license, with feedback continually sent to the traffic department.

The Internet developed in the United States as if all the world spoke English and will do so forever. This is far from the truth, although English will be the dominant language for the English-speaking nations, most professionals, and big businesses.

Communications among multinational corporations and their principal suppliers will be in English. But when one gets down to the nitty-gritty, consumers' side of life, it seems unlikely that people who speak Turkish or Polish will search for and buy a washing machine using English rather than their native tongue.

A large expansion in new languages on the Internet is already under way. Keyboards will become more complex. In his book *Alpha Beta*, John Man points out that there is a universal Unicode, which stores 143 characters to represent the alphabets in all languages. Complex graphic languages such as Arabic will have keyboards that can be flipped back and forth between the local language and English.

The Chinese will use a Roman keyboard for email, using a script called Pinyin, which converts the sounds of Chinese into Roman letters. The system can even take into account the tonal differences that are so important in Chinese.

The lexicographer David Crystal claims that Netspeak is emerging as a third form of communication, the other two types presumably being speech and text. The Internet will steadily change our ideas of grammar, syntax, and vocabulary. With regard to it, RUOK?

Health and Travel

Medicine is a favorite subject for discussions on the Internet now. New uses will offer a combination of speed and flexibility of response to an accident, disaster, or individual patients. The ability to incorporate broad-bandwidth imaging and interaction will allow the practitioner to examine and diagnose the patient at a distance. Routine data gathering and monitoring of patients will be transmitted to the physician's database.

A wireless Internet will transform sightseeing, eliminating the need to carry heavy guidebooks. It will allow you to call up anything you want, with the right level of detail to satisfy your needs.

You will not need to know the name of a building since GPS, the Global Positioning Satellite system, will automatically take care of that. The Internet will facilitate getting around in strange cities, minimizing the possibility of getting lost with no ready way of calling for help.

Taking Care of Home

The Internet will be the core of the most important information-technology development in the home, the electronic home work-study center. It will bring together all of the information technologies connected with the house and all of their functions: work at home, entertainment, recreation, and socialization.

A typical home will have seven or eight flat screens. The kitchen appliances will be connected to each other and networked to the Internet, allowing you to instruct them remotely from another room, your car, or your office. The ability to communicate internally with wireless will cost less than rewiring your house. Safety and security will cease to be concerns of the middle class and wealthy. The smart house will alert one to the presence of intruders, photograph them, and even capture them physically in many circumstances. The Internet will retain all the information it automatically sends to the police or fire department.

The Internet will allow you to participate remotely in celebrations, weddings, births, and funerals as you interact with other people through life-size wall screens. It will be the closest thing to being at the event, which may be 15 or 5,000 miles away.

The Internet will bring familiar forms of recreation into the home, but it will also lead to new types of entertainment and recreation. Socially, your contacts may be briefer but their numbers will be greater, and, on average, each will give satisfaction greater than you ever experienced before.

The boundless credible expectations of the Internet will enhance our lives, improve our work, free up our time, expand our contacts, and give most of us greater satisfaction in our activities.

Periodical Bibliography

The following articles have been selected to supplement the diverse views presented in this chapter.

Rodney Brooks — "Toward a Brain-Internet Link," *Technology Review*, November 2003.

Marcel Bullinga — "The Internet of the Future," *Futurist*, May 2002.

Economist — "A Brief History of Wi-Fi," June 12, 2004.

Economist — "Digital Dilemmas," January 25, 2003.

Jonah Goldberg — "Vote.con: The Perils of 'Cyber-Democracy,'" *National Review*, December 20, 1999.

Steven Levy — "Something in the Air," *Newsweek*, June 7, 2004.

Lawrence Lessig — "Control and Creativity: The Future of Ideas Is in the Balance," *American Spectator*, January/February 2002.

Charles C. Mann — "A Remote Control for Your Life," *Technology Review*, July/August 2004.

Michael I. Niman — "A Brave New World of Voting," *Humanist*, January/February 2004.

Wade Roush — "The Internet Reborn," *Technology Review*, October 2003.

Gene Rowe and John G. Gammack — "Promise and Perils of Electronic Public Engagement," *Science and Public Policy*, February 2004.

David Pearce Snyder — "Five Meta-Trends Changing the World," *Futurist*, July/August 2004.

Brad Stone et al. — "Your Next Computer," *Newsweek*, June 7, 2004.

Jesse Walker — "Cyberspace's Legal Visionary," *Reason*, June 2002.

For Further Discussion

Chapter 1

1. David Weinberger argues that the Internet increases social interaction, while Norman H. Nie and Lutz Erbring argue the opposite. Which viewpoint best describes your own experiences with the Internet? Explain your answer using examples from your own life.

2. Weinberger writes in very broad terms and cites a few examples to illustrate his points, while Nie and Erbring base their viewpoint on a set of survey results. Which approach do you find more persuasive, and why?

3. What do Steve Davis and his coauthors believe is the biggest problem in politics today? What does William A. Galston believe is the major problem of modern politics? How do these two differing views lead the authors to different conclusions about the Internet's effect on politics? Explain your answer.

Chapter 2

1. After reading the viewpoints by John G. Malcolm and Koleman Strumpf, do you believe the government should take stronger measures to control Internet gambling? Why or why not?

2. Steve Marks believes that the illegal downloading of music from the Internet is a serious problem, while Orson Scott Card believes the issue has been overblown. Whose viewpoint do you find more persuasive, and why? How does each author's background affect your reaction to their viewpoint?

3. After reading the viewpoints by Dan Verton and James Lewis, do you feel that the threat of cyberterrorism is a serious one? Would you consider it more or less of a problem than the other issues discussed in this chapter? Explain your answer.

Chapter 3

1. Do you feel that the Online Personal Privacy Act, as described by Ernest Hollings, is a good one? Why or why not? Why does Jeremy D. Mishkin oppose the law?

2. Do you feel that the Child Online Protection Act, as described in the viewpoints by the American Center for Law and Justice and Mike Himowitz, is a good one? Explain your answer. What other measures do you feel might be appropriate in dealing with the problem of pornography on the Internet?

3. Jay Nordlinger suggests that laws against spam may be necessary, while Clyde Wayne Crews Jr. feels that individuals should use

antispam software and other technologies to combat spam. Based on what you read in the two viewpoints, do you feel that the government should regulate spam, or leave individuals and the private sector to deal with the problem? Explain your answer.

Chapter 4

1. Based on the viewpoints by the *Economist* and Lawrence Lessig, do you think the Internet will benefit the public, corporations, or both? Defend your answer with examples from the viewpoints.

2. Do you feel that the virtual-nations scenario described by Mike Dillard and Janet Hennard is realistic? Why or why not?

3. Joseph F. Coates describes many ways in which information technology might become more a part of daily life. Of the many scenarios he presents, which do you think would be positive developments, and which might have a negative effect on daily life? Explain your answers.

Organizations to Contact

The editors have compiled the following list of organizations concerned with the issues debated in this book. The descriptions are derived from materials provided by the organizations. All have publications or information available for interested readers. The list was compiled on the date of publication of the present volume; the information provided here may change. Be aware that many organizations take several weeks or longer to respond to inquiries, so allow as much time as possible.

American Center for Law and Justice (ACLJ)
PO Box 64429, Virginia Beach, VA 23467
(757) 226-2489
Web site: www.aclj.org
The center is a national network of attorneys who are committed to the defense of Judeo-Christian values. ACLJ engages in litigation, provides legal services, renders advice and counsels clients, and supports attorneys who are involved in defending the religious and civil liberties of Americans. ACLJ supports laws to restrict pornography on the Internet. The ACLJ Web site offers news updates and position papers on a wide variety of issues.

American Library Association (ALA)
50 E. Huron, Chicago, IL 60611
(800) 545-2433
Web site: www.ala.org
A trade organization representing America's librarians, the ALA provides leadership for the development, promotion, and improvement of library and information services and the profession of librarianship. The ALA supports free access to library materials and resources and opposed the Children's Internet Protection Act, which went into effect on July 1, 2004, and requires public libraries to install content filtering software on computers with Internet access. The ALA publishes the magazine *American Libraries* and the *Newsletter on Intellectual Freedom*.

Berkman Center for Internet and Society
Harvard Law School, Baker House
1587 Massachusetts Ave., Cambridge, MA 02138
(617) 495-7547
e-mail: cyber@law.harvard.edu
Web site: http://cyber.law.harvard.edu

The Berkman Center is a research program founded to explore cyberspace, share in its study, and help pioneer its development. Intellectual property issues on the Internet are among the program's main topics of interest. The program's Web site offers a wealth of papers and news stories on Internet piracy, copyright, and Internet regulation issues.

Bridges.org
1424 Sixteenth St. NW, Suite 502, Washington DC 20036
(202) 299-0120
e-mail: info@bridges.org • Web site: www.bridges.org

Bridges.org is an international nonprofit organization that works to help span the digital divide. Bridges.org researches, tests, and promotes best practices for sustainable, empowering use of information and communication technology. The organization publishes reports, research, and position papers.

Cato Institute
1000 Massachusetts Ave. NW, Washington, DC 20001
(202) 842-0200 • fax: (202) 842-3490
Web site: www.cato.org

The Cato Institute is a libertarian public policy research foundation. It opposes government regulation of the Internet, including government efforts to tax the Internet and to restrict Internet gambling and e-mail spam. Cato publishes the magazine *Regulation*, and its Web site includes several reports on Internet issues, such as *The Digital Dirty Dozen: The Most Destructive High-Tech Legislative Measures of the 107th Congress* and *Internet Privacy and Self-Regulation: Lessons from the Porn Wars*, along with many shorter opinion pieces.

Center for Democracy and Technology (CDT)
1634 I St. NW, Suite 1100, Washington, DC 20006
(202) 637-9800
e-mail: feedback@cdt.org • Web site: www.cdt.org

CDT's mission is to develop public policy solutions that advance constitutional civil liberties and democratic values in the new computer and communications media. Pursuing its mission through policy research, public education, and coalition building, the center works to increase citizens' privacy and the public's control over the use of personal information held by government and other institutions. Its publications include the reports *Why Am I Getting All This Spam?*, *Considering Consumer Privacy*, and *Broadband Access:*

Maximizing the Democratic Potential of the Internet, as well as issue briefs and policy papers.

Computer Professionals for Social Responsibility (CPSR)

PO Box 717, Palo Alto, CA 94302

(650) 322-3778

e-mail: cpsr@cpsr.org • Web site: www.cpsr.org

CPSR works to provide the public and policy makers with realistic assessments of the power, promise, and problems of information technology. CPSR members work to direct public attention to critical choices concerning the applications of information technology and how those choices affect society. It publishes the quarterly *CPSR Journal* and the *PING!* newsletter.

Digital Promise Project

c/o Century Foundation

41 E. Seventieth St., New York, NY 10021

(212) 535-4441

e-mail: info@digitalpromise.org • Web site: www.digitalpromise.org

Digital Promise's goal is to unlock the potential of the Internet and other new information technologies for education. It funds efforts to train teachers in the use of information technology and to digitize educational resources. The report *Creating the Digital Opportunity Investment Trust (DO IT), A Proposal to Transform Learning and Training for the Twenty-First Century* is available for download on the organization's Web site.

Electronic Frontier Foundation (EFF)

454 Shotwell St., San Francisco CA 94110-1914

(415) 436-9333

e-mail: information@eff.org • Web site: www.eff.org

EFF is an organization of students and other individuals that aims to promote a better understanding of telecommunications issues. It fosters awareness of civil liberties issues arising from advancements in computer-based communications media and supports litigation to preserve, protect, and extend First Amendment rights in computing and Internet technologies. EFF publishes a comprehensive archive of digital civil liberties information on its Web site.

Electronic Privacy Information Center (EPIC)

1718 Connecticut Ave. NW, Suite 200, Washington, DC 20009

(202) 483-1140

Web site: www.epic.org

EPIC is a public interest research center that works to focus public attention on emerging civil liberties issues and to protect privacy, the First Amendment, and constitutional values. It supports privacy-protection legislation and provides information on how individuals can protect their online privacy. EPIC publishes the *EPIC Alert* newsletter and the *Privacy Law Sourcebook*.

Free Expression Policy Project (FEPP)
Brennan Center for Justice at NYU School of Law
Democracy Program Free Expression Policy Project
161 Avenue of the Americas, 12th Fl., New York, NY 10013
(212) 992-8847
Web site: www.fepproject.org

The project provides research and analysis on difficult censorship issues and seeks free speech–friendly solutions to the concerns that drive censorship campaigns. It opposes the restriction of information and free speech on the Internet that could result from copyright and antipornography legislation. FEPP policy reports include *Internet Filters* and *The Progress of Science and Useful Arts*, which deals with Internet copyright.

Morality in Media
475 Riverside Dr., Suite 239, New York, NY 10115
(212) 870-3222 • fax: (212) 870-2765
e-mail: mim@moralityinmedia.org
Web site: www.moralityinmedia.org

Morality in Media is a national, not-for-profit organization established in 1962 to combat obscenity and uphold decency standards in the media. It maintains the National Obscenity Law Center, a clearinghouse of legal materials on obscenity law, and conducts public information programs to educate and involve concerned citizens. It supports efforts to restrict pornography on the Internet, including pornographic spam. The Morality in Media Web site offers several articles and issue overviews.

Pew Internet and American Life Project
1100 Connecticut Ave. NW, Suite 710, Washington, DC 20036
(202) 296-0019
Web site: www.pewinternet.org

The project produces original, survey-based reports that explore the impact of the Internet on families, communities, work and home, daily life, education, health care, and civic and political life. The project also aims to be an authoritative source on the evolution of the Internet through collection of data and timely discussions of real-world developments as they affect the virtual world. Its many reports include *The Internet as a Unique News Source, Faith Online, Older Americans and the Internet,* and *Spam: How It Is Hurting Email and Degrading Life on the Internet.*

P2P United
Adam Eisgrau, Executive Director
c/o Flanagan Consulting LLC
1317 F St. NW, Suite 800, Washington, DC 20004
Web site: www.p2punited.org

P2P United is the unified voice of the peer-to-peer technology industry's leading companies and proponents. P2P United represents and champions the P2P industry and technology to policy makers, opinion leaders, the media, and the public. The organization does not support Internet piracy, and disputes the idea that Internet file sharing is mainly a tool for illegal copying. The organization's Web site offers issue overviews and news updates on legal and technological developments in the P2P field.

World Future Society
7910 Woodmont Ave., Suite 450, Bethesda, MD 20814
(800) 898-8274
Web site: www.wfs.org

The society is an association of people interested in how social and technological developments are shaping the future. It serves as a clearinghouse for ideas about the future. The WFS publishes the *Futurist,* a bimonthly magazine, and hosts the Cyber Society Forum on its Web site, where participants submit essays on the future of information technology.

Web Sites

Americans for Computer Privacy (ACP)
www.computerprivacy.org

ACP is a broad-based coalition that supports policies that advance the rights of American citizens to encode information without fear of government intrusion and opposes government efforts to increase widespread monitoring or surveillance.

Chilling Effects
www.chillingeffects.org

A joint project of several Internet law organizations, this Web site aims to help visitors understand the protections that the First

Amendment and intellectual property laws give to individuals' online activities.

Democracy 2.0
www.democracy2.org

This Web site seeks to enhance and expand democratic participation and to educate people about the potential for more widespread direct democracy via the Internet.

E-Fairness Coalition
www.e-fairness.org

The coalition represents brick-and-mortar and online retailers, retail corporations and associations, publicly and privately owned shopping centers, outlet centers and independently owned shops and a total of over 350,000 retail stores nationwide. It opposes special tax exemptions for online business.

Music United for Strong Internet Copyright
www.musicunited.org

Music United for Strong Internet Copyright (MUSIC) is a coalition of more than twenty trade organizations within the music industry. Its mission is to promote public awareness of the legal and moral issues surrounding online music sharing.

Pro-Music
www.pro-music.org

This site is part of the music industry's campaign to raise awareness about the illegality and harm of Internet piracy. It provides information of the copyright law as well as numerous links to sites that sell digital music legally.

Bibliography of Books

Alan B. Albarran and David H. Goff, eds. — *Understanding the Web: Social, Political, and Economic Dimensions of the Internet.* Ames: Iowa State University Press, 2000.

John Alderman — *Sonic Boom: Napster, MP3, and the New Pioneers of Music.* Cambridge, MA: Perseus, 2001.

Cynthia J. Alexander and Leslie A. Pal, eds. — *Digital Democracy: Policy and Politics in the Wired World.* New York: Oxford University Press, 1998.

David M. Anderson and Michael Cornfield — *The Civic Web: Online Politics and Democratic Values.* Lanham, MD: Rowman & Littlefield, 2003.

David B. Bolt and Ray A.K. Crawford, eds. — *Digital Divide: Computers and Our Children's Future.* New York: TV Books, 2000.

Frances Cairncross — *The Death of Distance: How the Communications Revolution Is Changing Our Lives.* Boston: Harvard Business School Press, 2001.

Martin Carnoy — *Sustaining the New Economy: Work, Family, and Community in the Information Age.* New York: Russell Sage Foundation, 2000.

Benjamin M. Compaine, ed. — *The Digital Divide: Facing a Crisis or Creating a Myth?* Cambridge, MA: MIT Press, 2001.

Richard Davis — *The Web of Politics: The Internet's Impact on the American Political System.* New York: Oxford University Press, 1999.

Steve Davis, Larry Elin, and Grant Reeher — *Click on Democracy: The Internet's Power to Change Political Apathy into Civic Action.* Cambridge, MA: Westview Press, 2002.

Bosa Ebo, ed. — *Cyberimperialism?: Global Relations in the New Electronic Frontier.* Westport, CT: Praeger, 2001.

Simson Garfinkel — *Database Nation: The Death of Privacy in the Twenty-first Century.* Cambridge, MA: O'Reilly, 2001.

Wendy Grossman — *From Anarchy to Power: The Net Comes of Age.* New York: New York University Press, 2001.

Bruce Haring — *Beyond the Charts: MP3 and the Digital Music Revolution.* Los Angeles: Jim Northern Media, 2000.

Philip N. Howard and Steve Jones — *Society Online: The Internet in Context.* Thousand Oaks, CA: Sage, 2004.

Charles Jennings et al. *The Hundredth Window: Protecting Your Privacy and Security in the Age of the Internet.* New York: Free Press, 2000.

Rosabeth Moss Kanter *Evolve!: Succeeding in the Digital Culture of Tomorrow.* Boston: Harvard Business School Press, 2001.

James E. Katz and Ronald E. Rice *Social Consequences of Internet Use: Access, Involvement, and Interaction.* Cambridge, MA: MIT Press, 2002.

Robert J. Klotz *The Politics of Internet Communication.* Lanham, MD: Rowman & Littlefield, 2004.

Lawrence Lessig *The Future of Ideas: The Fate of the Commons in a Connected World.* New York: Random House, 2001.

Alex Lightman, with William Rojas *Brave New Unwired World: The Digital Big Bang and the Infinite Internet.* New York: John Wiley & Sons, 2002.

Jessica Litman *Digital Copyright: Protecting Intellectual Property on the Internet.* Amherst, NY: Prometheus Books, 2001.

Christopher May *The Information Society: A Sceptical View.* Malden, MA: Blackwell, 2002.

Graham Meikle *Future Active: Media Activism and the Internet.* New York: Routledge, 2002.

Trevor Merriden *Irresistible Forces: The Business Legacy of Napster and the Growth of the Underground Internet.* New York: John Wiley/Capstone, 2001.

Vincent Mosco *Digital Sublime: Myth, Power, and Cyberspace.* Cambridge, MA: MIT Press, 2004.

Robert R. Reich *The Future of Success: Working and Living in the New Economy.* New York: Knopf, 2000.

Marc J. Rosenberg *E-Learning: Strategies for Delivering Knowledge in the Information Age.* New York: McGraw-Hill, 2001.

Diana Saco *Cybering Democracy: Public Space and the Internet.* Minneapolis: University of Minnesota Press, 2002.

Andrew L. Shapiro *The Control Revolution: How the Internet Is Putting Individuals in Charge and Changing the World We Know.* New York: Public Affairs, 1999.

Cass Sunstein *Republic.com.* Princeton, NJ: Princeton University Press, 2001.

Don Tapscott *Growing Up Digital: The Rise of the Net Generation.* New York: McGraw-Hill, 1998.

Siva Vaidhyanathan

Copyrights and Copywrongs: The Rise of Intellectual Property and How It Threatens Creativity. New York: New York University Press, 2001.

Jonathan Wallace
and Mark Mangan

Sex, Laws, and Cyberspace: Freedom and Censorship on the Frontiers of the Online Revolution. New York: M&T Books, 1996.

David Weinberger

Small Pieces Loosely Joined. Cambridge, MA: Perseus, 2002.

Anthony G. Wilhelm

Democracy in the Digital Age: Challenges to Political Life in Cyberspace. New York: Routledge, 2000.

Index

Negra, Mike, 74
network broadcasting, 53–54
Newsweek (magazine), 152
New Yorker (magazine), 40
New York Times (newspaper), 115
Nie, Norman H., 28, 31
Nordlinger, Jay, 140
Norris, Pippa, 155

online communities. *See* Web groups
Online Personal Privacy Act
  (proposed), 113
  provisions of, 117–20
open-source code, 169–70
organizations
  single-issue, rise of, 53–54
  traditional, decline of membership
   in, 38
organized labor, Internet and future of,
  182, 184
Ornery American (online newspaper),
  82

Patriot Act. *See* USA Patriot Act
PayPal, 66
peer-to-peer (P2P) networks, 72, 127,
  164
  filtering technology and, 75–78
  legal actions against, 76–78
policy-based routing, 164–65
politics
  Internet conversations on, 36–37
  Internet use for, in 2000 election, 40,
   42–43, 45
  negative views of, 45–46
  online communities and, 37–39
  protest of, Internet and, 155–56
  single-interest groups and, 48
  proliferation of, 53–54
polls. *See* public opinion polling
pornography
  in e-mail, 141, 144
  government should regulate, 130–34
  con, 135–39
  prevalence of chance encounters
   with, 132
Posey, Julie, 142–43, 144
privacy
  FTC on, 117
  legislation on, 122
   in EU, 118
    downside of, 128–29
   needs to be strengthened, 113–20
   con, 121–29
   as threat to First Amendment,
    127–29
  state regulation of, 120
  survey on, 115, 116

public opinion polling, 156
  deliberative, 159–60
  see also surveys
Putnam, Robert, 38, 41, 42

al Qaeda
  technological sophistication of,
   97–99
  use of Internet by, 104–105
  as virtual nation, 171, 174–75

Rabun, John, 142
radio, digital, 79–80
railroads, cyberterrorism and, 95–96
Rauch, Jonathan, 53
Recording Industry Association of
  America (RIAA), 72
Reeher, Grant, 35
referendums, 156–57
  support for, 157–58
  see also voting
Rheingold, Howard, 44
Rice, Ronald E., 23
Robertson, Cliff, 83
Roe v. Wade, 122

Schmidt, Howard, 93
Schumer, Charles, 147–49
Schwartz, Paul, 126
September 11, 2001, attacks, 174
Shapiro, Andrew L., 12, 54
Shostak, Arthur, 182
Skocpol, Theda, 53
Smith, Lamar, 138
Snyder, David Pierce, 152
social life
  survey on Web use and, 31
  Web use has negative effect on,
   32–34
spam (unsolicited e-mail)
  government should ban, 140–45
  con, 146–49
  pornographic, 141, 144
sports
  illegal betting on, prevalence of,
   68–69
  Internet and future of, 185
spyware, 126
Stanford Law Review (journal), 128
Staten, Mich'l E., 128
states
  online privacy regulated by, 120
  regulation of Internet gambling by,
   66
Strumpf, Koleman, 67
Sunstein, Cass, 52, 56
Supervisory Control and Data
  Acquisition (SCADA) systems, 95, 98

THE MIDDLE EAST

OPPOSING VIEWPOINTS®

Other Books of Related Interest

THE MIDDLE EAST

O P P O S I N G   V I E W P O I N T S ®

William Dudley, *Book Editor*

Daniel Leone, *President*
Bonnie Szumski, *Publisher*
Scott Barbour, *Managing Editor*
Helen Cothran, *Senior Editor*

OPPOSING
VIEWPOINTS®
SERIES

GREENHAVEN
PRESS®

THOMSON
™
GALE

San Diego • Detroit • New York • San Francisco • Cleveland
New Haven, Conn. • Waterville, Maine • London • Munich

© 2004 by Greenhaven Press. Greenhaven Press is an imprint of The Gale Group, Inc., a division of Thomson Learning, Inc.

Greenhaven® and Thomson Learning™ are trademarks used herein under license.

For more information, contact
Greenhaven Press
27500 Drake Rd.
Farmington Hills, MI 48331-3535
Or you can visit our Internet site at http://www.gale.com

Cover credit: AP/Wide World Photos

LIBRARY OF CONGRESS CATALOGING-IN-PUBLICATION DATA

The Middle East / William Dudley, book editor.
    p. cm. — (Opposing viewpoints series)
  Includes bibliographical references and index.
  ISBN 0-7377-1806-4 (pbk. : alk. paper) — ISBN 0-7377-1805-6 (lib. : alk. paper)
    1. Ethnic conflict—Middle East. 2. Arab-Israeli conflict. 3. Islam and
politics—Middle East. 4. Violence—Religious aspects—Islam. 5. Peace—Religious
aspects—Islam. 6. Middle East—Foreign relations—United States. 7. United
States—Foreign relations—Middle East. I. Dudley, William. II. Series.
  HM1121.M53 2004
  305.8'00956—dc21   2003049020

Printed in the United States of America

"Congress shall make
no law...abridging the
freedom of speech, or of
the press."

First Amendment to the U.S. Constitution

The basic foundation of our democracy is the First
Amendment guarantee of freedom of expression.
The Opposing Viewpoints Series is dedicated to the
concept of this basic freedom and the idea that it is
more important to practice it than to enshrine it.

Contents

Why Consider
Opposing Viewpoints?

"The only way in which a human being can make some approach to knowing the whole of a subject is by hearing what can be said about it by persons of every variety of opinion and studying all modes in which it can be looked at by every character of mind. No wise man ever acquired his wisdom in any mode but this."

John Stuart Mill

In our media-intensive culture it is not difficult to find differing opinions. Thousands of newspapers and magazines and dozens of radio and television talk shows resound with differing points of view. The difficulty lies in deciding which opinion to agree with and which "experts" seem the most credible. The more inundated we become with differing opinions and claims, the more essential it is to hone critical reading and thinking skills to evaluate these ideas. Opposing Viewpoints books address this problem directly by presenting stimulating debates that can be used to enhance and teach these skills. The varied opinions contained in each book examine many different aspects of a single issue. While examining these conveniently edited opposing views, readers can develop critical thinking skills such as the ability to compare and contrast authors' credibility, facts, argumentation styles, use of persuasive techniques, and other stylistic tools. In short, the Opposing Viewpoints Series is an ideal way to attain the higher-level thinking and reading skills so essential in a culture of diverse and contradictory opinions.

In addition to providing a tool for critical thinking, Opposing Viewpoints books challenge readers to question their own strongly held opinions and assumptions. Most people form their opinions on the basis of upbringing, peer pressure, and personal, cultural, or professional bias. By reading carefully balanced opposing views, readers must directly confront new ideas as well as the opinions of those with whom they disagree. This is not to simplistically argue that everyone who reads opposing views will—or should—change his or her opinion. Instead, the series enhances readers' understanding of their own views by encouraging confrontation with opposing ideas. Careful examination of others' views can lead to the readers' understanding of the logical inconsistencies in their own opinions, perspective on why they hold an opinion, and the consideration of the possibility that their opinion requires further evaluation.

Evaluating Other Opinions

To ensure that this type of examination occurs, Opposing Viewpoints books present all types of opinions. Prominent spokespeople on different sides of each issue as well as well-known professionals from many disciplines challenge the reader. An additional goal of the series is to provide a forum for other, less known, or even unpopular viewpoints. The opinion of an ordinary person who has had to make the decision to cut off life support from a terminally ill relative, for example, may be just as valuable and provide just as much insight as a medical ethicist's professional opinion. The editors have two additional purposes in including these less known views. One, the editors encourage readers to respect others' opinions—even when not enhanced by professional credibility. It is only by reading or listening to and objectively evaluating others' ideas that one can determine whether they are worthy of consideration. Two, the inclusion of such viewpoints encourages the important critical thinking skill of objectively evaluating an author's credentials and bias. This evaluation will illuminate an author's reasons for taking a particular stance on an issue and will aid in readers' evaluation of the author's ideas.

It is our hope that these books will give readers a deeper understanding of the issues debated and an appreciation of the complexity of even seemingly simple issues when good and honest people disagree. This awareness is particularly important in a democratic society such as ours in which people enter into public debate to determine the common good. Those with whom one disagrees should not be regarded as enemies but rather as people whose views deserve careful examination and may shed light on one's own.

Thomas Jefferson once said that "difference of opinion leads to inquiry, and inquiry to truth." Jefferson, a broadly educated man, argued that "if a nation expects to be ignorant and free . . . it expects what never was and never will be." As individuals and as a nation, it is imperative that we consider the opinions of others and examine them with skill and discernment. The Opposing Viewpoints Series is intended to help readers achieve this goal.

David L. Bender and Bruno Leone,
Founders

Greenhaven Press anthologies primarily consist of previously published material taken from a variety of sources, including periodicals, books, scholarly journals, newspapers, government documents, and position papers from private and public organizations. These original sources are often edited for length and to ensure their accessibility for a young adult audience. The anthology editors also change the original titles of these works in order to clearly present the main thesis of each viewpoint and to explicitly indicate the opinion presented in the viewpoint. These alterations are made in consideration of both the reading and comprehension levels of a young adult audience. Every effort is made to ensure that Greenhaven Press accurately reflects the original intent of the authors included in this anthology.

Introduction

"The Middle East has often been left behind in the political and economic advancement of the world. That is the history of the region. But it need not and must not be its fate."
—President George W. Bush, April 4, 2002.

The *Middle East*, a term first used in a 1902 article by American naval historian Alfred Thayer Mahan, refers to a geographic region of southwestern Asia that also includes parts of northern Africa and southeastern Europe. Although there is some scholarly disagreement on exactly which countries are part of the Middle East, one generally accepted definition includes the countries of Bahrain, Egypt, Iran, Iraq, Israel, Jordan, Kuwait, Lebanon, Oman, Qatar, Saudi Arabia, Sudan, Syria, Turkey, United Arab Emirates, and Yemen. These countries cover an area of approximately 3.7 million square miles and are home to a population of about 350 million people. Situated between three continents, the region has been the site of human civilization for more than five thousand years.

Unfortunately, the region's recent history has been most notable for its political instability, conflict, and war. The endemic political violence occurring in the area in the twentieth century has carried over into the twenty-first; in March 2003, for example, an invasion force consisting of American and British forces entered the Middle Eastern nation of Iraq. The stated goal of the invasion was to forcibly end the regime of Saddam Hussein, president of Iraq since 1979. Hussein, who had previously involved his country in war when he attacked Iran in 1980 and Kuwait in 1990, had been accused of threatening American and world security by developing weapons of mass destruction and supporting terrorist groups. U.S. president George W. Bush and others feared that terrorists, assisted by Iraq, would attack the United States with such weapons.

Both before and after the commencement of war, however, various Bush administration officials, including the president himself, voiced the hope that the invasion could have beneficial changes in addition to Iraqi disarmament. They predicted that a successful U.S.-instigated "regime change" in Iraq could result in the creation of a democratic government there, much as Germany and Japan became democracies following World War II. Some even ventured to predict that such a development would in turn inspire democratic reforms throughout the Middle East. Most of the countries in the region are ruled by authoritarian governments in which dissent is suppressed and people have little say in how they are governed—a situation that has persisted despite the post–Cold War wave of democracy that transformed much of Europe, Africa, and South America in the 1980s and 1990s. But, as President Bush stated in a February 2003 speech, "a new regime in Iraq would serve as a dramatic and inspiring example of freedom for other nations in the region. It is presumptuous and insulting to suggest that a whole region of the world . . . is somehow untouched by the most basic aspirations of life." Bush and his supporters have held out the possibility that American military power, coupled with the democratic aspirations of the peoples of the region, might give birth to a new political era for the Middle East.

The American and British military effort to oust Saddam Hussein in 2003 was a quick success; within a month the regime was finished and American troops were met by cheering crowds in the Iraqi capital of Baghdad. Whether or not Bush's broader vision of Middle East democratization is realizable is a matter of debate. Indeed, much in the region's troubled history seems to argue against success. The creation of Iraq and its neighbors was itself the product of a war involving foreign powers. In World War I (1914–1918) the Turkish Ottoman Empire, which had ruled most of the Middle East since the 1500s, collapsed. The empire's demise set the stage for the genesis of new states that constitute the present-day map of the region—a genesis that was aided and abetted by the victorious World War I nations, especially Great Britain and France. The two nations divided much of the region between them and fostered the creation of states to protect their interests. Iraq, for example, was cobbled together by the British from three Ottoman provinces populated by an amalgam of peoples, including ethnic Kurds, Shiite Arabs, and Sunni Arabs.

Creating democratic sovereign nations was not the goal of the French and British after World War I. They instead wanted stable regimes whose governments would protect British and French interests. To that end, for example, Great Britain created a monarchy in Iraq and arranged for the accession of an Arab tribal leader (and World War I ally) to rule Iraq as King Faisal. The discovery of oil in large quantities in the Middle East during the 1920s and 1930s added to foreign interest in the region. Following World War II the United States and the Soviet Union replaced Great Britain and France as the leading foreign powers in the Middle East. During the long Cold War (1945–1989), both superpowers courted governments, built alliances, and protected arrangements for oil exploration and development; neither was overly concerned about creating democracies in the region.

The attempts by Great Britain and other countries to cre-

ate and manage Middle East nations is one reason, many believe, for the region's history of violence. For much of the twentieth century the people of the Middle East have struggled in various ways against foreign control. Opposition to foreign intervention in the Middle East has taken several forms. As early as 1920 the people of Iraq revolted against British rule and were forcibly suppressed. In the 1950s and 1960s, Arab nationalism was an important force. A new generation of military officers took over the governments of many Arab states, in some cases violently overthrowing governments that had cooperated with Great Britain and France. King Faisal II of Iraq was deposed and killed in 1958, for example, and replaced by a series of military dictators that culminated with Saddam Hussein. Arab nationalism was also directed at Israel, a nation founded in 1948 as a homeland for Jews. Many Arab leaders condemned Israel's Jewish emigrants from Europe and other places as alien invaders and viewed Israel's creation as something forced on them by the United States and other outside powers. A coalition of Arab nations immediately attacked Israel in 1948 in what was to be the first of several wars between Israel and its neighbors.

In the 1970s and later, Middle East resistance to foreign and American influence became more explicitly religious in nature. The religion of Islam, which has been inextricably linked to the region's society and culture for hundreds of years, emerged as a strong political force in many Middle East countries, in some cases superseding Arab nationalism. For example, Muslims demanded more political power in Lebanon's government, leading to civil war and conflict in that country in the 1970s and 1980s that in turn caused Lebanon's neighbors, Syria and Israel, to intervene militarily. In 1979 Muslim religious leader Ayatollah Ruhollah Khomeini successfully led a revolution that toppled Iran's U.S.-supported government. In addition, Islamic-sponsored terrorist groups based in the Middle East have engaged in numerous acts of terrorism against Israel, and more recently, the United States—including the September 11, 2001, attacks.

As many commentators have pointed out, the region's history of resistance to foreign designs may complicate, if not prevent, American efforts to spread democracy in the Middle East, despite America's initial military success in the 2003 Iraq war. "Such grandiose visions," writes political columnist Walter Shapiro, "are fraught with danger if . . . we ignore the sway of nationalism and historical memory." Historian Mark Mazower argues that "American troops would have to remain in the region for a very long time" for any realistic chance at creating a democratic and pro-American government in Iraq. But the longer they stay, he points out, the more likely they will be viewed as an unwelcome foreign (and non-Muslim) occupation force rather than as democratic liberators. Even if the United States were to succeed in helping Iraq create a functioning democratic regime, many observers believe that other Middle East nations may view Iraq not as a model to emulate, but as a weak victim of foreign conquest. As a team of scholars from the Carnegie Endowment for International Peace puts it, the idea that people in the region "would respond to the establishment of a U.S.-installed, nominally democratic Iraqi regime by rising up in a surge of pro-democratic protests, . . . and installing pro-western, pluralist regimes is far-fetched."

The political future of the Middle East is one of several key questions debated in *The Middle East: Opposing Viewpoints* in the following chapters: Why Is the Middle East a Conflict Area? How Does Islam Affect the Middle East? What Role Should the United States Play in the Middle East? Is Peace Between Israel and the Palestinians Possible? The wide-ranging viewpoints in this volume can help readers better understand some of the issues facing the Middle East and gain insight into whether a lasting peace in the region can be achieved.

CHAPTER 1

Why Is the Middle East a Conflict Area?

Chapter Preface

The Middle East has long been a center of ethnic, religious, and political rivalries. One issue that illustrates the persistent nature of these conflicts is the Arab-Israeli dispute. After World War I, Palestine, a former province of the Turkish Ottoman Empire, came under British administrative rule. At this time, Palestine was primarily populated by Arabs—both Muslims and Christians—and by Jews, who comprised 10 percent of the population. The number of Jews in Palestine increased, however, after World War II, during which 6 million European Jews were killed in the Nazi Holocaust. This calamity bolstered efforts on the part of Zionists to establish a Jewish homeland in Palestine. Responding in part to Zionist demands, the United Nations in 1947 voted to divide Palestine into Jewish and Arab states—a decision that was rejected by neighboring Arab nations. Jewish nationalists proclaimed the establishment of the state of Israel in 1948, accepting the boundaries delineated by the UN resolution. The armies of Egypt, Iraq, Jordan, and Lebanon immediately invaded Israel, but were defeated in 1949.

Subsequent wars between Arab nations and Israel erupted in 1956, 1967, 1973, and 1982. In addition, in 1987, 1996, and 2000 widespread civil violence broke out within Israel between Israelis and Palestinians—violence that has continued to this day. Much of this conflict concerns the large number of Palestinian refugees displaced when Israel was formed. After 1948 large numbers of Palestinians—some uprooted by war, some fearing for their safety in a new Jewish state, and some trying to escape extremist groups on both sides—fled Israel. Most of these refugees—and their descendants—are now living in camps in the West Bank and the Gaza Strip, territories that Israel has occupied since the 1967 Six-Day War. Palestinian demands for Israel to give up these lands to Palestinian control, and Israeli efforts to protect Israel from Palestinian militant violence, are a continuing source of friction in the region.

The Arab-Israeli dispute is not the only cause of conflict in the Middle East, of course. The region's role as a vital supplier of oil increases its potential for political, territorial, and economic strife as nations vie for control over this precious resource. Iraq's 1990 invasion of Kuwait, for example, was largely seen as motivated by Iraq's desire to obtain its neighbor's vast petroleum resources. Prior to that, territorial and religious animosities between Iraq and Iran erupted into the region's bloodiest twentieth-century war, which lasted from 1980 to 1988 and resulted in more than 1 million casualties. The causes of such wars and conflict in the region are analyzed in the following chapter.

*"In the long-run, the only hope for a
normal, peaceful life for the people of
Israel is for their government to end
their occupation of Palestinian land."*

Israeli Occupation of Palestinian Lands Is a Source of Conflict

A Jewish Voice for Peace

Many observers have argued that a key cause of conflict in
the Middle East has been Israel's occupation of territories it
conquered in the 1967 war. These territories include the
West Bank (formerly held by Jordan), Gaza and the Sinai
Peninsula (held by Egypt) and the Golan Heights (held by
Syria). Israel signed a peace agreement with Egypt in 1978
and returned Sinai in 1982, annexed the Golan Heights in
1981, and allowed some Palestinian self-rule in parts of the
remaining occupied territories in Gaza and the West Bank in
the 1990s. In the following viewpoint by A Jewish Voice for
Peace, the authors contend that violence will be inevitable in
the Middle East as long as Israel continues to occupy Palestinian territory. They contend that Israel's occupation bru-
talizes Palestinians, is condemned by the world, and is unnecessary for Israel's security. A Jewish Voice for Peace is a
California-based activist organization.

As you read, consider the following questions:

1. Why are Jewish settlements in territories outside Israel's
   1967 boundaries illegal, according to the authors?
2. What human rights violations against the Palestinian
   people do the authors describe and condemn?

A Jewish Voice for Peace, *From Jew to Jew: Why We Should Oppose the Israeli
Occupation of the West Bank and Gaza.* Berkeley, CA: A Jewish Voice for Peace,
2002. Copyright © 2002 by A Jewish Voice for Peace. Reproduced by permission.

B ased in the San Francisco Bay Area, A JEWISH VOICE FOR PEACE is the oldest and largest of a growing number of Jewish groups that are convinced that the Israeli occupation of Palestinian territory must end. There are two compelling reasons for this. First, we wish to preserve the best part of our Jewish heritage—a deeply-ingrained sense of morality—and pass it on to the next generation, unsullied by the mistreatment of another people. We were brought up to believe that, as Jews, we are obligated to always take the moral high road and we can't imagine letting this proud ethical tradition die now.

Second, we are convinced that the only way to ensure the security of the people of Israel is for their government to conclude a just peace with the Palestinians. Without some reasonable version of justice being done, there will never be peace, and so we oppose any Israeli government policy that denies the Palestinians their legitimate rights. . . .

In the interest of peace, and with an open heart and mind, please consider the following facts.

1. The Occupation

The international community, through the United Nations and other forums, has made it clear that virtually the entire world considers the Israeli occupation of territories it captured in the 1967 war to be wrong and contrary to basic principles of international law. Every year since 1967 (up until the Oslo Process started [in 1993]), the UN General Assembly passed the same resolution (usually by lopsided votes like 150-2), stating that Israel is obligated to vacate the West Bank, Gaza and East Jerusalem, in exchange for security guaranteed by the international community, in accordance with UN Resolution 242.

While the circumstances were much different, the legal basis of these resolutions is the same principle used to force Iraq out of Kuwait [in 1991]—i.e., a country cannot annex or indefinitely occupy territory gained by force of arms. The only reason that Israel is able to maintain its occupation of Palestinian land is that the US routinely vetoes every Security Council resolution that would insist that Israel live up to its obligations under international law.

One of the original goals of Zionism was to create a Jewish state that would be just another normal country. If that is what Israel wants (and that is a reasonable goal), then it must be held to the same standards as any other country, including the prohibition against annexing territory captured by force of arms.

2. The Settlements

Similarly, all Jewish settlements, every single one, in territories outside Israel's 1967 boundaries, are a direct violation of the Geneva Conventions, which Israel has signed and is obligated to abide by, as well as UN Security Council Resolutions 446 and 465. As John Quigley, a professor of international law at Ohio State has written, "The Geneva Convention requires an occupying power to change the existing order as little as possible during its tenure. One aspect of this obligation is that it must leave the territory to the people it finds there. It may not bring its own people to populate the country. This prohibition is found in the convention's Article 49 which states, 'The Occupying Power shall not deport or transfer parts of its own civilian population into the territory it occupies.'". . .

In fact, on December 5, 2001, Switzerland convened a conference of 114 nations that have signed the Fourth Geneva Convention (a conference boycotted by the US and Israel). The assembled nations decided *unanimously* that the Convention did indeed apply to the occupied territories, that Israel was in gross violation of their obligations under that Convention, that Jewish-only settlements in those territories were illegal under the rules of the Convention, and that it was the responsibility of the other contracting parties to stop these violations of international law.

To be in such flagrant violation of the norms of international behavior is bad for Israel's standing in the world, bad for the Jewish people as a whole and, as we shall see, totally unnecessary.

3. Israel's Security

It is sometimes argued that the settlements are necessary for Israel's security, to protect Israel from terrorism and the threat of violence. But the reality is that the settlements are a major cause of Israel's current security problems, not the cure for them. *New York Times* columnist Anthony Lewis pointed out the aggressive nature of the settlements as follows, "It is false to see the settlements as ordinary villages or towns where Israelis only want to live in peace with their Palestinian neighbors. They are in fact imposed by force—superior Israeli military force—on Palestinian territory. Many have been built precisely to assert Israeli power and ownership. They are not peaceful villages but militarized encampments . . . The settlement policy is not just a political but a moral danger to the character of the state."

Palestinian Actions

"But wouldn't the Palestinians use their own state as a base for even more attacks against Israel?", it might be asked. For one, the Palestinians have long agreed that their future state would be non-militarized, no foreign forces hostile to Israel would be allowed in, and international monitors could be stationed on Palestinian land in order to verify these conditions.

Terrorism and Hope

As for individual acts of terrorism, there is an historical precedent that gives a realistic answer to this question. During the first years after the Oslo agreements were signed [in 1993], Hamas[1] tried to disrupt the peace process but, because of the prevailing optimism, their influence in Palestinian society diminished and their armed attacks fell off sharply. What that means for the future is that if the Palestinian people feel that even a rough version of justice has been done, they will not support the more extreme elements in their political spectrum. This is not just guesswork; it already happened with just the hope of justice being done.

Another aspect of this is that if Israel had internationally recognized borders, then they could be defended much more easily than the current situation where every hill in Palestine is a potential bone of contention because of Jewish settlements encroaching on Palestinian land. If they and their settlers and the military apparatus they require were gone, and the Palestinians were given enough aid by the in-

1. Hamas is a militant Palestinian group, formed in 1987, that seeks to replace Israel with an Islamic Palestinian state. Hamas has been classified as a terrorist organization by the United States.

ternational community to create a viable economy in their own state, they would naturally be overjoyed and a positive turn of events would be the inevitable result.

4. "But Don't They Just Want to Drive the Jews into the Sea?"

Officially since 1988, and unofficially for years before that, the Palestinian position has been that they recognize Israel's right to exist in peace and security within their 1967 borders. Period. At the same time, they expect to be allowed to establish a truly independent, viable, contiguous, non-militarized state in all of the West Bank, Gaza and East Jerusalem. This is what UN Resolution 242 says: "Land for Peace"—and the Palestinian Authority has stated repeatedly that UN Resolution 242 has to be the basis for any long-lasting solution to the conflict.

It is true that some Palestinians advocate that all of historic Palestine should be under Arab control, but there is no support for this position, either in the international community, nor among most Palestinians. Statements to that effect are just hyperbole and do not represent the official Palestinian position. Similarly, statements by some Palestinians inciting people to violence against Israelis can easily be matched by statements from Orthodox rabbis and fundamentalist settlers calling for death to the Arabs. There are *meshuganahs* [crazy people] aplenty on both sides.

But since the Palestinians' official position is clear, why shouldn't Israel take the Palestinians up on this offer and withdraw from the occupied territories? Israel is far stronger militarily than all the Arab armies combined and would face no credible military threat from a Palestinian state. And the threat of individual terrorist acts would, of necessity, be much less once the Palestinians felt that they had received a modicum of justice.

What would Israel lose by this obvious solution of just ending the occupation, which they could do tomorrow if they wanted to (or if the US insisted that they do so)? The only thing it would "lose" is the dream of some of its citizens for a "Greater Israel", where Israel's boundaries are expanded to its biblical borders. The problem with that dream is that it totally ignores the legitimate rights of the Palestinian people, and the will of virtually the entire international community. As long as the right-wing settlers and their supporters in the Israeli government insist on pursuing this dream, there will be nothing but bloodshed forever. The Palestinian people have lived in Palestine for thousands of years and they are not going away. Israel must conclude a just peace with them or innocent blood will continue to be shed indefinitely.

5. *Negotiations Leading up to the Current Intifada*

It has often been asked, "But didn't [Israeli prime minister Ehud] Barak offer 95% of the Occupied Territories to [Palestinian leader Yassar] Arafat at Camp David [in 2000] and

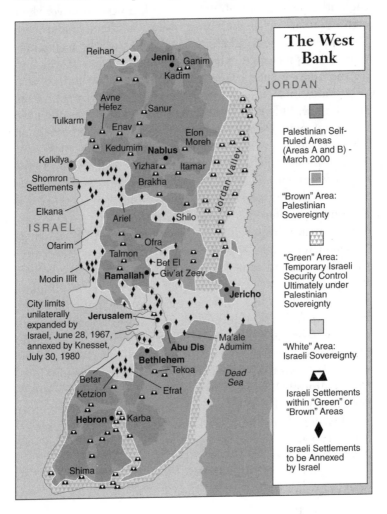

The West Bank

JORDAN

Reihan
Jenin Ganim
Kadim

Avne Hefez
Sanur
Tulkarm
Enav
Elon Moreh
Kedumim **Nablus**
Kalkilya
Yizhar Itamar
Shomron Settlements
Brakha
Elkana
Ariel Shilo
ISRAEL
Ofarim
Ofra
Talmon
Bet El
Modin Illit
Ramallah Giv'at Zeev

Jordan Valley

Jericho

City limits unilaterally expanded by Israel, June 28, 1967, annexed by Knesset, July 30, 1980

Jerusalem

Ma'ale Adumim
Abu Dis
Bethlehem
Tekoa

Dead Sea

Betar
Ketzion
Efrat

Hebron Karba

Shima

Palestinian Self-Ruled Areas (Areas A and B) - March 2000

"Brown" Area: Palestinian Sovereignty

"Green" Area: Temporary Israeli Security Control Ultimately under Palestinian Sovereignty

"White" Area: Israeli Sovereignty

Israeli Settlements within "Green" or "Brown" Areas

Israeli Settlements to be Annexed by Israel

doesn't his rejection of that offer mean that they don't want peace?" There are several crucial things to understand here. First, prisoners may occupy 95% of a prison's space, but it is the other 5% that determines who is in control. Similarly, the offer Barak made at Camp David II would have left the main settlement blocks and their Jewish-only bypass roads in place. Along with the extensive areas Israel planned on retaining indefinitely for its military use, this would have dissected Palestinian territory into separate bantustans ("native reservations"), isolated from each other, each surrounded by Israeli-controlled territory, having no common borders with each other or other Arab nations, with no control over their own air-space, with their main water aquifers (underneath the settlement blocs) taken by Israel, and with the Israeli military able to surround and blockade each enclave at will.

Jerusalem would have been similarly dissected so that each Palestinian island would be surrounded by an Israeli sea. This wouldn't be an acceptable "end of the conflict" to you if you were Palestinian, would it? Please see the map on [the previous page] and see for yourself what this "most generous" offer actually looked like. (Israel actually presented no maps at Camp David itself, but this was their offer of two months previous, and only marginal additional territory was theoretically offered at Camp David.)

The other important question here is 95% of what? "Greater Jerusalem" was unilaterally annexed by Israel after the 1967 war and so it was not included as West Bank territory in Barak's offer, even though it takes up a large chunk of the West Bank, most of it having no municipal connection with the actual city of Jerusalem. The international community has never recognized Israeli sovereignty over "Greater Jerusalem" and has repeatedly declared that Israel should withdraw from this and all territories it conquered by force of arms in 1967. Barak's offer also excluded large swaths of the Jordan Valley which the Israeli military would control indefinitely. Thus the Foundation for Middle East Peace estimates that the actual percentage of occupied land offered to the Palestinians was more like 80%, not 95%. . . .

6. *Looking at Cause and Effect*

"What about Palestinian crimes? Why don't you lay equal

blame on them?" Certainly, Palestinians have committed grave crimes, and in any process of reconciliation, both sides will have much to answer for. But as Jews, we are responsible to look at Israel objectively, and not just when Israelis are victims of violence.

Must Understand History

In order to understand why there is the level of violence we see today, it is necessary to understand how we got to this point.

a) Before the 1967 war. Before the Israeli occupation of the West Bank and Gaza, there was little organized Palestinian resistance. The majority of the tension was between Israel and the neighboring states. For the most part, violence between Israel and the Palestinians was limited to isolated Palestinian "infiltrations", as Israel generally referred to them.

The Israeli population may certainly have believed that they were in mortal danger from the armies of their Arab neighbors. But by the mid-1960s, Israeli leaders had a good deal of confidence that they could defeat a combination of Arab forces similar to that which they acomplished in 1948, and with greater ease. History, of course, proved them correct, which calls into question the myth that Israel was fighting a self-defensive war for its very existence in 1967.

The 1967 War

b) The 1967 war itself. The myth that the 1967 war was a purely defensive one is further weakened by statements of Israeli leaders themselves. For example, the *New York Times* published an article on May 11, 1997 quoting Moshe Dayan's[2] own diaries, in which he admits that the kibbutz residents who pressed the Government to take the Golan Heights in 1967 did so less for security than for the farmland. "They didn't even try to hide their greed for that land . . . The Syrians, on the fourth day of the war, were not a threat to us", Dayan wrote.

Or again from Professor John Quigley's landmark book, *Palestine And Israel*, "Mordecai Bentov, a cabinet minister who attended the June 4 (1967) cabinet meeting and sup-

2. Moshe Dayan was Israel's defense minister during the 1967 war.

ported the decision to invade Egypt, said Israel's 'entire story' about 'the danger of extermination' was 'invented of whole cloth and exaggerated after the fact to justify the annexation of new Arab territories'."

Even Menachem Begin[3] said, "The Egyptian army concentrations in the Sinai approaches do not prove that [Egyptian leader Gamal Abdel] Nasser was really about to attack us. We must be honest with ourselves. We decided to attack him." In short, the argument of self-defense does not stand up to a close examination of the historical record.

c) Peace Proposals after the 1967 war. In 1969, [Richard] Nixon's Secretary of State, William Rogers, proposed a peace plan based on UN Resolution 242, which would have guaranteed Israel's security within her pre-1967 borders. Israel rejected it out-of-hand. In 1971, Egyptian President Anwar Sadat offered Israel a similar proposal (which did not mention Palestinian rights at all). This was also rejected by Israel.

In 1976, Egypt, Syria, Jordan and the PLO [Palestine Liberation Organization] supported a resolution in the UN Security Council affirming Israel's right to exist in peace and security, as in UN Resolution 242, but with a Palestinian state created alongside Israel. Israel opposed it and the US vetoed it. Arafat personally reaffirmed his support of a two-state solution in statements made to Senator Adlai Stevenson in 1976, and Representative Paul Findley and *New York Times* columnist Anthony Lewis in 1978. The Saudis made similar proposals in 1979 and 1981, which were reiterated in their 2002 peace proposal, adopted by the entire Arab League.

Not a Defensive War

Yet Israel rejected all these peace proposals, and more, even though Israel's security was guaranteed in each one of them. Why? The historical record is clear that Israel's desire for additional land has been the single most important factor behind its expansionist policies. As David Ben-Gurion[4] said in 1938, "I favor partition of the country because when we become a strong power after the establishment of the state, we

---

3. Manachem Begin was Israel's prime minister from 1977 to 1983. 4. David Ben-Gurion was a Zionist leader who became Israel's first prime minister in 1948.

will abolish partition and spread throughout all of Palestine."

In sum, the 1967 war was not a purely defensive war on Israel's part, as Begin told us. The Israeli army met very little Palestinian resistance during the early years of the occupation. In the '60s and '70s, most Palestinian violence came from groups outside of the Occupied Territories. It is the Israeli desire to retain control over the West Bank, its expanding settlements and land appropriations that have sown the seeds of the situation we have today.

Israeli Actions

d) The Israeli occupation as the root cause of the violence. The main hallmark of the Israeli occupation has been the forcible expropriation of over half of the West Bank and Gaza for Jewish-only settlements, Jewish-only by-pass roads and Israeli closed military areas. These expropriations are possible only because of overwhelming Israeli military might and are, in and of themselves, acts of violence—just as armed robbery is an act of violence, even if no one is hurt. Can we really expect that no violent reaction to it would have occurred?

Israel's former Attorney General, Michael Ben-Yair stated point-blank in [the Israel newspaper] *Ha'aretz* (3/3/02) that, "We enthusiastically chose to become a colonial society, ignoring international treaties, expropriating lands, transferring settlers from Israel to the occupied territories, engaging in theft and finding justification for all these activities . . . In effect, we established an apartheid regime in the occupied territories immediately following their capture. That oppressive regime exists to this day."

e) How did the current level of violence come about? Palestinian attacks on Israeli civilians are well documented in our own media. And, while major Israeli incursions have gotten a good deal of attention, day-to-day excesses of the Israeli military have not been so widely reported. To get an accurate picture of the chain of events, let's look at the reports issued by human rights groups near the beginning of the current intifada.

Human Rights Violations

Human Rights Watch, for example, stated that, "Israeli security forces have committed by far the most serious and systematic violations. We documented excessive and indiscriminate use of lethal force, arbitrary killings, and collective punishment, including willful destruction of property and severe restrictions on movement that far exceed any possible military necessity."

B'Tselem is Israel's leading human rights group and their detailed analyses of the current intifada can be found at www.btselem.org. They concluded early on that, "In spite of claims to the contrary, Israel has not adopted a policy of restraint in its response to events in the Occupied Territories . . . Israel uses excessive and disproportionate force in dispersing demonstrations of unarmed Palestinians . . . Collective punishment, in the form of Israel's severe restrictions on Palestinians' movement in the Occupied Territories, makes life unbearable for hundreds of thousands with no justification." Collective punishment is illegal under international law.

The United Nations Commission on Human Rights reported the following, "There is considerable evidence of indiscriminate firing at civilians in the proximity of demonstrations and elsewhere (by Israeli troops) . . . The live ammunition employed includes high-velocity bullets which splinter on impact and cause the maximum harm. Equally disturbing is the evidence that many of the deaths and injuries inflicted were the result of head wounds and wounds to the upper body, which suggests an intention to cause serious bodily injury rather than restrain demonstrations . . . The measures of closure, curfew or destruction of property constitute violations of the Fourth Geneva Convention and human rights obligations binding upon Israel.". . .

The overwhelming consensus of these reports means that Israeli demands for the Palestinians to "stop the violence" turns reality on its head. The Palestinians have suffered almost four times the fatalities that Israel has in the current fighting, as well as tens of thousands of serious injuries. Furthermore, answering stone throwing with M-16 military weapons designed for battlefield use, or ineffective Molotov cocktails with very effective armored tanks and attack helicopters is simply not morally justifiable.

It is also important to keep in mind that many of Israel's current actions have been going on, in various degrees, for the last 35 years—systematic torture of Palestinians in Israeli jails, the forcible and illegal appropriation of over half the West Bank and Gaza by Israel for Jewish-only uses, daily humiliations and abuse at Israeli military checkpoints all over Palestinian land—these have combined to bring Palestinian anger to a boiling point.

Obstacles to Peace

In sum, we have seen that Israeli actions have served to seriously escalate the violence, and that Israel's stubborn refusal to end its occupation of the West Bank and Gaza Strip, even to the extent of just stopping its settlement activity, has been a major obstacle to any progress towards peace.

To be sure, Palestinian attacks on Israeli civilians have also been major obstacles towards such progress. Occupation and repression can never justify terrorism against civilians, but neither do terrorist acts by a few negate the Palestinian people's right to self-determination.

The best way to address these crimes is to end the occupation which inspires the Palestinians to commit them. Recent history has demonstrated clearly that support for such crimes, and the number of Palestinians willing to commit them, drops precipitously when the Palestinians have had hope for independence, and risen sharply in response to the intensifying occupation and expansion of settlements. . . .

End the Occupation

Any country has the right and the responsibility to protect its citizens, and Israel is no exception. But its policies for the last 35 years, and especially during the current intifada, have been based on the old adage, "the best defense is a good offense". While that's OK in football, in Israel that has translated into systematic torture or ill-treatment of literally hundreds of thousands of Palestinians in Israeli prisons, according to *B'Tselem* and other reputable groups. It means wanton cruelty being inflicted every day at military checkpoints, wanton destruction of Palestinian homes, and illegal strangling of Palestinian economic life, leading to extreme deprivation. And there is no other phrase than "war crimes" to accurately describe many of the actions of the IDF [Israeli

Defense Forces] during the attacks against the Palestinian civilian population in the spring of 2002. In short, the Israeli occupation of Palestinian territory is simply wrong—brutal, illegal and unnecessary.

We do agree that both sides have done poorly in advancing the cause of peace. As Jews, however, it is incumbent upon us to put our own house in order, above all else. As Americans, our responsibility is doubled. Our government has, through unprecedented financial and political support, allowed Israel to maintain its occupation and commit human rights violations with complete impunity. Thus, we are both responsible for the escalation and in a unique position to do something about it.

In the long-run, the only hope for a normal, peaceful life for the people of Israel is for their government to end their occupation of Palestinian land, allow the creation of a viable Palestinian state, and live and let live. The only other alternative is the current situation of endless bloodshed, which our silence, among other things, makes possible.

"It is not the 1967 occupation that led to the Palestinians' rejection of peaceful coexistence and their pursuit of violence."

Israeli Occupation of Palestinian Lands Is Not a Source of Conflict

Efraim Karsh

Efraim Karsh is professor and director of Mediterranean studies at King's College, University of London. His books include *The Arab-Israeli Conflict: The Palestine War 1948*. In the following viewpoint, he rejects the view that Israel's occupation of the territories it acquired in the 1967 Six-Day War has been brutal or oppressive, or that it is the cause of violence between Palestinians and Israelis. Palestinian terrorism predates 1967, he argues, and has intensified even after Israel took steps in the 1990s to withdraw from the territories and permit Palestinian self-rule. It is Arab and Palestinian opposition to the existence of Israel itself that is a root cause of regional conflict, Karsh concludes.

As you read, consider the following questions:

1. What different meanings does the term "occupation" have regarding Israel, according to Karsh?
2. How have the living standards and conditions of Palestinians improved under Israeli rule, according to the author?
3. Why does Karsh attribute an increase in Palestinian terrorist attacks in the 1990s to an *"absence* of occupation"?

Efraim Karsh, "What Occupation?" *Commentary*, vol. 114, July/August 2002, pp. 46–51. Copyright © 2002 by the American Jewish Committee. Reproduced by permission of the publisher and the author.

No term has dominated the discourse of the Palestinian-Israeli conflict more than "occupation." For decades now, hardly a day has passed without some mention in the international media of Israel's supposedly illegitimate presence on Palestinian lands. This presence is invoked to explain the origins and persistence of the conflict between the parties, to show Israel's allegedly brutal and repressive nature, and to justify the worst anti-Israel terrorist atrocities. The occupation, in short, has become a catchphrase, and like many catchphrases it means different things to different people.

Different Conceptions of Occupation

For most Western observers, the term "occupation" describes Israel's control of the Gaza Strip and the West Bank, areas that it conquered during the Six-Day war of June 1967. But for many Palestinians and Arabs, the Israeli presence in these territories represents only the latest chapter in an uninterrupted story of "occupations" dating back to the very creation of Israel on "stolen" land. If you go looking for a book about Israel in the foremost Arab bookstore on London's Charing Cross Road, you will find it in the section labeled "Occupied Palestine." That this is the prevailing view not only among Arab residents of the West Bank and Gaza but among Palestinians living within Israel itself as well as elsewhere around the world is shown by the routine insistence on a Palestinian "right of return" that is meant to reverse the effects of the "1948 occupation"—i.e., the establishment of the state of Israel itself. . . .

Hanan Ashrawi, the most articulate exponent of the Palestinian cause, has been . . . forthright in erasing the line between post-1967 and pre-1967 "occupations." "I come to you today with a heavy heart," she told the now-infamous World Conference Against Racism in Durban last summer (2002), "leaving behind a nation in captivity held hostage to an ongoing *naqba* [catastrophe]":

> In 1948, we became subject to a grave historical injustice manifested in a dual victimization: on the one hand, the injustice of dispossession, dispersion, and exile forcibly enacted on the population. . . . On the other hand, those who remained were subjected to the systematic oppression and bru-

tality of an inhuman occupation that robbed them of all their rights and liberties.

This original "occupation"—that is again, the creation and existence of the state of Israel—was later extended, in Ashrawi's narrative, as a result of the Six-Day war:

> Those of us who came under Israeli occupation in 1967 have languished in the West Bank, Jerusalem, and the Gaza Strip under a unique combination of military occupation, settler colonization, and systematic oppression. Rarely has the human mind devised such varied, diverse, and comprehensive means of wholesale brutalization and persecution.

Taken together, the charges against Israel's various "occupations" represent—and are plainly intended to be—a damning indictment of the entire Zionist enterprise. In almost every particular, they are also grossly false.

The Creation of Israel

In 1948, no Palestinian state was invaded or destroyed to make way for the establishment of Israel. From biblical times, when this territory was the state of the Jews, to its occupation by the British army at the end of World War I, Palestine had never existed as a distinct political entity but was rather part of one empire after another, from the Romans, to the Arabs, to the Ottomans. When the British arrived in 1917, the immediate loyalties of the area's inhabitants were parochial—to clan, tribe, village, town, or religious sect—and coexisted with their fealty to the Ottoman sultan-caliph as the religious and temporal head of the world Muslim community.

Under a League of Nations mandate explicitly meant to pave the way for the creation of a Jewish national home, the British established the notion of an independent Palestine for the first time and delineated its boundaries. In 1947, confronted with a determined Jewish struggle for independence, Britain returned the mandate to the League's successor, the United Nations, which in turn decided on November 29, 1947, to partition mandatory Palestine into two states: one Jewish, the other Arab.

The state of Israel was thus created by an internationally recognized act of national self-determination—an act, moreover, undertaken by an ancient people in its own homeland.

In accordance with common democratic practice, the Arab population in the new state's midst was immediately recognized as a legitimate ethnic and religious minority. As for the prospective Arab state, its designated territory was slated to include, among other areas, the two regions under contest today—namely, Gaza and the West Bank (with the exception of Jerusalem, which was to be placed under international control).

As is well known, the implementation of the UN's partition plan was aborted by the effort of the Palestinians and of the surrounding Arab states to destroy the Jewish state at birth. What is less well known is that even if the Jews had lost the war, their territory would not have been handed over to the Palestinians. Rather, it would have been divided among the invading Arab forces, for the simple reason that none of the region's Arab regimes viewed the Palestinians as a distinct nation. As the eminent Arab-American historian Philip Hitti described the common Arab view to an Anglo-American commission of inquiry in 1946, "There is no such thing as Palestine in history, absolutely not.". . .

No Conception of Palestinian Nationhood

Neither Egypt nor Jordan ever allowed Palestinian self-determination in Gaza and the West Bank—which were, respectively, the parts of Palestine conquered by them during the 1948–49 war. Indeed, even UN Security Council Resolution 242, which after the Six-Day war of 1967 established the principle of "land for peace" as the cornerstone of future Arab-Israeli peace negotiations, did not envisage the creation of a Palestinian state. . . .

At this time—we are speaking of the late 1960's—Palestinian nationhood was rejected by the entire international community, including the Western democracies, the Soviet Union (the foremost supporter of radical Arabism), and the Arab world itself. "Moderate" Arab rulers like the Hashemites in Jordan viewed an independent Palestinian state as a mortal threat to their own kingdom, while the Saudis saw it as a potential source of extremism and instability. Pan-Arab nationalists were no less adamantly opposed, having their own purposes in mind for the region. As late as 1974, Syrian President

Hafez al-Assad openly referred to Palestine as "not only a part of the Arab homeland but a basic part of southern Syria"; there is no reason to think he had changed his mind by the time of his death in 2000.

Nor, for that matter, did the populace of the West Bank and Gaza regard itself as a distinct nation. The collapse and dispersion of Palestinian society following the 1948 defeat had shattered an always fragile communal fabric, and the subsequent physical separation of the various parts of the Palestinian diaspora prevented the crystallization of a national identity. Host Arab regimes actively colluded in discouraging any such sense from arising. . . .

The Period After 1967

What, then, of the period after 1967, when these territories passed into the hands of Israel? Is it the case that Palestinians in the West Bank and Gaza have been the victims of the most "varied, diverse, and comprehensive means of wholesale brutalization and persecution" ever devised by the human mind?

At the very least, such a characterization would require a rather drastic downgrading of certain other well-documented 20th-century phenomena, from the slaughter of Armenians during World War I and onward through a grisly chronicle of tens upon tens of millions murdered, driven out, crushed under the heels of despots. By stark contrast, during the three decades of Israel's control, far fewer Palestinians were killed at Jewish hands than by King Hussein of Jordan in the single month of September 1970 when, fighting off an attempt by Yasir Arafat's PLO [Palestine Liberation Organization] to destroy his monarchy, he dispatched (according to the Palestinian scholar Yezid Sayigh) between 3,000 and 5,000 Palestinians, among them anywhere from 1,500 to 3,500 civilians. . . .

Such crude comparisons aside, to present the Israeli occupation of the West Bank and Gaza as "systematic oppression" is itself the inverse of the truth. It should be recalled, first of all, that this occupation did not come about as a consequence of some grand expansionist design, but rather was incidental to Israel's success against a pan-Arab attempt to destroy it.

Upon the outbreak of Israeli-Egyptian hostilities on June 5, 1967, the Israeli government secretly pleaded with King Hussein of Jordan, the de-facto ruler of the West Bank, to forgo any military action; the plea was rebuffed by the Jordanian monarch, who was loathe to lose the anticipated spoils of what was to be the Arabs' "final round" with Israel.

Thus it happened that, at the end of the conflict, Israel unexpectedly found itself in control of some one million Palestinians, with no definite idea about their future status and lacking any concrete policy for their administration. In the wake of the war, the only objective adopted by then-Minister of Defense Moshe Dayan was to preserve normalcy in the territories through a mixture of economic inducements and a minimum of Israeli intervention. The idea was that the local populace would be given the freedom to administer itself as it wished, and would be able to maintain regular contact with the Arab world via the Jordan River bridges. In sharp contrast with, for example, the U.S. occupation of postwar Japan, which saw a general censorship of all Japanese media and a comprehensive revision of school curricula, Israel made no attempt to reshape Palestinian culture. It limited its oversight of the Arabic press in the territories to military and security matters, and allowed the continued use in local schools of Jordanian textbooks filled with vile anti-Semitic and anti-Israel propaganda.

Economic and Social Progress

Israel's restraint in this sphere—which turned out to be desperately misguided—is only part of the story. The larger part, still untold in all its detail, is of the astounding social and economic progress made by the Palestinian Arabs under Israeli "oppression." At the inception of the occupation, conditions in the territories were quite dire. Life expectancy was low; malnutrition, infectious diseases, and child mortality were rife; and the level of education was very poor. Prior to the 1967 war, fewer than 60 percent of all male adults had been employed, with unemployment among refugees running as high as 83 percent. Within a brief period after the war, Israeli occupation had led to dramatic improvements in general well-being, placing the population of the territories ahead of most of their Arab neighbors.

In the economic sphere, most of this progress was the result of access to the far larger and more advanced Israeli economy: the number of Palestinians working in Israel rose from zero in 1967 to 66,000 in 1975 and 109,000 by 1986, accounting for 35 percent of the employed population of the West Bank and 45 percent in Gaza. Close to 2,000 industrial plants, employing almost half of the work force, were established in the territories under Israeli rule.

Asay. © 1996 by Creators Syndicate, Inc. Reprinted with permission.

During the 1970's, the West Bank and Gaza constituted the fourth fastest-growing economy *in the world*—ahead of such "wonders" as Singapore, Hong Kong, and Korea, and substantially ahead of Israel itself. . . .

Under Israeli rule, the Palestinians also made vast progress in social welfare. Perhaps most significantly, mortality rates in the West Bank and Gaza fell by more than two-thirds between 1970 and 1990, while life expectancy rose from 48 years in 1967 to 72 in 2000 (compared with an average of 68 years for all the countries of the Middle East and North Africa). Israeli medical programs reduced the infant-mortality rate of 60 per 1,000 live births in 1968 to 15 per 1,000 in 2000 (in Iraq the rate is 64, in Egypt 40, in Jordan 23, in Syria 22). And under a systematic program of inoculation, childhood diseases like polio, whooping cough, tetanus, and measles were eradicated.

No less remarkable were advances in the Palestinians' standard of living. By 1986, 92.8 percent of the population in the West Bank and Gaza had electricity around the clock, as compared to 20.5 percent in 1967; 85 percent had running water in dwellings, as compared to 16 percent in 1967; 83.5 percent had electric or gas ranges for cooking, as compared to 4 percent in 1967; and so on for refrigerators, televisions, and cars.

Finally, and perhaps most strikingly, during the two decades preceding the *intifada* of the late 1980's, the number of schoolchildren in the territories grew by 102 percent, and the number of classes by 99 percent, though the population itself had grown by only 28 percent. Even more dramatic was the progress in higher education. At the time of the Israeli occupation of Gaza and the West Bank, not a single university existed in these territories. By the early 1990's, there were seven such institutions, boasting some 16,500 students. Illiteracy rates dropped to 14 percent of adults over age 15, compared with 69 percent in Morocco, 61 percent in Egypt, 45 percent in Tunisia, and 44 percent in Syria.

Rise of the PLO

All this, as I have noted, took place against the backdrop of Israel's hands-off policy in the political and administrative spheres. Indeed, even as the PLO (until 1982 headquartered in Lebanon and thereafter in Tunisia) proclaimed its ongoing commitment to the destruction of the Jewish state, the Israelis did surprisingly little to limit its political influence in the territories. The publication of pro-PLO editorials was permitted in the local press, and anti-Israel activities by PLO supporters were tolerated so long as they did not involve overt incitement to violence. . . . As a result, the PLO gradually established itself as the predominant force in the territories, relegating the pragmatic traditional leadership to the fringes of the political system. . . .

But these things were not to be. By the mid-1970's, the PLO had made itself into the "sole representative of the Palestinian people," and in short order Jordan and Egypt washed their hands of the West Bank and Gaza. Whatever the desires of the people living in the territories, the PLO had vowed from the moment of its founding in the mid-1960's—well *before* the Six-Day war—to pursue its "revolution until victory," that is, until the destruction of the Jewish state. Once its position was secure, it proceeded to do precisely that.

By the mid-1990's, thanks to [the 1993] Oslo [accords], the PLO had achieved a firm foothold in the West Bank and Gaza. Its announced purpose was to lay the groundwork for Palestinian statehood but its real purpose was to do what it knew best—namely, create an extensive terrorist infrastructure and use it against its Israeli "peace partner." At first it did this tacitly, giving a green light to other terrorist organizations like Hamas and Islamic Jihad; then it operated openly and directly.

Israel's Withdrawal

But what did all this have to do with Israel's "occupation"? The declaration signed on the White House lawn in 1993 by the PLO and the Israeli government provided for Palestinian self-rule in the entire West Bank and the Gaza Strip for a transitional period not to exceed five years, during which Israel and the Palestinians would negotiate a permanent peace settlement. During this interim period the territories would be administered by a Palestinian Council, to be freely and democratically elected after the withdrawal of Israeli military forces both from the Gaza Strip and from the populated areas of the West Bank.

By May 1994, Israel had completed its withdrawal from the Gaza Strip (apart from a small stretch of territory containing Israeli settlements) and the Jericho area of the West Bank. On July 1, [PLO chairman] Yasir Arafat made his triumphant entry into Gaza. On September 28, 1995, despite Arafat's abysmal failure to clamp down on terrorist activities in the territories now under his control, the two parties signed an interim agreement, and by the end of the year Israeli forces had been withdrawn from the West Bank's populated areas with the exception of Hebron (where redeployment was completed in early 1997). On January 20, 1996, elections to the Palestinian Council were held, and shortly afterward both the Israeli civil administration and military government were dissolved.

The geographical scope of these Israeli withdrawals was relatively limited; the surrendered land amounted to some 30 percent of the West Bank's overall territory. But its impact on the Palestinian population was nothing short of revolutionary. At one fell swoop, Israel relinquished control over virtually all of the West Bank's 1.4 million residents. Since that time, nearly 60 percent of them—in the Jericho area and in the seven main cities of Jenin, Nablus, Tulkarm, Qalqilya, Ramallah, Bethlehem, and Hebron—have lived entirely under Palestinian jurisdiction. Another 40 percent live in towns, villages, refugee camps, and hamlets where the Palestinian Authority exercises civil authority but, in line with the Oslo accords, Israel has maintained "overriding responsibility for security." Some two percent of the West Bank's population—tens of thousands of Palestinians—continue to live in areas where Israel has complete control, but even there the Palestinian Authority maintains "functional jurisdiction."

In short, since the beginning of 1996, and certainly following the completion of the redeployment from Hebron in January 1997, 99 percent of the Palestinian population of the West Bank and the Gaza Strip have not lived under Israeli occupation. By no conceivable stretching of words can the anti-Israel violence emanating from the territories during these years be made to qualify as resistance to foreign occupation. In these years there has *been* no such occupation.

Terrorism and the Peace Process

If the stubborn persistence of Palestinian terrorism is not attributable to the continuing occupation, many of the worst outrages against Israeli civilians likewise occurred—contrary to the mantra of Palestinian spokesmen and their apologists—not at moments of breakdown in the Oslo "peace process" but at its high points, when the prospect of Israeli withdrawal appeared brightest and most imminent.

Suicide bombings, for example, were introduced in the atmosphere of euphoria only a few months after the historic Rabin-Arafat handshake on the White House lawn[1]: eight people were murdered in April 1994 while riding a bus in the town of Afula. Six months later, 21 Israelis were murdered on a bus in Tel Aviv. In the following year, five bombings took the lives of a further 38 Israelis. During the short-lived government of the dovish Shimon Peres (November 1995–May 1996), after the assassination of Yitzhak Rabin, 58 Israelis were murdered within the span of one week in three suicide bombings in Jerusalem and Tel Aviv.

Further disproving the standard view is the fact that terrorism was largely *curtailed* following Benjamin Netanyahu's election [as Israel's prime minister] in May 1996 and the consequent slowdown in the Oslo process. During Netanyahu's three years in power, some 50 Israelis were murdered in terrorist attacks—a third of the casualty rate during the Rabin government and a sixth of the casualty rate during Peres's term.

There was a material side to this downturn in terrorism as well. Between 1994 and 1996, the Rabin and Peres governments had imposed repeated closures on the territories in order to stem the tidal wave of terrorism in the wake of the Oslo accords. This had led to a steep drop in the Palestinian economy. With workers unable to get into Israel, unemployment rose sharply, reaching as high as 50 percent in Gaza. The movement of goods between Israel and the territories, as well as between the West Bank and Gaza, was seriously disrupted, slowing exports and discouraging potential private investment.

The economic situation in the territories began to improve during the term of the Netanyahu government, as the steep fall in terrorist attacks led to a corresponding decrease in closures. Real GNP per capita grew by 3.5 percent in 1997, 7.7 percent in 1998, and 3.5 percent in 1999, while unemployment was more than halved. By the beginning of 1999, ac-

1. Israeli Prime Minister Yitzhak Rabin and Palestinian leader Yasir Arafat made the historic handshake at the signing ceremony for the Oslo Accords on September 13, 1993.

cording to the World Bank, the West Bank and Gaza had fully recovered from the economic decline of the previous years.

Then, in still another turnabout, came Ehud Barak, who in the course of a dizzying six months in late 2000 and early 2001 offered Yasir Arafat a complete end to the Israeli presence, ceding virtually the entire West Bank and the Gaza Strip to the nascent Palestinian state together with some Israeli territory, and making breathtaking concessions over Israel's capital city of Jerusalem. To this, however, Arafat's response was war. Since its launch, the Palestinian campaign has inflicted thousands of brutal attacks on Israeli civilians—suicide bombings, drive-by shootings, stabbings, lynching, stonings—murdering more than 500 and wounding some 4,000.

In the entire two decades of Israeli occupation preceding the Oslo accords, some 400 Israelis were murdered; since the conclusion of that "peace" agreement, twice as many have lost their lives in terrorist attacks. If the occupation was the cause of terrorism, why was terrorism sparse during the years of actual occupation, why did it increase dramatically with the prospect of the end of the occupation, and why did it escalate into open war upon Israel's most far-reaching concessions ever? To the contrary, one might argue with far greater plausibility that the *absence* of occupation—that is, the withdrawal of close Israeli surveillance—is precisely what facilitated the launching of the terrorist war in the first place.

Palestinian Leadership Does Not Want Peace

There are limits to Israel's ability to transform a virulent enemy into a peace partner, and those limits have long since been reached. To borrow from Baruch Spinoza, peace is not the absence of war but rather a state of mind: a disposition to benevolence, confidence, and justice. From the birth of the Zionist movement until today, that disposition has remained conspicuously absent from the mind of the Palestinian leadership.

It is not the 1967 occupation that led to the Palestinians' rejection of peaceful coexistence and their pursuit of violence. Palestinian terrorism started well before 1967, and continued—and intensified—after the occupation ended in all but name. Rather, what is at fault is the perduring Arab view that the creation of the Jewish state was itself an original act of "inhuman occupation" with which compromise of any final kind is beyond the realm of the possible. Until that disposition changes, which is to say until a different leadership arises, the idea of peace in the context of the Arab Middle East will continue to mean little more than the continuation of war by other means.

"The Western nations have committed a litany of crimes against the Muslim world according to the Islamic opposition."

Foreign Intervention Is the Primary Cause of Conflict in the Middle East

William O. Beeman

The following viewpoint was written shortly after the September 11, 2001, terrorist attacks in which nineteen people from Saudi Arabia and other Middle Eastern nations hijacked jetliners and crashed them into the World Trade Center towers in New York and the Pentagon in Washington, D.C. In the following viewpoint, William O. Beeman argues that this act of terrorism has causes stemming from decades of meddling by Western nations, including the United States, in the Middle East. These actions, he argues, have led to divisiveness between Middle Eastern regimes and their people, initiated wars between Middle Eastern nations, and created in the region widespread antipathy toward the West. Beeman is an anthropology professor and specialist in Middle Eastern culture at Brown University in Rhode Island.

As you read, consider the following questions:

1. Who was the original leader of Islamic opposition to the West, according to Beeman?
2. How was the Middle East affected by the Cold War between the United States and the Soviet Union, in the author's view?
3. What role did the United States play in the creation of Saddam Hussein and the Taliban, according to Beeman?

William O. Beeman, "Why a Military Response Won't Work—Historic Roots of Middle East Grievances," *Pacific News Service*, September 19, 2001. Copyright © 2001 by *Pacific News Service*. Reproduced by permission.

The Bush administration's projected war on terrorism is designed to eradicate and delegitimize terrorists. Both aims are futile. The grievances of the terrorists who committed the horrendous attacks on New York and Washington on September 11 [2001] have deep and persistent roots going back more than 150 years. The terrorists harbor a hatred that will not die, and their grievances cannot be delegitimized through military attacks.

Middle Eastern opposition to the West is far from being a phenomenon invented by Osama bin Laden,[1] or the Taliban,[2] or for that matter Iran, Iraq or the Palestinians. It has grown consistently since the beginning of the 19th Century as an effective oppositional force both to the West and to local secular rulers. Western powers were blind to Middle Eastern opposition forces throughout the 20th Century because they were preoccupied with their own great power rivalry during this period.

The original leader of the opposition to the West was Jalal al-Din al-Afghani (1838–1897). Called the "Father of Islamic Modernism," Al-Afghani was educated in Iran, Afghanistan and India. He traveled throughout the Islamic world promulgating an "Islamic reform movement." Using an Islamic ideology helped him to transcend ethnic differences in the region, and preach a message all would understand. He sought to mobilize Muslim nations to fight against Western imperialism and gain military power through modern technology. Al-Afghani claimed that Britain, France and Russia in particular were operating in collusion with Middle Eastern rulers to rob the people of their patrimony through sweetheart deals for exploitation of natural and commercial resources in the region.

As a direct result of the efforts of Al-Afghani and his followers, groups such as the Muslim Brotherhood evolved throughout the region. These groups generally espoused three methods in their political and religious activity: personal piety coupled with evangelism, modernization without sacrificing core Islamic beliefs, and political resistance to secular regimes.

1. Osama bin Laden is the terrorist leader believed responsible for the September 11, 2001, terrorist attacks.   2. The Taliban is an Islamic regime in Afghanistan that harbored Osama bin Laden's terrorist network.

Crimes of Western Nations

The Western nations have committed a litany of crimes against the Muslim world according to the Islamic opposition. After World War I, the Middle Eastern peoples were treated largely as war prizes to be divided and manipulated for the good of the militarily powerful Europeans. The British and the French without consent or consultation on the part of the residents created every nation between the Mediterranean Sea and the Persian Gulf for their own benefit. This increased the resentment of the fundamentalists against the West and against the rulers installed by Westerners.

Remapping the Middle East

During the past two centuries, Western empires have mapped and re-mapped the Middle East repeatedly. They appointed, promoted, demoted, and dethroned local leaders to suit their strategic interests. One thing remained consistent and was omnipresent in their successive attempts to readjust borders and consolidate hegemonies: the availability of local demons to justify the frequent strategic reshaping and remapping.

One hundred and seventy years ago, Mohamed Ali of Egypt was declared a threat to free trade and was overthrown in favor of weak successors. Four decades later, Ahmed Urabi was removed from office and Egypt became a British occupied country (1882). A long line of successors, who pursued an independent course, provided the empire the necessary pretext to intervene. . . . A sense of threat kept the West busy fine tuning the empire to insure the perpetual dependency of the natives. Irrespective of their level of rationality, the Arab demons were declared a threat either to their own people, to their neighbors, to regional stability, to America's standard of living or even to US national security.

Naseer Aruri, *Counterpunch*, October 28, 2002.

During the Cold War, the United States and the Soviet Union fought over the Middle East nations like children over toys. Governments such as those of Egypt, the Sudan, Iraq, and Syria were constantly pressed to choose between East and West. The choice was often prompted by "gifts" of military support to sitting rulers. With ready sources of money and guns in either Washington or Moscow, Middle Eastern rulers could easily oppress the religious fundamentalists who opposed them. This added to the anger of the religious reformers. At this point the oppositionists abandoned political action through conventional political processes and turned to extra-governmental methods—terrorism—to make their dissatisfaction felt.

The United States became the sole representative of the West after 1972, when Great Britain, poor and humbled, could no longer afford to maintain a full military force in the region. Anxious to protect oil supplies from the Soviet Union, Washington propped up the Shah of Iran and the Saudi Arabian government in the ill-fated "Twin Pillars" strategy. This ended with the Iranian revolution, leaving America with a messy patchwork of military and political detritus. When Iran went to war with Iraq, the U.S. supported [Iraqi leader] Saddam Hussein to prevent Iran from winning. Anxious about Soviet incursions into Afghanistan, it propped up the Taliban. These two forces—Saddam and the Taliban—are very much an American creation.

The Final Blow

The final blow came when America finally had to confront its former client, Iraq, in the Gulf War. Americans established a military base on Saudi Arabian soil—considered sacred by pious Muslims. Saudi officials had been resisting this move for years, knowing that it would be politically dangerous both for them and for the United States. This action was the basis for Osama bin Laden's opposition to the United States.

All of this meddling only confirms the century-old assertion that the West was out to rob the people of the Middle East of their prerogatives and patrimony. The current revolutionaries in the region, including bin Laden, have political pedigrees leading directly back to the original reformer, Al-Afghani. Willy-nilly, the United States keeps reinforcing these old stereotypes. It is essential that we find a way to break this pattern, or we will be mired in these troubled relations forever.

"Water is returning as the likeliest cause of conflict in the Middle East."

Scarce Water Could Cause Conflict in the Middle East

Adel Darwish

Fighting over scarce natural resources is often a cause of war and conflict between nations. In the following viewpoint Adel Darwish maintains that future water shortages are likely to create conflicts among the nations of the Middle East. The aridity of the region—as well as the area's growing population and political instability—will cause strife unless various nations agree to work together on water projects, the author contends. Darwish, a journalist, is coauthor of *Water Wars: Coming Conflict in the Middle East.*

As you read, consider the following questions:

1. According to Darwish, what percentage of renewable water supplies does the Middle East use annually?
2. According to the author, which world leaders have suggested that water will be a likely cause of war in the Middle East.
3. How has the High Dam on the Nile affected development in Egypt, according to Darwish?

Adel Darwish, "Arid Waters," *Our Planet*, vol. 17, 1995. Copyright © 1995 by the United Nations Environment Programme. Reproduced by permission.

A lone figure dressed all in black materializes out of the mirage where the dry sky glare meets the desert. As he moves closer, his attitude becomes tense. His eyes blaze as he reaches the well where a man is drinking, and with a single stroke of his sword, he strikes off the stranger's head.

That opening scene from the film *Lawrence of Arabia*—based on a story told by Lawrence himself—provides a stark warning that water in the arid environment of the Middle East is a matter of life and death.

Since the first oil well—discovered during drilling for water—gushed in Bahrain in 1932, countries have argued over borders in the hope of getting access to new riches. Now that most borders have been set, oil fields mapped and reserves accurately estimated, history is coming full circle. Water is returning as the likeliest cause of conflict in the Middle East. Whoever controls water or its distribution can dominate the region.

Searching for Water

From Turkey, the southern bastion of the North Atlantic Treaty Organization (NATO), down to Oman on the Indian Ocean, from the snow-helmeted Atlas Mountains in Morocco, to the depths of the Jordan valley, governments are searching for more water.

The population of the region will rise by 34 million within 30 years, and will then need 470 billion cubic metres of water annually—132 billion more than the total available supplies based on current levels of consumption (even assuming that there will be a 2 per cent improvement in conservation each year.

Water is being used faster than nature can replace it. On average the region uses 155 per cent of its renewable water supplies each year. Individual countries' consumption ranges from the Libyan Arab Jamahiriya at 374 per cent to Bahrain at 102 per cent.

In 1994, the World Bank estimated that renewable per capita water supplies would fall fivefold in the space of one lifetime—1960–2025—to 667 cubic metres per year (well below the official level of water scarcity). In several countries this will barely cover basic human needs into the twenty-first century.

When President Anwar Sadat signed the peace treaty with Israel, he said that Egypt will never go to war again, except to protect its water resources. King Hussein of Jordan has said he will never again go to war with Israel, except over water. [Former] United Nations Secretary-General Boutros Boutros-Ghali has warned bluntly that water will cause the next war in the area.

In 1989 Israel withdrew hydrologists and surveyors who were investigating building a dam in Ethiopia on the Blue Nile, which provides 85 per cent of Egypt's water, amid threats of war in the People's Assembly in Cairo. In 1990 Turkey stopped the flow of the Euphrates altogether to fill its Ataturk Dam. The media of the two downstream nations, the Syrian Arab Republic and Iraq, united in denouncing the stoppage and there were threats of armed retaliation. The CIA gave its opinion in 1992 that trouble between Turkey and the Syrian Arab Republic over water was the likeliest prospect for a full-scale war in the region.

Few agreements have been reached about sharing such cross-border water resources as international aquifers or the rivers of the region. Two of the three main aquifers lie for the most part under the West Bank of the Jordan. Muslim fundamentalists have recently made it *Jihad*—a sacred mission—to recover water used by Israeli settlers, for the use of Muslims.

Limits to International Law

International law on shared water courses, rivers or cross-border aquifers is unclear. Governments and organizations negotiate agreements using a mixture of customary use and local and traditional laws, and the established right of use over an unspecified period of time. Such mixtures are often contradictory and in themselves a cause of conflict. There are few, if any, precedents that the United Nations International Law Commission or the International Court of Justice could cite to establish rules to arbitrate on water sharing.

Since the late 1940s, the World Bank has insisted that agreements are concluded between riparian nations on sharing the benefits of the water projects that it helps to finance. It also commissions independent studies to modify plans and alter designs to minimize the harm that the project might inflict on neighbouring peoples.

But when governments finance their own water schemes, there is no provision in international law to stop them imposing their will on neighbours, uprooting ethnic minorities or inflicting far reaching and lasting effects on the environment.

Israel, Palestinians and Water

[In the] bloody Israeli-Palestinian conflict, the region's competing actors are jockeying to maintain control of the available water. The combination of a naturally arid environment, years of drought, and poor planning is proving to be dry tinder in a combustible atmosphere.

Take Israel's far Right infrastructure minister Effie Eitam's order halting all Palestinian well drilling in the West Bank in October 2002, alleging that Palestenians were runing a 'water Intifada' against Israel through unauthorized tapping. Besides endangering the crippled Palestinian farming sector, the move threatened the tens of millions of dollars of foreign aid money spent on unfinished water infrastructure.

The next day Fatil Qawash, the head of Palestinian Water Authority, was irate. 'Year by year, we have less and less water. No more water in the springs, no more water from the weather and at the same time the Israeli side has applied a policy to reduce the water that they supply us, he said. 'Now they are blaming us for stealing water. This is not stealing water. This is our water.'

There lies the crux of the problem. Israel has access to both high-tech solutions and water from the occupied West Bank. Palestinians, on the other hand, have far less water to work with and remain caught in the terms of agreements signed with Israel years ago. Palestinian long-term planning remains tentative as long as the issue of their regional water rights is unresolved.

Charmaine Seitz, *New Internationalist*, 2003.

To taunt the late Egyptian leader Colonel Gamal Abdel Nasser in the 1950s, Britain unwisely induced the World Bank to turn down Egypt's request to finance the building of the High Dam on the Nile near Aswan. The Soviet Union was only too happy to finance and construct instead, winning a foothold in the region. The dam was built away from international supervision and Colonel Nasser turned down alternative projects, which would have been environmentally and economically more sound. 'Here are joined the political, national and military battles of the Egyptian people, welded together like the gigantic mass of rock that has blocked the course of the ancient Nile,' he told the crowds in May 1964 when the first phase of the project was complete.

The dam is providing multiple benefits to farmers and generating about twice the national requirement for electricity. But it has also had less benign effects. It has damaged valuable ecosystems and fishing grounds (the sardines that once bred in the Nile have almost disappeared from the Mediterranean), eroded beaches by changing the hydrology of the area (the coastal defences built on the Mediterranean coast in the 1940s have been overwhelmed since the dam was built) and deprived the Nile Valley and delta of the silt and natural fertilizers which had nourished its agriculture for thousands of years.

An Ultimate Solution

The ultimate solution to the water problems of the region is to shift production and economic patterns away from agriculture, the major user of water, and import food supplies instead—which would be cheaper than building unrealistic water projects—or to grow crops that consume less water for exports. But political insecurity and distrust of neighbours make this difficult for governments to do.

Similar problems dog plans for a joint Jordanian-Israeli Canal from the Red Sea to the Dead Sea, which would use the 100 metre drop between the seas to generate electricity for desalination: it can only work when all neighbours agree to cooperate on peaceful terms. Even if it happens, demand will soon outstrip supply if the nations in the region continue to abuse its water resources.

It remains likely that water conflict will add to the troubles of the region. 'A time may well come,' one leading politician of the area said privately, 'when we have to calculate whether a small swift war might be economically more rewarding than putting up with a drop in our water supplies'.

Periodical Bibliography

The following articles have been selected to supplement the diverse views presented in this chapter.

Fouad Ajami	"The Endless Claim (Palestinian State)," *U.S. News & World Report*, January 8, 2001.
Mohammed Aldouri	"Iraq States Its Case," *New York Times*, October 17, 2002.
Perry Anderson	"Scurrying Towards Bethlehem (Zionism and the Israeli-Palestinian Conflict)," *New Left Review*, July/August 2001.
Arnaud De Borchgrave	"Terrorism Is a Common Threat in Struggles for Independence," *Insight on the News*, May 6, 2002.
Larry Derfner et al.	"Spiral of Violence," *U.S. News & World Report*, March 18, 2002.
James O.C. Jonah	"The Middle East Conflict: The Palestinian Dimension," *Global Governance*, October–December 2002.
Avi Jorisch	"The Middle East Explodes—The Recent Troubles," *World & I*, February 2002.
Joe Klein	"How Israel Is Wrapped Up in Iraq," *Time*, February 10, 2003.
Dennis Kucinich	"The Bloodstained Path," *The Progressive*, November 2002.
Johanna McGeary	"Dissecting the Case: The Administration's Rationale for War with Iraq Is Based on New and Old Evidence—as Well as Passionate Conviction," *Time*, February 10, 2003.
New Statesman	"Middle East: No Goodies or Baddies," March 18, 2002.
Fiamma Nirenstein	"How Suicide Bombers Are Made," *Commentary*, September 2001.
John Pilger	"If You Got Your News Only from the Television, You Would Have No Idea of the Roots of the Middle East Conflict, or That the Palestinians Are Victims of an Illegal Military Occupation," *New Statesman*, July 1, 2002.
Danny Rubenstein	"Israel at Fifty," *Nation*, May 4, 1998.
Jonathan Schanzer	"Palestinian Uprisings Compared," *Middle East Quarterly*, Summer 2002.

Somini Sengupta	"In Israel and Lebanon, Talk of War over Water," *New York Times*, October 16, 2002.
Joseph C. Wilson	"A 'Big Cat' with Nothing to Lose; Leaving Hussein No Hope Will Trigger His Worst Weapons," *Los Angeles Times*, February 6, 2003.
Mortimer B. Zuckerman	"Clear and Compelling Proof," *U.S. News & World Report*, February 10, 2003.

How Does Islam Affect the Middle East?

Chapter Preface

In July 2002 the United Nations Development Programme (UNDP) published a report that examined the development of twenty-two Arab nations (as well as Palestinians in Israel) using measurements ranging from per capita income growth to Internet usage statistics. Written by Arab scholars, the *Arab Human Development Report 2002* concluded that while the region, blessed with natural resources, has made much progress in some areas, including poverty reduction, these nations lagged behind the rest of the world in their social, political, and economic development. One of the report's striking findings was that more than half of Arab youth polled expressed a desire to leave their country and move to Europe or North America. The report's authors identified three main areas in which modern Arab culture was lacking: political freedom, knowledge development, and the treatment and status of women.

The report did not directly discuss or implicate Islam as a cause of these social problems, yet many argue that the role of this religion in hampering development cannot be overlooked. Of the three major world religions that originated in the Middle East—Judaism, Christianity, and Islam—it is Islam, founded by the Arabian prophet Muhammad in the 600s, that became the dominant religion in the region. Presently more than 90 percent of the Middle East's people, including most Arabs, Iranians, and Turks, are Muslims (Christians of various sects make up about 7 percent of the region's population, while Jews, most of whom live in Israel, make up 1 percent). Islam is not only the religion of most of the people, but it is the official state religion of many Middle East nations. As a result, Islamic clerics play a major role in the politics of these countries. In Saudi Arabia, for example, other religions are forbidden, and Islamic law or *sharia*—based on the Koran, Islam's holy book—is the foundation of its legal system.

Whether and how Islam contributes to underdevelopment is a matter of debate. The fact that women in most Arab countries lack equal political and civil rights—one of the problems identified in the UNDP report—has served as a flash-point issue for those debating the role of Islam in Middle East development. Saudi Arabia serves as a good example. In Saudi Arabia, women face serious gender discrimination, including segregation in public areas, lack of freedom of movement (including the right to drive automobiles), less rights in criminal trials, and limited participation in government. Some observers argue that Islam is the primary cause of these gender inequities. Author Ibn Warraq asserts that "Islam is the fundamental cause of the repression of Muslim women. . . . Islam has always considered women as creatures inferior in every way: physically, intellectually, and morally." But others argue that gender discrimination is more a product of Arab culture and customs rather than Islamic teachings. "Many of the most repressive practices ascribed to Islam are based on cultural traditions . . . or contested interpretations," writes religion journalist Teresa Watanabe. "Even Saudi-trained scholars, for instance, agree that the kingdom's ban on women driving is not grounded in the Koran or the prophet's traditions."

Islam's role in determining the status of women in the Middle East is one of several issues discussed in the following chapter. Authors examine how Islam will shape future development of the region.

*"For the Middle East today, moderate Islam
may be democracy's last hope."*

Islam Can Be Compatible with Democracy

Ray Takeyh

Of all the nations in the Middle East, only Israel fully quali-
fies as a democracy in which its citizens have the right to elect
or vote out governments. Other Middle East countries are
ruled by hereditary monarchs, military rulers, or lifetime
presidents. Some people have speculated that longstanding
cultural traditions, including the Islamic religion, prevent the
region from becoming more democratic. In the following
viewpoint Ray Takeyh takes issue with the view that Middle
East Muslims are not capable of democracy. Many people in
the region have been inspired by the emergence of democracies in other parts of the world, he argues, and a new generation of Islamic thinkers is attempting to formulate ways of
replacing existing Middle East regimes with democratic governments that are consistent with Islamic values. Takeyh is a
research fellow at the Washington Institute for Near East
Policy; his works include *The Receding Shadow of the Prophet:
Radical Islamic Movements in the Modern Middle East.*

As you read, consider the following questions:
1. Why is the choice between "Islam" and "modernity" a
   simplistic one, according to Takeyh?
2. Why does the author consider extremist militant Islam
   to be on the decline?
3. How might future Islamic democracies differ from those
   in Western nations, according to the author?

The televised footage of an airliner crashing into the World Trade Center [during the September 11, 2001, terrorist attacks on America] is now the prevailing image of Islam. Media pundits decry anti-Muslim bigotry and hasten to remind the public that Islam is a religion of peace and tolerance, notwithstanding the actions of an extremist minority. But in the same breath many of those pundits warn of a clash of civilizations—a war that pits the secular, modernized West against a region mired in ancient hatreds and fundamentalist rage.

A Third Option

This simplistic choice between "Islam" and "modernity" ignores a third option that is emerging throughout the Middle East. Lost amidst the din of cultural saber-rattling are the voices calling for an Islamic reformation: A new generation of theological thinkers, led by figures such as Iranian President Muhammad Khatami and Tunisian activist Rached Ghannouchi, is reconsidering the orthodoxies of Islamic politics. In the process, such leaders are demonstrating that the region may be capable of generating a genuinely democratic order, one based on indigenous values. For the Middle East today, moderate Islam may be democracy's last hope. For the West, it might represent one of the best long-term solutions to "winning" the war against Middle East terrorism.

Militant Islam continues to tempt those on the margins of society (and guides anachronistic forces such as Afghanistan's Taliban and Palestine's Islamic Jihad), but its moment has passed. In Iran, the Grand Ayatollah's autocratic order[1] degenerated into corruption and economic stagnation. Elsewhere, the Islamic radicals' campaign of terror—such as Gamma al-Islamiyya in Egypt and Hezbollah in Lebanon—failed to produce any political change, as their violence could not overcome the brutality of the states they encountered. The militants' incendiary rhetoric and terrorism only triggered public revulsion, not revolutions and mass uprisings. Indeed, the Arab populace may have returned to reli-

---

1. Ayatollah Khomeini led a revolution and established an Islam-based government in Iran in 1979.

gion over the last two decades, but they turned to a religion that was tolerant and progressive, not one that called for a violent displacement of the existing order with utopias.

Political Islam as a viable reform movement might have petered out were it not for one minor detail: The rest of the world was changing. The collapse of the Soviet Union and the emergence of democratic regimes in Eastern Europe, Latin America, and East Asia electrified the Arab populace. Their demands were simple but profound. As one Egyptian university student explained in 1993, "I want what they have in Poland, Czechoslovakia. Freedom of thought and freedom of speech." In lecture halls, street cafes, and mosques, long dormant ideas of representation, identity, authenticity, and pluralism began to arise.

A New Generation

The task of addressing the population's demand for a pluralistic society consistent with traditional values was left to a new generation of Islamist thinkers, who have sought to legitimize democratic concepts through the reinterpretation of Islamic texts and traditions. Tunisia's Ghannouchi captures this spirit of innovation by stressing, "Islam did not come with a specific program concerning life. It is our duty to formulate this program through interaction between Islamic precepts and modernity." Under these progressive readings, the well-delineated Islamic concept of *shura* (consultation) compels a ruler to consider popular opinion and establishes the foundation for an accountable government. In a modern context, such consultation can be implemented through the standard tools of democracy: elections, plebiscites, and referendums. The Islamic notion of *jima* (consensus) has been similarly accommodated to serve as a theological basis for majoritarian rule. For Muslim reformers, Prophet Mohammed's injunction that "differences of opinion within my community is a sign of God's mercy" denotes prophetic approbation of diversity of thought and freedom of speech.

The new generation of Islamists has quickly embraced the benefits wrought by modernization and globalization in order to forge links between Islamist groups and thinkers in the various states of the Middle East. Through mosques, Islamists easily distribute pamphlets, tracts, and cassettes of Islamic thinkers and writers. In today's [2001] Middle East, one can easily find the Egyptian Brotherhood's magazine *Al-Dawa* in bookstores in the Persian Gulf while the Jordanian Islamist daily *Al-Sabil* enjoys wide circulation throughout the Levant. The advent of the Internet has intensified such cross-pollination, as most Islamist journals, lectures, and conference proceedings are posted on the Web. The writings of Iranian philosopher Abdol Karim Soroush today appear in Islamic curricula across the region, and Egypt's Islamist liberal Hassan Hanafi commands an important audience in Iran's seminaries.

Islamic Democracy

In the future, such Islamists will likely vie to succeed the region's discredited military rulers and lifetime presidents. But what will a prospective Islamic democracy look like? Undoubtedly, Islamic democracy will differ in important ways from the model that evolved in post-Reformation Europe. Western systems elevated the primacy of the individual above the community and thus changed the role of religion from that of the public conveyor of community values to a private guide for individual conscience. In contrast, an Islamic democracy's attempt to balance its emphasis on reverence with the popular desire for self-expression will impose certain limits on individual choice. An Islamic polity will support fundamental tenets of democracy—namely, regular elections, separation of powers, an independent judiciary, and institutional opposition—but it is unlikely to be a libertarian paradise.

The question of gender rights is an excellent example of the strengths—and limits—of an Islamic democracy. The Islamists who rely on women's votes, grass-roots activism, and participation in labor markets cannot remain deaf to women's demands for equality. Increasingly, Islamic reformers suggest the cause of women's failure to achieve equality is not religion but custom. The idea of black-clad women passively accepting the dictates of superior males is the province of Western caricatures. Iran's parliament, cabinet, and universities are populated with women, as are the candidate lists for Islamic opposition parties in Egypt and

Cause for Optimism

There is . . . cause for cautious optimism. Recent polls show that Arabs and Muslims, while more culturally conservative and religious than most of the democratic world, share many of the same aspirations for freedom and democracy that we do. It's also a positive that the Arab countries tend to be ethnically homogenous: It's easier to make democracy work in societies that don't have violent ethnic animosities. A number of Arab countries possess significant wealth and have achieved relatively high levels of economic development, making it possible to avoid the instability that often arises from grinding poverty. Moreover, these societies possess the immense untapped potential of women, who have long been denied their proper place in political and economic life.

The West has a crucial role to play in these developments. For many years the U.S. and the rest of the democratic world were hesitant to apply to Arab countries the kind of pressure for democratic change that was so helpful in Central and Eastern Europe, Latin America, and parts of Asia. But this policy is beginning to change. . . .

Our strategy will become stronger if it emphasizes that there is nothing inherently Islamic or Arabic about dictatorship and tyranny—that, just like the citizens of Europe, today's Muslims have the prerequisites for entering the democratic community of nations.

Adriar Karatnycky, *National Review*, Decmber 31, 2002.

Turkey. But while an Islamic democracy will not impede women's integration into public affairs, it will impose restrictions on them, particularly in the realm of family law and dress codes. In such an order, women can make significant progress, yet in important ways they may still lag behind their Western counterparts. Moderate Islamists are likely to be most liberal in the realm of economic policy. The failure of command economies in the Middle East and the centrality of global markets to the region's economic rehabilitation have made minimal government intervention appealing to Islamist theoreticians. Moreover, a privatized economy is consistent with classical Islamic economic theory and its well-established protection of market and commerce. The Islamist parties have been among the most persistent critics of state restrictions on trade and measures that obstruct opportunities for middle-class entrepreneurs.

International Implications

The international implications of the emergence of Islamic democracies are also momentous. While revolutionary Islam could not easily coexist with the international system, moderate Islam can serve as a bridge between civilizations. The coming to power of moderate Islamists throughout the Middle East might lead to a lessening of tensions both within the region and between it and other parts of the world. Today, security experts talk of the need to "drain the swamps" and deprive terrorists of the state sponsorship that provides the protection and funding to carry out their war against the West. Within a more open and democratic system, dictatorial regimes would enjoy less freedom to support terrorism or engage in military buildups without any regard for economic consequences.

Ultimately, however, the integration of an Islamic democracy into global democratic society would depend on the willingness of the West to accept an Islamic variant on liberal democracy. Islamist moderates, while conceding that there are in fact certain "universal" democratic values, maintain that different civilizations must be able to express these values in a context that is acceptable and appropriate to their particular region. Moderate Islamists, therefore, will continue to struggle against any form of U.S. hegemony, whether in political or cultural terms, and are much more comfortable with a multipolar, multi-"civilizational" international system. Khatami's call for a "dialogue of civilizations" presupposes that there is no single universal standard judging the effectiveness of democracy and human rights.

Certainly, the West should resist totalitarian states who use the rhetoric of democracy while rejecting its essence through false claims of cultural authenticity. But even though an Islamic democracy will resist certain elements of post-Enlightenment liberalism, it will still be a system that features regular elections, accepts dissent and opposition parties, and condones a free press and division of power between branches of state. As such, any fair reading of Islamic democracy will reveal that it is a genuine effort to conceive a system of government responsive to popular will. And this effort is worthy of Western acclaim.

"Democratic values do not slumber in the subconsious of the Islamic world."

Islam May Not Be Compatible with Democracy

Milton Viorst

The following viewpoint was written shortly after U.S.-led military action ended the dictatorship of Iraqi leader Saddam Hussein in April 2003. Journalist and author Milton Viorst argues that if free elections were to be held in Iraq, Hussein's regime could well be replaced by an Islamic theocracy in which democratic freedoms as practiced in the West would be restricted. He argues that similar results would occur throughout the Middle East from attempts to democratize Middle Eastern nations. Viorst raises the question of whether Islam—the dominant religion in the region—is compatible with democracy. Viorst is a veteran Middle East journalist and the author of *In the Shadow of the Prophet: The Struggle for the Soul of Islam.*

As you read, consider the following questions:
1. What distinction does Viorst draw between countries in Europe and the Middle East?
2. What was so important about the Renaissance to the development of democracy, according to the author?
3. What conclusions does Viorst draw about the American government's vision of a transformed Middle East?

I raq's Shiites,[1] 60% of the population, most of them fervently religious, have stunned U.S. officials who gave us the [2003] war to overthrow Saddam Hussein. Not only do they reject our occupation, but they also dismiss the Western-style democracy that we were assured they would welcome.

It took hardly more than recent [April 2003] full-color pictures in newspapers and on television of Shiite men flagellating themselves until blood streamed from their flesh to make the case that we are dealing with people we don't know. Ironically, Hussein's regime had barred self-flagellation as barbaric. For believers, his fall did not mean freedom to adopt a constitution and elect a parliament; it meant freedom to suffer the stings of whips for a martyr who died 13 centuries ago[2] and to demand an Islamic state.

When communism died at the end of the 1980s, Vaclav Havel, the poet who became president of Czechoslovakia, declared that "democratic values slumbered in the subconscious of our nations." His words suggest that these nations waited only for the sunshine of spring to awake to the democracy that had lain dormant within them. Indeed, societies liberated from communism, including Russia, navigated the currents of Western values to adopt democratic systems, though they sometimes perilously scraped the rocks. So did the European countries delivered from fascism after World War II—Italy and Germany, then Spain and Portugal.

But democratic values do not slumber in the subconscious of the Islamic world. Free elections threaten to bring religious extremists to power in Egypt, Jordan, Pakistan and even Turkey, which has been working at democracy for nearly a century. Were free elections held in Saudi Arabia, fanatics would surely triumph. In 1992, elections brought Algeria to the edge of Islamic rule, triggering a civil war that still rages. Given the substantial divisions in Iraq's population, and the power of religion within its Shiite majority, free elections there would probably produce the same outcome.

Years ago, I asked an elderly philosopher in Damascus,

---

1. Shiites are followers of the Shia branch of Islam. They have long been suppressed in Iraq by Saddam Hussein's Sunni-dominated regime.   2. Imam Hussein bin Ali, the grandson of the prophet Mohammed.

Syria, to explain the difficulty the Arabs have in mastering democracy, and he answered, ruefully: "The Islamic world never had a Renaissance." What he meant, I later understood, was that the steps toward secularism that Western society first took in mid-millennium are yet to be taken—or, at best, have been taken only hesitantly—within Islam.

The Renaissance's Importance

The seminal notion that the Renaissance introduced to the West was that mankind, not God, is at the hub of the social universe. It held reason as important as faith, and urged men and women to claim responsibility, free of clergy, for their own lives.

Under the influence of texts from ancient Greece, Muslims in their Golden Age considered and rejected these ideas before passing the texts on to Europe. After triggering the Renaissance, the ideas led, over quarrelsome centuries, to the Reformation, the Enlightenment and the Scientific Revolution. While Islam remained wedded to desert tradition, Europe created a civilization imbued with a sense of individual identity, in which men and women asserted rights apart from those of the community. These ideas, for better or worse, became the foundation of the secular culture that characterizes Western civilization today.

Religion by no means disappeared. Instead, it was redefined as a personal bond, a relationship of choice, between the individual and God. The redefinition made Westerners comfortable separating worship from the state. True, segments of the Catholic Church, Orthodox Jewry and evangelical Protestantism still question this arrangement. But the secular idea constitutes the foundation of mainstream Western values. Without it, democracy—and the civil society that, along with the press, supports it—would be impossible.

Islam and Everyday Life

This process has largely bypassed Islamic society. Muslims like to say that "Islam isn't just a religion; it's a way of life." What they mean is that there is no barrier between faith and the everyday world, between what is sacred and what is profane. It is not so much that Muslims are more pious than

Westerners. It is that the imperatives of the culture impose limits on diversity of outlook, whether religious or social. These imperatives suppress the demand for personal identity, leaving believers with little tolerance for the free and open debate necessarily at democracy's core.

Ironically, Hussein's Baath regime once promised to introduce Iraq to secularism. It went further than any other Arab state in emancipating women, curbing clerical power, promoting literature and arts and advancing universal literacy within a framework of modern education. Its tragedy is that these seeds of democracy were subsumed under the world's most brutal tyranny, crushing their human potential. After 1,400 years of Islamic conservatism and 25 of Hussein, there is little likelihood that a disposition to democracy slumbers in Iraq's psyche.

From President [George W.] Bush on down, officials who are presiding over the rebuilding of Iraq would be wise to remember that the values at our system's heart have been a thousand years in the making. No doubt Iraq's Shiite majority is happy at Hussein's downfall, but American lectures on the virtues of replacing him with democratic rule fall on uncomprehending ears. So much must first be done to lay a groundwork of individual freedom and responsibility, values that Iraqis must willingly embrace. At the moment, the majority is more comfortable with the familiar idea of Islamic government. Would that it were otherwise, but the administration's vision of a Middle East reshaped by Western democracy, starting with Iraq, is naive and, moreover, delusive.

"*Resort to political violence . . . became the preferred option after Iran's revolution emboldened [Islamic] fundamentalists everywhere.*"

Islamic Fundamentalism Fosters Violence in the Middle East

Martin Kramer

Martin Kramer, a senior associate and former director of the Moshe Dayan Center for Middle Eastern and African Studies at Tel Aviv University in Israel, has written numerous articles and books on the Middle East and Islam. In the following viewpoint he argues that fundamentalist Islam has led to political violence in the Middle East. Islamic fundamentalists believe that the tenets of Islam should govern all facets of life, from private conduct to state and public affairs. Although they often claim that their beliefs do not justify violence, Kramer contends, fundamentalists have resorted to war, assassination, and terrorism in an attempt to spread the influence of Islam throughout the Middle East and the world.

As you read, consider the following questions:
1. According to Kramer, what evidence led an Arab critic to compare Sayyid al-Afghani's thinking to fascism?
2. What is the "double identity" of the Muslim Brethren, according to the author?
3. What doctrine of Ruhollah Khomeini's led to the success of an Islamic revolution in Iran, according to Kramer?

Martin Kramer, "The Drive for Power," *Middle East Quarterly*, June 1996.
Copyright © 1996 by Transaction Publishers. Reproduced by permission.

As the twentieth century closes, two words, Islam and fundamentalism, have become intimately linked in English usage. *The Concise Oxford Dictionary of Current English* now defines *fundamentalism* as the "strict maintenance of ancient or fundamental doctrines of any religion, especially Islam." However problematic this formula, it does acknowledge that fundamentalism in Islam is today the most visible and influential of all fundamentalisms.

The nature of fundamentalist Islam, and even the use of the term, is hotly debated. But this debate is largely a self-indulgent exercise of analysts. Within Islam, there are Muslims who have created an "-ism" out of Islam—a coherent ideology, a broad strategy, and a set of political preferences. They do not defy definition. They defy the world.

The Contradictions of Fundamentalist Islam?

What is fundamentalist Islam? Its contradictions seem to abound. On the one hand, it manifests itself as a new religiosity, reaffirming faith in a transcendent God. On the other hand, it appears as a militant ideology, demanding political action now. Here it takes the form of a populist party, asking for ballots. There it surges forth as an armed phalanx, spraying bullets. One day its spokesmen call for a *jihad* (sacred war) against the West, evoking the deepest historic resentments. Another day, its leaders appeal for reconciliation with the West, emphasizing shared values. Its economic theorists reject capitalist materialism in the name of social justice, yet they rise to the defense of private property. Its moralists pour scorn on Western consumer culture as debilitating to Islam, yet its strategists avidly seek to buy the West's latest technologies in order to strengthen Islam.

Faced with these apparent contradictions, many analysts in the West have decided that fundamentalism defies all generalization. Instead they have tried to center discussion on its supposed "diversity." For this purpose, they seek to establish systems of classification by which to sort out fundamentalist movements and leaders. The basic classification appears in many different terminological guises, in gradations of subtlety.

We need to be careful of that emotive label, 'fundamentalism', and distinguish, as Muslims do, between revivalists, who choose to take the practice of their religion most devoutly, and fanatics or extremists, who use this devotion for political ends.

So spoke the Prince of Wales in a 1993 address, summarizing the conventional wisdom in a conventional way. The belief that these categories really exist, and that experts can sort fundamentalists neatly into them, is the sand on which weighty policies are now being built.

Radical Islamic Movements

Radical Islamic movements in general have clearly identified their enemy: the regimes in the Islamic worlds which practice non-Islamic law: the West which has been undermining Islam from within and corrupting it with its norms of permissiveness in order to totter it and replace it; and Israel-Zionism—the Jews, who are intrinsically the enemies of Allah and humanity, in addition to their being an arm of the West in the heart of the islamic world. The enemy must be depicted in evil terms so as to make it a free prey for Muslims to attack and destroy. Rhetorical delegitimation of their enemy is an essential step towards making the use of violence permissible, even desirable, against him. Hence the systematic and virulent onslaughts of those movements against what they perceive as their enemies, domestic and external.

Raphael Israeli, *Terrorism and Political Violence*, Autumn, 1997.

Fundamentalist Islam remains an enigma precisely because it has confounded all attempts to divide it into tidy categories. "Revivalist" becomes "extremist" (and vice versa) with such rapidity and frequency that the actual classification of any movement or leader has little predictive power. They will not stay put. This is because fundamentalist Muslims, for all their "diversity," orbit around one dense idea. From any outside vantage point, each orbit will have its apogee and perigee. The West thus sees movements and individuals swing within reach, only to swing out again and cycle right through every classification. Movements and individuals arise in varied social and political circumstances, and have their own distinctive orbits. But they will not defy the gravity of their idea.

The idea is simple: Islam must have power in this world. It is the true religion—the religion of God—and its truth is manifest in its power. When Muslims believed, they were powerful. Their power has been lost in modern times because Islam has been abandoned by many Muslims, who have reverted to the condition that preceded God's revelation to the Prophet Muhammad. But if Muslims now return to the original Islam, they can preserve and even restore their power.

That return, to be effective, must be comprehensive; Islam provides the one and only solution to all questions in this world, from public policy to private conduct. It is not merely a religion, in the Western sense of a system of belief in God. It possesses an immutable law, revealed by God, that deals with every aspect of life, and it is an ideology, a complete system of belief about the organization of the state and the world. This law and ideology can only be implemented through the establishment of a truly Islamic state, under the sovereignty of God. The empowerment of Islam, which is God's plan for mankind, is a sacred end. It may be pursued by any means that can be rationalized in terms of Islam's own code. At various times, these have included persuasion, guile, and force.

What is remarkable about fundamentalist Islam is not its diversity. It is the fact that this idea of power for Islam appeals so effectively across such a wide range of humanity, creating a world of thought that crosses all frontiers. Fundamentalists everywhere must act in narrow circumstances of time and place. But they are who they are precisely because their idea exists above all circumstances. Over nearly a century, this idea has evolved into a coherent ideology, which demonstrates a striking consistency in content and form across a wide expanse of the Muslim world.

The Thought of Sayyid al-Afghani

The pursuit of power for Islam first gained some intellectual coherence in the mind and career of Sayyid Jamal al-Din "al-Afghani" (1838–97), a thinker and activist who worked to transform Islam into a lever against Western imperialism. His was an age of European expansion into the heartlands of

Islam, and of a frenzied search by Muslims for ways to ward off foreign conquest. . . .

A contemporary English admirer described Afghani as the leader of Islam's "Liberal religious reform movement." But Afghani—not an Afghan at all, but a Persian who concealed his true identity even from English admirers—was never what he appeared to be. While he called for the removal of some authoritarian Muslim rulers, he ingratiated himself with others. While he had great persuasive power, he did not shrink from conspiracy and violence. A disciple once found him pacing back and forth, shouting: "There is no deliverance except in killing, there is no safety except in killing." These were not idle words. On one occasion, Afghani proposed to a follower that the ruler of Egypt be assassinated, and he did inspire a supple disciple to assassinate a ruling shah of Iran in 1896. Afghani was tempted by power, and believed that "power is never manifested and concrete unless it weakens and subjugates others." Quoting this and other evidence, one Arab critic has argued that there is a striking correspondence between Afghani's thought and European fascism. . . .

Between Afghani and the emergence of full-blown fundamentalism, liberal and secular nationalism would enjoy a long run in the lands of Islam. Europe had irradiated these lands with the idea that language, not religion, defined nations. In the generation that followed Afghani, Muslims with an eye toward Europe preferred to be called Arabs, Turks, and Persians. "If you looked in the right places," wrote the British historian Arnold Toynbee in 1929, "you could doubtless find some old fashioned Islamic Fundamentalists still lingering on. You would also find that their influence was negligible." Yet that same year, an Egyptian schoolteacher named Hasan al-Banna (1906–49) founded a movement he called the Society of the Muslim Brethren. It would grow into the first modern fundamentalist movement in Islam.

Fundamentalists in Egypt and Iran

The Muslim Brethren emerged against the background of growing resentment against foreign domination. The Brethren had a double identity. On one level, they operated openly, as a membership organization of social and political awakening. Banna preached moral revival, and the Muslim Brethren engaged in good works. On another level, however, the Muslim Brethren created a "secret apparatus" that acquired weapons and trained adepts in their use. Some of its guns were deployed against the Zionists in Palestine in 1948, but the Muslim Brethren also resorted to violence in Egypt. They began to enforce their own moral teachings by intimidation, and they initiated attacks against Egypt's Jews. They assassinated judges and struck down a prime minister in 1949. Banna himself was assassinated two months later, probably in revenge. The Muslim Brethren then hovered on the fringes of legality, until Gamal Abdel Nasser, who had survived one of their assassination attempts in 1954, put them down ruthlessly. Yet the Muslim Brethren continued to plan underground and in prison, and they flourished in other Arab countries to which they were dispersed.

At the same time, a smaller and more secretive movement, known as the Devotees of Islam, appeared in Iran, under the leadership of a charismatic theology student, Navvab Safavi (1923–56). Like the Muslim Brethren, the Devotees emerged at a time of growing nationalist mobilization against foreign domination. The group was soon implicated in the assassinations of a prime minister and leading secular intellectuals. The Devotees, who never became a mass party, overplayed their hand and were eventually suppressed. Navvab himself was executed, after inspiring a failed assassination attempt against another prime minister. But the seed was planted. One of those who protested Navvab's execution was an obscure, middle-aged cleric named Ruhollah Khomeini, who would continue the work of forging Islam and resentment into an ideology of power. . . .

Islamic fundamentalists sought to replace weak rulers and states with strong rulers and states. Such a state would have to be based on Islam, and while its precise form remained uncertain, the early fundamentalists knew it should not be a constitutional government or multiparty democracy. . . . This preference for a strong, authoritarian Islamic state, often rationalized by the claim that Islam and democracy are incompatible, would become a trademark of fundamentalist thought and practice.

The pursuit of this strong utopian state often overflowed into violence against weak existing states. These "reformers" were quick to disclaim any link to the violence of their followers, denying that their adepts could read their teachings as instructions or justifications for killing. Afghani set the tone, following the assassination of Iran's shah by his disciple. "Surely it was a good deed to kill this bloodthirsty tyrant," he opined. "As far as I am personally concerned, however, I have no part in this deed." Banna, commenting on the assassinations and bombings done by the Muslim Brethren, claimed that "the only ones responsible for these acts are those who commit them." Navvab, who failed in his one attempt at assassination, sent young disciples in his stead. For years he enjoyed the protection of leading religious figures while actually putting weapons in the hands of assassins. (Only when abroad did he actually boast. "I killed Razmara," he announced on a visit to Egypt in 1954, referring to the prime minister assassinated by a disciple three years earlier.) But despite the denials, violence became the inescapable shadow of fundamentalist Islam from the outset—and the attempt to separate figure from shadow, a problematic enterprise at best.

A Transnational Movement

The fundamentalist forerunners also determined that fundamentalist Islam would have a pan-Islamic bent. The peripatetic Afghani took advantage of steamship and train, crossing political borders and sectarian divides to spread his message of Islamic solidarity. His Paris newspaper circulated far and wide in Islam, through the modern post. Egypt's Muslim Brethren also looked beyond the horizon. In 1948, they sent their own volunteers to fight the Jews in Palestine. Over the next decade, branches of the Muslim Brethren appeared across the Middle East and North Africa, linked by publications and conferences. Egyptian Brethren fleeing arrest set up more branches in Europe, where they mastered the technique of the bank transfer.

The fundamentalist forerunners even laid bridges over the historic moat of Sunni prejudice that surrounded Shi'i Iran. Iran's Devotees of Islam mounted massive demonstrations for Palestine, and recruited 5,000 volunteers to fight Israel. They were not allowed to leave for the front, but Navvab himself flew to Egypt and Jordan in 1953, to solidify his ties with the Muslim Brethren. Visiting the Jordanian-Israeli armistice line, he had to be physically restrained from throwing himself upon the Zionist enemy. Navvab presaged those Iranian volunteers who arrived in Lebanon thirty years later to wage Islamic jihad against Israel.

From the outset, then, fundamentalists scorned the arbitrary boundaries of states, and demonstrated their resolve to think and act across the frontiers that divide Islam. The jet, the cassette, the fax, and the computer network would later help fundamentalists create a global village of ideas and action—not a hierarchical "Islamintern" but a flat "Islaminform"—countering the effects of geographic distance and sectarian loyalty. Not only has the supposed line between "revivalist" and "extremist" been difficult to draw. National and sectarian lines have been erased or smudged, and fundamentalists draw increasingly on a common reservoir for ideas, strategies, and support.

A resolute anti-Westernism, a vision of an authoritarian Islamic state, a propensity to violence, and a pan-Islamic urge: these were the biases of the forerunners of fundamentalist Islam. No subsequent fundamentalist movement could quite shake them. Indeed, several thinkers subsequently turned these biases into a full-fledged ideology. . . .

Iran's Revolution

It was Ruhollah Khomeini (1902–89) who wrote the ideological formula for the first successful fundamentalist revolution in Islam. Khomeini added nothing to fundamentalist ideology by his insistence on the need for an Islamic state, created if necessary by an Islamic revolution, but he made a breakthrough with his claim that only the persons most learned in Islamic law could rule: "Since Islamic government is a government of law, knowledge of the law is necessary for the ruler, as has been laid down in tradition." The ruler "must surpass all others in knowledge," and be "more learned than everyone else." Since no existing state had such a ruler, Khomeini's doctrine constituted an appeal for region-wide revolution, to overturn every extant form of authority and replace it with rule by Islamic jurists. In Iran, where such jurists had maintained their independence from the state all along, this doctrine transformed them into a revolutionary class, bent on the seizure and exercise of power. Much to the astonishment of the world—fundamentalists included—the formula worked, carrying Khomeini and his followers to power on a tidal wave of revolution in 1979. . . .

Khomeini's delegitimation of rule by nominal Muslim kings and presidents found a powerful echo, and he demonstrated how a revolution might succeed in practice. Khomeini also showed how cultural alienation could be translated into a fervid antiforeign sentiment, an essential cement for a broad revolutionary coalition. Later it would be assumed that only "extremists" beyond Iran were thrilled by Iran's revolution. In fact, the enthusiasm among fundamentalists was almost unanimous. As a close reading of the press of the Egyptian Muslim Brethren has demonstrated, even this supposedly sober movement approached the Iranian revolution with "unqualified enthusiasm and unconditional euphoria," coupled with an "uncritical acceptance of both its means and goals." Sunni doubts would arise about implementation of the Islamic state in Iran, but for the next decade, much of the effort of fundamentalists would be invested in attempts to replicate Khomeini's success and bring about a second Islamic revolution.

The attempts to make a second revolution demonstrated that fundamentalists of all kinds would employ revolutionary violence if they thought it would bring them to power. Frustrated by the drudgery of winning mass support, full of the heady ideas of Mawlana Mawdudi and Sayyid Qutb [early twentieth-century fundamentalist revolutionaries], and inspired by Khomeini's success, they lunged forward. From the wild-eyed to the wily, Sunni fundamentalists of all stripes began to conspire. A messianic sect seized the Great Mosque in Mecca in 1979. A group moved by Qutb's teachings assassinated Egyptian President Anwar Sadat in 1981. The Muslim Brethren declared a rebellion against the Syrian regime in 1982. Another path of violence paralleled this one—the work of the half-dozen Shi'i movements in Arab lands that had emerged around the hub of Islamic revolution in Iran. They targeted their rage against the existing order in Iraq, Saudi Arabia, Kuwait, Lebanon, and the smaller Gulf states. In Iraq, they answered Khomeini's appeal by seeking to raise the country's Shi'is in revolt in 1979. In Lebanon, they welcomed Iran's Revolutionary Guards in 1982, first to help drive out the Israelis, then to send suicide bombers to blow up the barracks of U.S. and French peacekeepers there in 1983. Another Shi'i bomber nearly killed the ruler of Kuwait in 1985. Some of Khomeini's adepts went to Mecca as demonstrators, to preach revolution to the assembled pilgrims. Others hijacked airliners and abducted foreigners. Khomeini put a final touch on the decade when he incited his worldwide following to an act of assassination, issuing a religious edict demanding the death of the novelist Salman Rushdie in 1989.

This violence was not an aberration. It was a culmination. From the time of Afghani, fundamentalists had contemplated the possibility of denying power through assassination, and taking power through revolution. Because resort to political violence carried many risks, it had been employed judiciously and almost always surreptitiously, but it remained a legitimate option rooted firmly in the tradition, and it became the preferred option after Iran's revolution emboldened fundamentalists everywhere. For the first time, the ideology of Islam had been empowered, and it had happened through revolution. Power for Islam seemed within reach, if only the fundamentalists were bold enough to run the risk. Many of them were. They included not just the avowed revolutionaries of the Jihad Organization in Egypt, but the cautious and calculating readerships of the Muslim Brethren in Syria and the Shi'i Da'wa Party in Iraq.

It was a seesaw battle throughout the 1980s. Nowhere was Iran's experience repeated. The masses did not ignite in revolution, the rulers did not board jumbo jets for exile. Regimes often employed ruthless force to isolate and stamp out the nests of fundamentalist "sedition." Fundamentalists faced the gaol and the gallows in Egypt. Their blood flowed in the gutters of Hama in Syria, Mecca in Saudi Arabia, and Najaf in Iraq. Yet fundamentalists also struck blows in return, against government officials, intellectuals, minorities, and foreigners. While they did not take power anywhere, they created many semiautonomous pockets of resistance. Some of these pockets were distant from political centers, such as the Bekaa Valley in Lebanon and several governates of Upper Egypt, but fundamentalists also took root in urban quarters and on university campuses, where Islamic dress for women became compulsory and short-cropped beards for men became customary. From time to time, impatient pundits would proclaim that the tide of fundamentalist Islam had gone out, but its appeal obviously ran much deeper. Its straightforward solution to the complex crisis of state and society spoke directly to the poor and the young, the overqualified and the underemployed, whose numbers were always increasing faster than their opportunities.

Ideological Coherence

After Iran's revolution and the subsequent revolts, it was impossible to dismiss the ideological coherence fundamentalist Islam had achieved. It had succeeded in resurrecting in many minds an absolute division between Islam and unbelief. Its adherents, filled with visions of power, had struck at the existing order, turned against foreign culture, and rejected not only apologetics but politics—the pursuit of the possible through compromise. Fundamentalism mobilized its adherents for conflict, for it assumed that the power sought for Islam existed only in a finite quantity. It could only be taken at the expense of others: rulers, foreigners, minorities. Fundamentalists did not admit the sharing of this power, anymore than they admitted the sharing of religious truth, and although fundamentalists differed on the means of taking power, they were unanimous on what should be done with it. One observer has written that even in Egypt, where the fundamentalist scene seemed highly fragmented, the political and social program of the violent fringe groups "did not seem to differ much from that of the mainstream Muslim Brethren," and was shared by "almost the whole spectrum of political Islam." This was true, by and large, for fundamentalist Islam as a whole.

*"The Muslim Brotherhood dissociates itself
and denounces, without any hesitation, all
forms of violence and terrorism."*

Islamic Fundamentalism Does Not Foster Violence in the Middle East

Muhammad M. El-Hodaiby

Muhammad M. El-Hodaiby is a leader of the Muslim Brotherhood in Egypt, an Islamic political organization founded in 1928 (and which has been officially banned by the Egyptian government). In the following viewpoint he maintains that the tenets of Islam uphold justice, human dignity, pluralism, and nonviolence. Misleading Western interpretations of Islamic fundamentalism, he contends, have led many to conclude that Islamic renewal movements are inherently violent—a conclusion El-Hodaiby rejects. Those Muslims who do participate in violence are reacting, in a misguided way, to governmental attempts to suppress Islamic resurgence. In actuality, El-Hodaiby argues, most Islamic revival movements simply aim to help Muslims return to the principles of true Islam.

As you read, consider the following questions:
1. How did Western imperialism affect Muslim societies, in El-Hodaiby's opinion?
2. According to the author, why is "Political Islam" a misleading term?
3. According to the texts of the Koran [Qur'an], cited by El-Hodaiby, what rights do non-Muslims have in Muslim states?

E ver since the Egyptian people, along with other African and Asian peoples, embraced Islam in the deep-seated conviction that it is a true religion revealed to a true prophet, Islam has fully characterized the life and activities of those peoples. The two basic sources of Islam—the Holy Qur'an and the *sunna* (authentic traditions of the Prophet)—became the sole reference point for the life of the Muslim individual, family, and community as well as the Muslim state and all economic, social, political, cultural, educational, and legislative and judiciary activities. The Islamic creed and *shari'a* (law) ruled over the individual and society, the ruler and the ruled; neither a ruler nor a ruled people could change anything they prescribed.

Since the Islamic shari'a was revealed by God, judges applied its teachings and fulfilled its rules with no intervention from the rulers. A massive wealth of jurisprudence developed (*fiqh*) from the work of scores of scholars who devoted their lives to the interpretation of the Qur'an and sunna through the use of *ijtihad*, the exercise of independent judgment. Various schools of thought emerged, differing mainly on secondary matters, as well as on some points of application. Believers in religions other than Islam, meanwhile, lived in the Islamic homeland secure in their persons, honor, and property as well as everything they held dear. Except for isolated cases, history does not show Muslim persecution of non-Muslims.

The comprehensive Islamic system remained dominant in the Islamic states. This does not mean that the application was perfectly sound or that the rulers perpetrated no wrongs. In fact, many of the texts were abandoned or incorrectly interpreted. After the first three caliphs who succeeded the Prophet as leader of the Muslim community, disputes arose over the selection of head of state. Internal wars broke out, and the leadership of the state soon changed from a caliphate chosen through shura, a process of consultation, to a hereditary and tyrannical monarchy. This deviation from the tenets of Islam occurred even though the relevant text remained clear and unchanged in the Qur'an. Still, the rulers' tyranny was restricted by the jurisprudence of scholars based on the Qur'an and sunna, which left little room for the rulers to promulgate public laws out of character with the shari'a.

The Colonial Christian Invasion

In the period of colonial Christian invasion, the Islamic shari'a was excluded from serving as the constitution and law of the state. Egypt was occupied by the British in September 1882; less than a year later, in July 1883, Islamic religious courts were replaced by "national courts." Most of the new judges were non-Egyptians, and the law they applied were translated French laws, which became the dominant laws in civil, commercial, and criminal cases. The jurisdiction of Islamic religious courts was restricted to areas of personal status, marriage, divorce, and the related issues of establishing lineage, dowries, and alimonies. The Islamic economic system was replaced by a system of banks, despite the prohibition of the interest rate under Islamic shari'a. In the educational realm, new schools offered few opportunities for the young to learn the creed and tenets of their religion. The social system permitted alcohol, prostitution, gambling, and other activities forbidden in Islam.

The countries and peoples subjected to the armies, creed, and social, economic, and ethical systems of the West struggled for independence. After many years, they managed to regain some of their freedom, but they emerged from the age of imperialism with a weak social structure and a ruined economic system in which poverty, ignorance, disease, and backwardness prevailed. Consequently, the system of government became corrupt and weak. Tyrants emerged that were supported by the forces of imperialism, which withdrew their armies but retained much of their influence.

Since the overwhelming majority of these peoples in Muslim societies believed in Islam and embraced it as a full system of life, forces soon appeared among them that strove to awaken the spirit of faith and remove ideas that had emerged during the decadent era of imperialism. Movements of Islamic revival became active to spread correct Islamic thought and demand the application of the rulings of the Islamic shari'a, particularly the basic principles which ensure shura, freedom, justice, and socioeconomic balance.

Among the strongest of these movements is the Muslim Brotherhood, which originated in Egypt in 1928, during the waning years of military colonialism, and has continued its struggle to the present.

Key Principles of the Muslim Brotherhood

The call of the Muslim Brotherhood was based on two key pillars. First, the Muslim Brotherhood aimed to institute Islamic shari'a as the controlling basis of state and society. About 97 percent of the Egyptian people are Muslims, the majority of whom perform the rites of worship and the ethics enjoined by Islam. But in Egypt, legislation, the judiciary, and economic and social systems are founded on non-Islamic bases. The disjunction between government legislation and policy, on the one hand, and the Islamic shari'a on the other, led to the emergence of many social, economic, and political practices that are invalid under Islamic shari'a. Realizing that a government that is committed to Islam cannot be established without a popular base that believes in its teachings, the Muslim Brotherhood strove to provide a mechanism for the education of society in Islamic principles and ethics.

Second, the Muslim Brotherhood worked to help liberate Muslim countries from foreign imperialism and achieve unity among them, contributing to the struggle against the occupying British armies in Egypt while continuously backing liberation movements in many Arab and Islamic countries. The ruling powers in many of these countries are totalitarian, tyrannical, and personalist, denying popular will and elections, despite the extensive propaganda they finance to convince people otherwise. Because these governments rely on foreign influence, and in view of their special formation and military nature, there have been repeated clashes between them and the Muslim Brotherhood. In Egypt, three years after the assassination in 1949 of Hasan Al-Banna, the founder of the Brotherhood, clashes broke out between the Brotherhood and the military regime. In the era of Gamal Abdel-Nasser, thousands of group leaders and members were arrested, jailed, and tortured; six of the Brotherhood's top leaders were executed by Nasser in 1954 and many others killed in prisons and detention camps. Twelve years later, the famous intellectual Sayyid Qutb and two other leaders were also killed.

After a period of relative calm, the authorities in Egypt resumed their campaign against the Brotherhood. Shortly before the parliamentary elections of 1995, they arrested 62 of the most prominent Brotherhood leaders and brought them before military courts on the pretext of their political activity and preparations for running in elections. Despite these obstacles, the Muslim Brotherhood remains the largest and most effective political and doctrinal movement in Egypt.

Western Media Misinterpretations

In the West the rise of Islamic movements led to attempts, especially in the media, to characterize the nature of Islamic resurgence. The Western media usually tries to relate events in other parts of the world to historical experiences in the West, but their efforts to draw analogies often result in a mixing of fact and fantasy. Among the catch words in the Western media are the misnomer "Islamic fundamentalism" and the misleading term "political Islam."

In the Western experience, religious groups called "fundamentalists" have been characterized by narrow-minded and artificial interpretations of some of their holy books, interpretations which would petrify life and isolate society from thought and culture and even the natural sciences. When Western propaganda and media call some movements of Islamic renewal "fundamentalist," they aim to create a link in the mind of the public between those Islamic movements and the negative connotations of fundamentalism in the West.

As a result, the image of Islamic movements is distorted and their call made repulsive. The fact of the matter is that there is no similarity between the Western notion of fundamentalism and Islamic liberation and renewal movements. The majority of Islamic movements today accept all the exigencies of the modern age, and the natural sciences and technology, unlike the fundamentalisms of the Western experience.

The Western media also speaks of "Political Islam," a misleading term because it gives the false impression that there is a distinction between Islam as a religion, with its creed, rites, and ethics, and Islam as a political system. Groups reflective of political Islam are then seen as falsely attributing to themselves religious sanction in order to gain backing for their political views. But Islam is inherently political: there are categorical texts in the Qur'an making it mandatory to apply the shari'a and act in accordance with it. One verse declares: "O you who believe! Obey God, and obey the Apostle, and those charged with authority among you. If you differ in anything among yourselves, refer it to God and His Apostle, if you do believe in God and the Last Day: that is best, and most suitable for final determination" (Qur'an 4:59). Another one states: "But no, by the Lord, they can have no (real) faith, until they make you judge in all disputes between them, and find in their souls no resistance against your decisions, but accept them with the fullest conviction" (Qur'an 4:65). And there are others.

Shari'a

The teachings of the Islamic shari'a have introduced and regulated the principles of justice, fairness, equality, human dignity, and inviolability of person and property. The shari'a includes texts relating to systems which are now considered to be an integral part of politics. The Muslim Brotherhood demands that these particular shari'a injunctions be implemented. Their enforcement cannot be ignored. Scholars of Al-Azhar University in Cairo, the most important institution specializing in the study of Islam, and the scholars and jurisprudents of all Islamic institutions throughout the world are unanimous in upholding this view.

Muslim scholars are also agreed, however, that no one other than prophets of God are infallible: indeed, the first ruler to come after the Prophet, Abu Bakr Al-Siddiq, came to power saying: "I have become your ruler though I am not the best among you. Obey me as long as I obey God's injunctions regarding you. If I disobey, correct me." Rulers are no more than human beings. Therefore, while the government in Islam is required to abide by the principles of the Islamic shari'a, it is still a civil government that is subject to accountability.

The fixed and unchangeable tenets of the Islamic shari'a are very few, consisting of basic principles designed to achieve justice and social and economic equality, as well as protect human rights, dignity, soul, and property; and preserve and protect the teachings of religion and the system of state. There can always be access to ijtihad to deduce views that are appropriate to global, economic, and social changes. Islam knows no infallible religious government that speaks in the name of God. . . .

A Commitment to Nonviolent Methods

In past years, the Muslim Brotherhood has repeatedly stated that it is involved in political life and has committed itself to legal and nonviolent methods of bringing about change. Its only weapons are honest and truthful words and selfless dedication to social work. In following this course, it is confident that the conscience and awareness of the people are the rightful judges of all intellectual and political trends which compete honestly with one another. Thus, the Muslim Brotherhood reiterates its rejection of any form of violence and coercion as well as all types of coups which destroy the unity of the ummah [nation] because such plots would never give the masses the opportunity to exercise their free will. Furthermore, these methods would create a great crack in the wall of political stability and form an unacceptable assault on the true legitimacy in the society.

Indeed, the present atmosphere of suppression, instability, and anxiety has forced many young men of this nation to commit acts of terrorism which have intimidated innocent citizens and threatened the country's security, as well as its economic and political future. The Muslim Brotherhood dissociates itself and denounces, without any hesitation, all forms of violence and terrorism. In addition, it considers those who shed the blood of others or aid such bloodshed as complicit in sin. Hence, the Brotherhood requests all Muslims to abandon such actions and return to the right way, because "a Muslim is one who refrains from attacking others either physically or verbally." We invite all those who are involved in acts of violence to remember the advice of our Messenger (s.a.w.), in the farewell pilgrimage sermon when he commanded us to protect the sanctity of blood, honor, and property of every Muslim. (Muslims use "s.a.w.," meaning "peace and blessings of God be upon him," after the name of the Prophet).

The Muslim Brotherhood's continuous policy has been one of urging the government not to counter violence with violence, and to abide, instead, by the rules of law and jurisdiction. Some people deliberately and unfairly accuse the Muslim Brotherhood of being involved in terrorist acts. These accusations, stemming from the Brotherhood's unwillingness to support wholeheartedly the confrontational policies of the government, cannot be taken seriously in the light of the clear long-term record of the Muslim Brotherhood's contribution to political life, including its participation in general elections and representative bodies.

The Brotherhood has declared fifteen democratic principles, included in my political program for the November 1995 elections, which we invite all political parties and powers in Egypt to support as a National Charter. These principles declare that "it is not permissible for any one individual, party, group, or institution to claim the right to authority, or to continue in power except with the consent of the people." We upheld the principle "power exchange through free and fair general elections." We confirmed our complete commitment to freedom of religion, opinion, assembly, parliamentary representation and participation (for men and women), an independent judiciary, and an army free from political involvement.

Non-Muslims' Rights

The texts of the Qur'an and sunna obligate Muslims to ensure the safety and security of non-Muslims with revealed books preceding Islam (particularly Jews and Christians) as citizens in the Muslim state. These texts ensure for non-Muslims the freedom of belief and the freedom to abide by the laws in which they believe, not the Islamic shari'a. For example, non-Muslims marry under their own laws, and their marriages are recognized by the Muslim state. Nor are they bound by the dietary laws of Muslims. The Islamic texts allow Muslims to deal with those non-Muslims as long as the

Muslims observe the shari'a in such dealings.

The non-Muslims also have the right to own property, real estate, and all kinds of assets. They can engage in various professions like medicine, engineering, agriculture, and trade. They have the right to assume all offices of state that are not related to enforcing the Islamic shari'a in which they do not believe. In addition, they are free to take their disputes and litigation to competent and knowledgeable persons of their own law. A Muslim judge cannot examine or pass verdicts in these cases unless non-Muslims themselves refer these cases to him.

Islam is Not an Explanation

Islam is not an explanation for the Middle East's uniqueness. Religion is particularly important in the Middle East, and the region is the most autocratic in the world. Yet Islam cannot fully explain these findings; and the disporportionate importance of religion and the presence of autocracy in the region do not lead to the increased levels of ethnic conflict one would expect.

Jonathan Fox, *Middle East Quarterly*, Fall 2001.

The stand of the Muslim Brotherhood is based on the clear Qur'anic edict of no compulsion in religion: we do not wish to compel people to act against their faith or ideology. Our stance regarding our Christian compatriots in Egypt and the Arab world is not new and it is clear and well-known. The Christians are our partners in the country; they were our brothers in the long struggle to liberate the nation. They enjoy all rights of citizenship, financial, psychological, civil, or political. To care for and cooperate with them in every good cause is an Islamic obligation which no Muslim would dare to take lightly.

Honoring Humanity

Today, politicians and thinkers worldwide are raising the banner of pluralism, exhorting recognition of diversity in ideas and actions. However, when the Qur'an was revealed to Prophet Muhammad (s.a.w.) more than 1400 years ago, Islam accepted these differences as universal, and based its political, social, and cultural systems on such variation: "And we made you into nations and tribes, that you may know each other—not that you may depose each other . . ." (Qur'an 49:13). Pluralism according to Islam obliges the recognition of the "other" and requires the psychological and intellectual readiness to accept what truth and good others may possess: as Muslims believe, "wisdom is what a believer should be looking for; wherever he finds it, he should utilize it in the best possible way." Muslims do not hide behind an iron curtain, isolated from relationships with other nations.

The Muslim Brotherhood reaffirms its commitment to this enlightened and wise Islamic viewpoint and reminds all those who follow or quote the Muslim Brotherhood to be sincere in their words and actions. Every Muslim should befriend others and open his heart and mind to everyone, never look down on any person nor remind him of past favors, nor lose patience with him. Brothers' hands should always be extended to others in kindness and love. Their approach to the whole world is one of peace in words and actions, following the example of our Messenger (s.a.w.), a mercy sent to all the worlds. . . .

It is worthwhile to remind ourselves and others that Islam is the only ideological and political system that has honored man and humanity to the utmost degree. Islam is absolutely free from all forms of discrimination, whether based on race, color, or culture. From the beginning Islam has protected the lives, privacy, dignity, and property of all individuals and considered any violation of these sanctities a sin. It has also made their protection a religious duty and an Islamic act of devotion, even if non-Muslims do not follow such standards.

The Qur'an explains this as follows: ". . . And let not the hatred of others make you swerve to wrong and depart from justice. Be just: that is nearer to piety." (Qur'an 5:8). If some Muslims, now or in the past, have not committed themselves to this obligation, their misdeeds should not be attributed to Islam. It has been commonly accepted in writings on the philosophy of Islamic jurisprudence that "you can identify true men by seeing them stick to truth, but truth cannot be identified by seeing those who follow it."

Human Rights

The Muslim Brotherhood would like to proclaim to everyone that we are at the forefront of those who respect and work for human rights. We call for providing all safeguards for these rights, securing them for every human being and facilitating the practice of all liberties within the framework of ethical values and legal limits. We believe that human freedom is the starting point for every good cause, for progress and creativity. The violation of human freedom and rights under any banner, even Islam, is a degradation of man and a demotion from the high position in which God has placed him, and it prevents man from utilizing his initiative and powers to prosper and develop.

At the same time, we present to the world's conscience tragic acts of injustice afflicting those Muslims who have never hurt anyone. It is the duty of all wise men to protest loudly, calling for the universality of human rights and the enjoyment of human freedom on an equal footing. Such equality is the true way toward international and social peace and toward a new world order. This is our faithful testimony, and this is our call in all truth and sincerity. We invite everyone to turn over a new leaf in human and international relations, so that we may enjoy justice, liberty, and peace: "Our Lord! Decide between us and our people in truth for You are the best to decide." Praise be to Allah and His blessings upon Prophet Muhammad.

Periodical Bibliography

The following articles have been selected to supplement the diverse views presented in this chapter.

America	"Islam and Modernity," November 12, 2001.
Anthony Arnove	"Islam's Divided Crescent," *Nation*, July 8, 2002.
Kevin Baker	"The Upside to Radical Islam," *New York Times*, December 15, 2002.
Lisa Beyer	"Roots of Rage," *Time*, October 1, 2001.
Richard W. Bulliet	"The Crisis Within Islam," *Wilson Quarterly*, Winter 2002.
Stephanie Cronin	"Modernity, Power, and Islam in Iran: Reflections on Some Recent Literature," *Middle Eastern Studies*, October 2001.
Economist	"Democracy and Islam," April 17, 1999.
Dexter Filkins	"Can Islamists Run a Democracy?" *New York Times*, November 24, 2002.
Thomas L. Friedman	"An Islamic Reformation," *New York Times*, December 4, 2002.
Francis Fukuyama and Nadav Samin	"Can Any Good Come of Radical Islam?" *Commentary*, September 2002.
Adrian Karatnycky	"It's Not Islam: Muslims Can Be Free and Democractic," *National Review*, December 31, 2002.
Martin Kramer	"Ballots and Bullets: Islamists and the Relentless Drive for Power," *Harvard International Review*, Spring 1997.
Bernard Lewis	"The Revolt of Islam," *New Yorker*, November 19, 2001.
Valentine M. Moghadam	"Islamic Feminism and Its Discontents," *Signs*, Summer 2002.
Soli Ozel	"Islam Takes a Democratic Turn," *New York Times*, November 5, 2002.
Edward W. Said	"A Devil Theory of Islam," *Nation*, August 12, 1996.
Roger Scruton	"Religion of Peace?: Islam, Without the Comforting Cliches," *National Review*, December 31, 2002.
Gabriel Warburg	"Islam and Democracy," *Middle Eastern Studies*, July 1999.
Ibn Warraq	"Islam, the Middle East, and Fascism," *American Atheist*, Autumn 2001.

CHAPTER 3

What Role Should the United States Play in the Middle East?

Chapter Preface

In 1948 the United States became the first country to recognize the newly formed state of Israel. Since then it has been more involved in Middle Eastern affairs than any other country outside the region. This involvement can be seen in several areas. Militarily, the United States has stationed numerous troops and naval forces in and around the region to promote regional stability. When Iraq invaded Kuwait in 1990, the United States provided leadership and more than a half million troops in the subsequent 1991 Persian Gulf war that liberated Kuwait. For twelve years after that conflict America maintained economic sanctions and launched occasional military strikes against Iraq. In March 2003, after months of speaking of the necessity of "regime change" in Iraq, President George W. Bush ordered a concerted military action against that nation.

America has been heavily involved in the region in ways besides war. Much of the U.S. foreign aid budget goes to countries in the Middle East. Israel, which receives $3 billion in military and economic assistance, and Egypt, which receives $2 billion, lead the world in receiving American aid. Diplomatically, U.S. leaders have historically been heavily involved in peace efforts in the region, with special attention directed to the Arab-Israeli conflict. President Jimmy Carter's involvement was crucial in creating the 1978 peace agreement between Israel and Egypt, for example.

Many analysts identify two primary reasons for America's interest in the Middle East: oil and Israel. America is the world's largest importer of oil and has dwindling domestic reserves. The Middle East nations of Iran, Iraq, Kuwait, Qatar, Saudi Arabia, and the United Arab Emirates contain 65 percent of the world's proven oil reserves and account for 40 percent of the world's crude oil trade. The 1973 oil embargo, in which Saudi Arabia and other countries withheld their oil from the United States, sharply raised oil prices and demonstrated the potential power of Middle Eastern countries to dominate the world oil market in ways detrimental to the United States and other consumer nations. Much U.S. foreign policy is designed to maintain friendly relations

with Saudi Arabia and other countries in the region to ensure a stable supply of oil.

While America's interest in oil is based on economics, its
support of Israel is based on historical, moral, and geopolit-
ical concerns. After the Holocaust, in which millions of Jews
were killed by Nazi Germany during World War II, many
Americans supported the Jews' desire for a homeland in the
Middle East, which was seen as one way to prevent future
Jewish persecution. In addition, Israel is, in the words of political analyst Alon Ben-Meir, "the only democracy in an inherently unstable region," thus providing the United States
with a strategic military ally in the Middle East.

These two objectives—a stable oil supply and support of
Israel—are often in conflict. American attempts to cultivate
good relations with oil-rich Arab states have been compli-
cated by the United States's support of Israel, a country that
many Arab states view as an enemy. Because of these conflicts of interest, many commentators argue about whether
America is fair in how it treats the opposing parties in the
Arab-Israeli conflict. The viewpoints in this chapter debate
these and other issues pertaining to U.S. foreign policy in
the Middle East.

"Because outside intervention [to resolve the Palestinian-Israel conflict] is required, the only superpower capable of orchestrating it successfully is the United States."

The United States Should Intervene to End the Israeli-Palestinian Conflict

Sherwin Wine

Rabbi Sherwin Wine is a founder of the Society for Humanistic Judaism and the author of several books including *Judaism Beyond God*. In the following viewpoint he argues that the United States should take an active role in ending the endemic violence between Israelis and Palestinians, which he categorizes as a clash between Jewish and Arab nationalism. He argues that the ongoing conflict between Israelis and Palestinians is not only harming the people of the Middle East but is threatening the global economy. The conflict is so bitter and entrenched that outside intervention is required to end it, he asserts, and only the United States is powerful enough to do so.

As you read, consider the following questions:

1. What is the foundation of the war in Israel, according to Wine?
2. Why do both sides see themselves as victims, according to the author?
3. What elements of an imposed truce settlement does Wine outline?

Sherwin Wine, "Arabs and Jews," *Humanist*, vol. 62, September/October 2002, pp. 15–18. Copyright © 2002 by the American Humanist Association. Reproduced by permission.

The war between the Jews and the Arabs in former British Palestine has been going on for eighty-one years. In 1921, the first Arab explosion against the Zionist pioneers announced the beginning of the fray. Hatred and suspicion have undermined any successful resolution of the conflict.

After the Jewish War of Independence in 1948, the conflict became a war between the Jewish state and external Arab enemies. In that conflict, the Israelis were generally victorious. The Israeli triumph in 1967 crushed Gamal Abdel Nasser, the hero of Arab nationalism. But in 1987 the Palestinian Arabs chose a new kind of battle—internal rebellion. The infitada was born. And it has grown in fury ever since.

Zionist and Arab Nationalism

The foundation of the war is the power of nationalism. Jewish nationalism was born out of the defiance of the oppressed masses in czarist Russia. It was fed by racial anti-Semitism. Diaspora nationalism sought to liberate the Jews of eastern Europe and give them cultural autonomy. It was destroyed by native resistance and the Holocaust.

Zionist nationalism also saw itself as a national liberation movement. It naively proposed to solve anti-Semitism by returning the Jews to their ancient homeland. Reinforced by socialist idealism and the revival of Hebrew as a popular language, it led to the establishment of a Jewish settlement in Palestine. The closing of the doors to immigration in the United States, the support of the British government, and the rise of Adolf Hitler gave this nationalism the impetus that the slaughter of six million Jews was to make irresistible. Zionism became the most powerful movement to mobilize the Jewish masses in the twentieth century.

Arab nationalism was an import from the West and was cultivated initially by Christian Arabs as a way of countering their exclusion by Muslims. Propelled by Turkish oppression and by the humiliation of European conquest, the Arab nationalist movement was led by Westernized intellectuals who embraced secular values and placed nationhood above religion. Since the Arab world never fully experienced the secular revolution which had transformed European life, the Arab nationalism of the street had difficulty distinguishing between Arab loyalty and Muslim loyalty. Religion is inevitably part of the nationalist package in the Muslim world.

Since the Arab world is vast, divided by regional differences, cultural diversity, and the internal boundaries of twenty-two states created by colonial masters, the unification of the Arab nation hasn't been easy. Nasser tried and failed. He was defeated by both the Israelis and by the hostility of his political enemies and rivals within the Arab world.

The one issue that has the power to transcend the internal state boundaries of the Arab world and to mobilize the Arab masses is Zionism. Whether or not it deserves such designation, the Jewish state has become the symbol of Arab humiliation. Perceived as the last and most outrageous example of European colonialism, Israel is the object of almost universal Arab hate. The defeat of Israel has become the ultimate perceived means of restoring Arab honor. The hatred of Zionism is so intense that it is difficult for most Arabs to distinguish between their hostility to Israel and their hatred for Jews.

In fact, the suspicion and hatred between Arabs and Jews is so fierce that dialogue is condemned to failure. Most public and private encounters between conventional Arab and Jewish leaders degenerate into shouting matches. Each side insists on its rights. And, of course, both sides are "right." The Palestinian Arabs have been invaded, abused, and oppressed. The Israeli Jews are by now mainly native-born residents of the land they defend and the creators of a dynamic, modern, high-tech state; they have no place else to go.

From the Jewish point of view, the Arab hostility cannot easily be distinguished from anti-Semitism. The memories of the Holocaust hover over every response. Of course, the popular media in the Arab world reinforce this perception by aping the propaganda of European Jew hatred. From the perspective of the Arabs, Jewish voices are confused with the voices of Jewish extremists who advocate expulsion and deportation.

Extremists and Victims on Both Sides

There is an abundance of extremists on both sides. The Arab and Palestinian nationalist and fundamentalist worlds feature many militant groups that advocate terrorism and call for the destruction of the Jewish state. The Jewish and Israeli extremists are equally militant in their refusal to recognize the right of a Palestinian state to exist (beyond suggesting that Jordan is already a Palestinian state). To the credit of the Israelis, Israel features a peace movement that has no counterpart in the Arab world.

Both sides see themselves as victims. Jews see Israel as a small beleaguered state in a vast and petroleum-rich Arab world that does nothing to rescue its Palestinian brothers and sisters from poverty. Arabs see Israel as the agent of American imperialism, supported by the wealth and military technology of the world's only superpower—a nation that is beholden to Jewish political power.

What President George W. Bush Should Do

The president's basic approach to the Middle East is correct. He is horrified by the suicide bombings and understands Israel's need to respond to them. He also believes, however, that only a political settlement will resolve the problem. He endorses a Palestinian state and has announced an international conference to begin talking about all this. But words mean nothing in the Middle East. . . . The president must aggressively use his power and prestige—his political capital—to push the Palestinians, Israelis and Arabs toward substantive political talks. This is not going to bring peace tomorrow, but it might well lower the tensions, which is good for them—and for the United States.

Fareed Zakaria, *Newsweek*, May 20, 2002.

The failure of the Oslo peace process [a series of peace agreements reached between Israel and the Palestinians in the 1990s] is as much the result of intense hatred and suspicion as it is the incompatibility of vested interests. The issues of boundaries, Jerusalem, and refugees are shrouded by such levels of distrust that the normal compromises that negotiations bring can never emerge. No arrangements can provide the security that most Israelis want. And no "deal" can yield the sense of honor and vindication that most Palestinians and Arabs seek.

In searching for alternatives to endless war, certain realities need to be confronted. This war is not only bad for the Israelis and the Palestinians but also for Jews and Arabs. For the Jews, the war has already spread to Europe, where Muslim militants assault synagogues and vulnerable Jews. For the Arabs, the war prevents any real confrontation with the political, economic, and social issues that affect their world. War continues to justify government by military dictators.

This war is bad for the United States and the rest of the world. The Palestinian issue has provided the fuel whereby Muslim militants have won the allegiance of millions of Arabs and Muslims in their desire to wage war against the United States and Western culture. A war between the West and Islam is a world war. It is different from a war against Muslim fundamentalist terrorism; such a conflict would enjoy the support of most Muslim governments. The success of the United States' response to the attacks of September 11, 2001, lies in the ability to make such a distinction.

A Cycle of Vengeance

Jews and Arabs, Israelis and Palestinians by themselves cannot achieve peace—or even an effective truce—by relying on negotiations alone; the cycle of vengeance has its own logic. Every terrorist action incites retaliation; every retaliation incites counter-retaliation. No antagonist can allow itself to be seen as weak. Revenge is a necessary tactic in maintaining credibility. The cycle cannot stop itself without outside intervention.

The proposed Palestinian state [in 2000 and 2001 negotiations] is no more than 3,000 square miles in size—hardly a formula for viability. It is presently a series of urban "doughnut holes" within Israeli-occupied territory. The presence of the Israeli army is justified not only by the argument for security but also by the necessity to defend small Jewish settlements which have been established in the West Bank and Gaza by religious Jewish settlers laying claim to the land. These settlements prevent peace, add nothing to the security of Israel, and provide more provocation to Arabs to kill more Jews.

Jerusalem is already divided. Jewish Jerusalem (about two-thirds of the expanded city) has no Arabs, while Arab Jerusalem (the eastern sector) has no Jews. While some Arabs work in Jewish Jerusalem, almost no Jews even penetrate Arab Jerusalem unless they are on military duty. A unified city is more desirable than a divided city, but the division already exists.

A binational Israeli-Palestinian state—a dream of many peaceniks—is not politically viable even though it would be economically desirable. Jewish and Arab nationalism are realities; they cannot be wished away. Mutual hatred and suspicion are realities; they cannot be dismissed. Arguing against nationalism may work a hundred years from now but it doesn't fly today. A Jewish state—in which Jewish national culture is the dominant culture and most people speak Hebrew—is no more racist than would be an Arab state whose dominant culture and language reflected its people. Three million Palestinian refugees cannot return to the Jewish state without destroying the Jewish national character of the Jewish state.

U.S. Intervention

Because outside intervention is required, the only superpower capable of orchestrating it successfully is the United States. Since September 11, George W. Bush has mobilized an effective coalition of world powers, including Europe, Russia, China, and India—as well as many allies in the Muslim world. The war between the Israelis and the Palestinians has begun to undermine the coalition, especially with Bush's perceived support of the Ariel Sharon government in Israel. Joint intervention with the approval of the United Nations and with the support of moderate Muslim powers could restore the coalition. This intervention is no different from the intervention that the United States initiated in Bosnia and Kosovo [during their wars in the 1990s].

What would be the elements of such an intervention? The United States controls the process. The Israelis don't trust the United Nations and won't cooperate with an effort managed by the hostile nations of the developing world.

The United States acts as a neutral "parent." It doesn't always praise one side and condemn the other; it creates a setting for negotiations, with the presence of major members of the coalition. The format of such negotiations is only a pretense. In the "back room" the United States dictates the settlement and everybody knows that the United States has imposed the settlement. Both antagonists protest, but they yield because they have no choice. The imposition gives the leaders of both sides an excuse, a way to save face, and a scapegoat. They can justify their "surrender" to their constituencies by pleading helplessness. They may even shake hands reluctantly. Whether [Palestinian leader Yasser] Arafat will still be representing the Palestinians is the question.

All that can realistically be achieved at this time is an effective truce. Peace will have to await a reduction in the fury of hatred and suspicion. For now, an imposed settlement should include the following:

- the removal of all Jewish settlements from the West Bank and Gaza, except those settlements which function as contiguous communities for Tel Aviv and Jerusalem
- the digging of a ditch and construction of a fence between the Jews and Arabs along the adjusted 1967 boundaries
- the policing of this fence by the United States and its European allies
- the granting of Arab East Jerusalem to the Palestinians as their national capital
- the demilitarization of the new Palestinian state, with periodic inspections by the United States and its coalition partners
- compensation for Palestinian refugees who cannot return.

Such compensation may cost over $30 billion and would be covered by the United States, Japan, and European allies. If the compensation helps to bring about an effective truce, it would be worth the investment. Rescuing the global economy for peace justifies the expense.

Compensating Israel

Israel needs to be compensated for its "willingness" to shrink and to confront the wrath of its right-wing extremists. Since it won't in the foreseeable future be accepted by the Arab and Muslim worlds, it needs to be regarded as the European power it is. Israel's high-tech economy needs the European market, just as its European culture needs a European support system. The price that Europe pays for this necessary peace is that it accepts Israel as a member of the European Union. Such acceptance is no different than acceptance of Cyprus or Turkey, and Israelis will be better off trading in euros than shekels.

After this settlement is imposed, terrorist violence will likely continue. The war against Muslim fundamentalist terrorists will also continue. For the extremists in the Arab and Muslim world—and even in the Jewish world—hatred is a way of life. For moderates, an effective truce will enable them to join the forces of peace.

The ball is in Bush's court if he would only lead the way. The leaders of the Defense Department and the religious right will likely oppose this kind of proposal, but only such action can provide any light at the end of the tunnel that is the Middle East.

"The task of advancing confidence-building measures should be left to the Israelis and Palestinians, and other players in the region."

The United States Should Not Intervene to End the Israeli-Palestinian Conflict

Leon T. Hadar

Leon T. Hadar is the Washington bureau chief of the *Business Times* of Singapore and an adjunct professor at American University in Washington, D.C. His writings include the book *Quagmire: America in the Middle East*. In the following viewpoint he asserts that the United States should not interject itself into the Israeli-Palestinian dispute, arguing that America can do little to alter the dynamics of the conflict. It is up to the Israelis and Palestinians themselves to come up with the necessary compromises to secure peace, he concludes.

As you read, consider the following questions:
1. What actions by Israeli and Palestinian leaders led Hadar to conclude they do not want peace?
2. What harms would result from U.S. efforts to encourage negotiations in the Middle East, according to the author?
3. What steps does Hadar recommend that America take?

Leon T. Hadar, "Resist the Interventionist Impulse in the Middle East," *Christian Science Monitor*, June 15, 2001. Copyright © 2001 by *Christian Science Monitor*. Reproduced by permission.

The acceptance by Israel and the Palestinian Authority of the cease-fire plan put forth by CIA Director George Tenet [in 2001], has strengthened the hands of those at home and abroad who are arguing that a more-energized diplomatic role by the United States could help end the violence in the Middle East.

American pundits and US allies hope the White House is abandoning its posture of "benign neglect" toward the Israeli-Palestinian conflict, and is ready to adopt the more central role that previous administrations had played in trying to make peace between Arabs and Jews. More specifically, they are urging Washington to press the Israelis and Palestinians to implement the recommendations of the international commission headed by former Sen. George Mitchell, which called for the introduction of "confidence building" steps— including a freeze on the building of new Israeli settlements in the occupied territories, and an effort by Palestinian security forces to end anti-Israeli violence.

A Difference Between Expectations and Reality

But the fact that both sides have accepted the conclusions of the Mitchell report, and may be willing to back a fragile cease-fire brokered by the United States, reflects nothing more than short-term tactics by Israeli and Palestinian officials hoping to win brownie points with Washington and the "international community." That the Israelis and Palestinians cannot reconcile their opposing views on what constitutes "peace," and continue to engage in acts of violence, highlights the wide divergence between the expectations for diplomatic momentum among "peace processing" experts in Washington and the harsh political realities in the Middle East. It demonstrates why the Bush administration should resist the pressure for a new American-led "peace initiative."

Indeed, the election of ultra-nationalist Ariel Sharon as prime minister and the growing militancy on the Palestinian side, where Yasser Arafat seems unwilling or unable to put an end to the intifada, have been clear indications that there is no political support among the leaders and the people involved in this bloody ethnic and religious war for the kind of confidence-building measures proposed by the Mitchell commission.

If anything, Mr. Sharon is intent on increasing the number of Jewish settlers in the West Bank. He is confident that Israel's military power will force the Palestinians to bow to its dictates and give up their demand for full independence. Meanwhile, Arafat is strengthening his alliance with radical Islamic fighters, and hoping the growing violence will trigger a dramatic international response that would leave Washington no choice but to pressure Israel to withdraw from the West Bank and Gaza. Neither side will be willing to modify its position as long as it enjoys domestic support.

"REMIND ME AGAIN WHY I WANTED THIS GIG?.."

Thompson. © 2002 by Copley News Service. Reproduced by permission.

In that context, there is little that Washington could do to change these long-term strategic calculations. A new US effort to energize the "peace process" would only raise expectations among the Palestinians and the other Arabs that President [George W.] Bush could compel Israel to end its settlement policy. But the pro-Israeli disposition in Washington coupled with a weak Arab diplomatic hand make that an unlikely scenario. And the image of a US administration unable to force a change in the repressive Israeli policies would damage America's position in the Arab world, and strengthen Sharon.

Resisting the Interventionist Urge

By resisting the interventionist urge and encouraging the "localization" of the Palestinian-Israeli issue, the Bush administration will send a clear signal to the Palestinians that their only chance of winning political independence is through direct negotiations with the Israelis. Instead of complaining about US diplomatic passivity, Egypt, Jordan, and the European Union should use their power to persuade Arafat to end the violence.

At the same time, Mr. Bush could follow the footsteps of his father's administration by cutting economic aid to Israel by the amount of money it spends on the Jewish settlements in the occupied territories. He could make any continuing military aid to Israel conditional on its agreement to stop using American-made weapons against civilians in the occupied territories.

The task of advancing confidence-building measures should be left to the Israelis and Palestinians, and other players in the region. A successful outcome of such a process could encourage the United States to strengthen its diplomatic and economic ties with them. But Washington should not use its resources to promote such a strategy, so it will not have to pay the costs of its possible failure.

"Americans hope for constitutional governments in the Middle East not because we are naive, but because we seek democracy's practical dividends."

The United States Should Promote Democratic Regimes in the Middle East

Victor Davis Hanson

In 2002, when this article was originally published, the United States was engaged in debate on whether to use military action to effect a "regime change" in Iraq, a country suspected of hiding weapons of mass destruction. Some proponents of American military intervention, assuming that it would result in victory and temporary American occupation of Iraq, argued that such a course of events could well begin a new era in the Middle East. In the following viewpoint Victor Davis Hanson argues that the United States should seize the opportunity that military intervention in Iraq would provide to promote democracy in the Middle East. America's past policy of supporting autocratic Middle East regimes in the name of stability, he asserts, has resulted in endemic conflict, human rights abuses, and anti-American sentiment. Hanson, a professor of classics at California State University in Fresno, is the author of several books on military history.

As you read, consider the following questions:
1. What are the practical dividends of democracy in the Middle East, according to Hanson?
2. What past examples of U.S. democracy promotion and creation does the author cite?

What will our invasion of Iraq unleash? Our greatest challenge may be not the elimination of Iraq's weapons of mass destruction but the subsequent reconfiguration of the Middle East. What happens inside Iraq on the day [Iraqi leader] Saddam Hussein is gone will reveal American intentions, capabilities, and morality. What we do in Iraq will set the stage for success or failure in the entire region.

If we are to promote some quasi-democracy in post-Saddam Iraq, how will we do it? Iraq is a Muslim country with no tradition of consensual government or even an indigenous vocabulary for "democracy," "citizen," "secularism," or "referendum." The realists remind us that the seeds of constitutional government do not grow in soil that lacks a middle class and the rule of law. They point out that there has never been a truly free Arab democracy in 1,500 years. They are joined by the multicultural, moral relativist, and increasingly isolationist Left, which contends that we have no business dictating to any country the nature of its government.

Perhaps, then, we should allow Iraq to lapse into a purportedly pro-American despotism like Saudi Arabia and Egypt—permit some general, say, like [Pervez] Musharraf of Pakistan, to rise to power on promises to pump oil, rein in terrorists, curb the madrassas [religious schools that promote radical Islam], not threaten his neighbors, and reform at some future date. Or perhaps, if the postwar chaos grows overwhelming, we should do as we did in Afghanistan years ago—shrug, declare a victory of sorts, leave quietly, and hope that the feuding Shiites, Kurds, Baathists, and generals we leave behind turn out to be better and weaker than Saddam Hussein.

Conflicting advice comes daily from all sides, from Middle Eastern dissidents, Arabists, Islamic diplomats, and the Europeans. But we should decide for ourselves upon a course of action before we go to Iraq. If we profess support for democracy in Iraq now, before the bombs fall, this assurance to the Iraqi people may help our cause more than a European armored division or a Middle Eastern base. Our commitment to political reform—not to any individual or clique—will give us the military and ethical advantage of consistency, purpose, and clarity.

Americans hope for constitutional governments in the Middle East not because we are naive, but because we seek democracy's practical dividends. Modern democracies rarely attack America or each other. When they fight illiberal regimes, they win. The Falklands, Panama, Serbia, and the Middle East all demonstrate the power of legitimate governments over dictatorships. Yet this pragmatic consideration is often dismissed as starry-eyed idealism. Only belatedly have we advocated democratic reform for the Palestinians, as a remedy for our previous failed policy of appeasement of [Yasser] Arafat and his corrupt regime.

We are not talking of Jeffersonian democracy all at once. First, remove the dictator, to permit a more lawful society to evolve on the model of Panama, Grenada, Serbia, and the Philippines. Keep up the pressure of American and world opinion, international aid, the return of Westernized dissidents, the emancipation of women, and the occasional threat of American force. Let [the September 11, 2001, terrorist attacks] remind us that inaction can be as deadly as intervention.

Two Converging Camps

In the past, Americans were told that the Middle East was divided roughly into two camps (plus democratic Israel): the sometime sponsors of terror (Afghanistan, Algeria, Iran, Iraq, Lebanon, Libya, Syria, and Yemen) and the so-called moderate dictatorships (Egypt, the Gulf states, Jordan, Morocco, Saudi Arabia, and Tunisia). Although the latter group ruled without a popular mandate and made use of coercion and intimidation, they nevertheless curbed their brutality and either condemned or ignored but did not openly abet terrorists.

Our State Department has the unenviable task of maintaining workable relationships with these allegedly pro-Western regimes—at a time when some friends and foes are looking more and more alike. Lunatic Iran still pumps oil; the sober Saudis murmur of boycotts. Saudis in the United States are enraged at us; Iraqis living here lobby congressmen to liberate their country. Our tanks and planes can obliterate armies, but they can't stop suicide-murderers. Washington may assure us that Egypt and Saudi Arabia are our friends, yet their citizens comprise the majority of the September 11 terrorists and the detainees at Guantanamo—while Libyans, Syrians, and Iraqis are less likely to join al Qaeda.[1]

The events of the last year [2001] prove that both extremist and moderate governments in the Middle East are riding a tidal wave of resentment. Governments of both kinds seek to survive largely through bribery, oppression, and censorship, and by scapegoating Israel and America. This they hope will postpone an accounting with their people. In the absence of elections, free speech, or any public audit of government finances, our "friends" must divert the attention of their restless populations to the bogeyman of the West. Yet at root, the Arab masses probably hate us less than they abhor their own governments for lack of freedom and economic progress. If Islamic zeal were the cure for what ails these regimes, Saudi Arabia, Pakistan, and Iran would be pillars of stability.

Middle East Pathologies

The pathologies of the Middle East are urgent and will only get worse if left alone. The last two decades of ruined economies have brought nothing but disaster. The unusually candid "Arab Human Development Report 2002," issued by leading Arab intellectuals under the auspices of the United Nations, provides the details. An exploding population (38 percent is under 14 years of age) will have to fight for scarce resources: The 22 Arab countries have a combined gross domestic product less than Spain's. The wealthiest 85,000 Saudi families have overseas assets of $700 billion. Labor productivity fell between 1960 and 1990, while it soared elsewhere. Even Africa outperformed the Arab world in rates of economic growth and the incidence of constitutional government between 1975 and 1990. More foreign books were translated into Greek than into Arabic [in 2001]. The report speculates that half the youths in most Arab countries desire to emigrate—usually to the lands of the infidels, Europe or the United States.

In response to this depressing state of affairs, an exasper-

1. Al Qaeda is the terrorist network believed responsible for the September 11, 2001, terrorist attacks on America. Following America's subsequent military response in Afghanistan, where al Qaeda was headquartered, hundreds of suspected al Qaeda members were taken to America's naval base in Guantanamo Bay, Cuba.

ated United States has tried everything from appeasement to confrontation—everything except systematic, sustained, and unqualified support for democratic reform. On that score, our experience in Afghanistan is encouraging. [In 2001], no country in the Middle East was more lawless, anti-American, or brutal than Afghanistan under the Taliban [Afghanistan's former ruling regime]; today, our intervention has produced a more consensual government, and refugees are going home. A secular and democratic Turkey, meanwhile, proves that Islam is not intrinsically incompatible with liberal society. And reforms in Qatar promise hope for eventual elections; Qatar's liberality explains the absence of a Saudi-style backlash from the populace, as well as the regime's willingness to work with us on energy and defense.

The "realist" rejoinder is that elections in the Middle East are a onetime thing. In Iran, the ouster of the autocratic shah made way for an election, after which the mullahs destroyed democracy; Khomeini's death only brought in more fanatics.[2] Arafat rigged an election and hasn't held another. Jordan's parliament is a façade behind which King Abdullah rules by kowtowing to Iraq, Syria, the Palestinians, and the United States. The very idea of elections brought disaster in Algeria.

Yet even these dismal scenarios are instructive. The fact that the mullahs were elected in Iran has put an enormous burden of legitimacy upon them; their abject failure may better serve the long-term interests of the United States than the Saudi royal family's success. Palestinians too are talking more about the need for fair elections than the need to keep Arafat in office. America has much to gain when democracy works, while autocratic regimes profess stability but are volatile under the surface. Better to deal with a subverted democracy: At least its people will soon realize that they, not the United States, are responsible for their disasters.

Limits of Realpolitik

The problem with the old realpolitik is not just that it is occasionally amoral but also that it has been tried and found

---

2. Ayatollah Ruhollah Khomeini, the leader of Iran's 1979 Islamic Revolution, died in 1989.

wanting. Short-term stability has left unaddressed the fes-
tering long-term problem of Arab development. The rot
now overwhelms us.

Ending the Democratic Exception

The United States does play a large role on the world stage,
and our efforts to promote democracy throughout the Muslim world have sometimes been halting and incomplete. Indeed, in many parts of the Muslim world, and particularly in
the Arab world, successive U.S. administrations, Republican
and Democratic alike, have not made democratization a sufficient priority.

At times, the United States has avoided scrutinizing the internal workings of countries in the interests of ensuring a
steady flow of oil, containing Soviet, Iraqi and Iranian expansionism, addressing issues related to the Arab-Israeli conflict, . . . or securing basing rights for our military. Yet by failing to help foster gradual paths to democratization in many
of our important relationships—by creating what might be
called a "democratic exception"—we missed an opportunity
to help these countries become more stable, more prosper-
ous, more peaceful, and more adaptable to the stresses of a
globalizing world.

It is not in our interest—or that of the people living in the
Muslim world—for the United States to continue this exception. U.S. policy will be more actively engaged in supporting
democratic trends in the Muslim world than ever before.

Richard N. Haas, address before the Council on Foreign Relations, December 4, 2002.

We must try something new, out of self-interest. We need
to prevent more Egyptians, Kuwaitis, Pakistanis, Palestinians, and Saudis from murdering more Americans, as their
"shocked," subsidized, and protected governments shrug,
send condolences, and remind us that their "friendship"
should earn them immunity from U.S. bombs. The world is
not static. What worked for the last fifty years—a mixture of
concern for oil, opposition to communism, and profits from
weapons sales—no longer justifies supporting duplicitous
dictators who can scarcely feed their own people in a region
awash in petroleum. The end of Soviet-sponsored communism means we no longer need fear that elected socialists

will turn into Communist props.

We cannot continue to treat symptoms rather than the etiology of the disease. We have used restrained military force to send a message to the occasional megalomaniac who boasted of killing Americans. So we bombed [Libyan leader Muammar] Qaddafi; blasted the Sudanese; sent cruise missiles into Afghan caves; shelled Lebanon; and hit Iraq in the no-fly zones.[3] It was a tit-for-tat strategy, originated by [former president Ronald] Reagan, institutionalized by the elder Bush [former president George Bush], and popularized by [former president Bill] Clinton.

The advantage of a reactive strategy seemed to be that it let Americans go on living without much disruption or cost in lives and treasure. But September 11 taught us otherwise: The terrorists and their hosts saw that we offered no sustained threat to their operations, and they seized their chance. Now, they will not be content with blowing up an embassy or a ship. They deal in symbols and shock, and so will always, like carnival barkers or professional wrestlers, be seeking to meet or exceed their prior achievements.

A New Strategy

The alternative to the old realpolitik is a brand new strategy oriented toward ending the entire apparatus of autocracy and creating in its place the conditions for future political legitimacy and economic growth in the Middle East. Rather than fearing the uncertainty that this would entail, we should understand that sometimes temporary chaos may be better than enduring stasis.

Indeed, this is the course on which we have embarked in Afghanistan—as revolutionaries of sorts, rather than Pollyanna interventionists or cynical isolationists. The verdict is still out on the stability of the [Homid] Karzai government, much less the country's long-term prospects. Clearly, though, the present government gives Afghanistan its first ray of hope

---

3. Following the 1991 Gulf War, the United States, Great Britain, and France imposed no-fly zones in northern and southern parts of Iraq. Iraqi aircraft are forbidden to operate in these areas, ostensibly to protect ethnic and religious groups from Iraqi persecution. The United States and Great Britain have since enforced these zones through bombing missions against Iraqi air defense targets.

in three decades. Before September 11, Pakistan was considered a humane place compared with Afghanistan; now the Karzai government arguably holds more promise than Musharraf's dictatorship. And yet under American pressure, Pakistan today offers some improvement over a year ago, when we largely ignored its anti-democratic pathologies. Could the nascent, legitimate Afghanistan—backed by American and European aid, the return of dissidents and exiles from the West, an influx of social workers, the emancipation of women, the establishment of schools, and the threat of force—offer hope elsewhere in the Middle East?

History provides more encouragement than we might think. Cynics in 1945 warned us that Japanese terrorists would make an American occupation of mainland Japan impossible. The traditions of Japan were Asian and authoritarian, they said, and we should not confuse a desire for Western weapons and industry with any capacity for democracy. Yet we plunged in, and in five years Japan had become the sanest and most humane society between San Francisco and Beijing. Rather than search for a Westernized leader, we took on the greater burden of establishing institutions in a completely foreign landscape. Simultaneously, Germany and Italy, both historically unstable republics, were transmogrified from fascist killer states into liberal republics almost overnight.

We poured in aid, brought their rehabilitated governments into the world community, interfered with their school systems, empowered women, stationed troops to monitor recidivism, sought out moderates, dissidents, and exiles, helped to draft constitutions, tried the guilty—then crossed our fingers that the people's inclusion in decision-making and enjoyment of personal freedom would bring a new maturity and responsibility to society. Today, without the specter of a global and nuclear Soviet Union to make "regime change" difficult and distort elections, we are once again free to promote democracy in unlikely places.

There are now millions of exiles from the Middle East residing in Western countries who want Western liberalism to take root in their native lands. Democracy has no rival in French Marxism, Communist nostalgia, or Baathist nonsense. Unlike communism, Islamic fundamentalism does not even purport to bring progress and equality. Nor has it a nuclear patron with global reach, like the old Soviet Union. We need not fear a universal Islamic fundamentalism. It may thrive in Saudi Arabia, where fanaticism of one sort or another is the only way to foment revolution, but it has alienated the masses in theocratic Iran, now that the extremists have lost the romance of tormented idealists and are seen as accountable for their institutionalized oppression. We also have an ally in global popular culture. However crass, free expression subverts theocracy and dictatorship.

Costs and Dangers

We must not be naive. Establishing lawful rule in lawless places entails real costs and dangers. Thus, war or the threat of force may be the necessary catalyst. Germany and Japan did not abandon fascism voluntarily. . . . Armed resistance can bring profound change because defeat brings humiliation, and humiliation sometimes precipitates a collective change of heart. The Eastern Europeans, and eventually the Russians, broke free because they saw the Soviet Union was exhausted, had lost the Cold War, and was near collapse. When the generals and colonels of Greece and Argentina brought military ruin and embarrassment to their countries, they fled. South Korea and Taiwan were born out of war; they survived and eventually democratized because America vowed to protect them with force.

In the Middle East, there will be no change until Saddam Hussein is defeated and what he stands for is shown to lead only to oblivion. The use of military power must be decisive, producing a rout, not a stalemate. Were we to intervene and then hesitate or otherwise lose, we might achieve the opposite result from that desired—encouraging strongmen to "stand up to" the United States.

A second price we must be willing to pay is the lengthy presence of American troops. They are still in Germany, Italy, Japan, and South Korea. All that prevents the violent overthrow of democracies in Latin America and their replacement with dictatorships is fear of the Marines. Taiwan remains free only because of the proximity of American carriers and submarines. We already have thousands of soldiers in the Gulf states and Saudi Arabia: They could just as well protect democracies as keep a watch on or support tyrants.

A third burden we must assume is that we must expect and not fear anti-Americanism. Newly created democracies will not necessarily love us. Look at postwar France, which resented the United States mere months after it was liberated. Arabs may feel some identification with Europe, given their former colonial relationships, geographical proximity, and shared distrust of American power, even as their children may prefer the American way. Regardless, we must remember that, while we are at war with no democracy, we have had to intervene in a lot of autocracies in the last twenty years. Far better to suffer the chastisements of a democratically elected Saudi parliament for, say, our rejection of [the] Kyoto [greenhouse gas emissions treaty] than to stand by while the Saudi royal family bankrolls the spread of extremism around the world.

Finally, with the Cold War a thing of the past, we must rethink our dealings with caretaker dictators who make noises about moving toward the rule of law, press freedom, and markets but deliver little meaningful reform. The old rationale for bearing with mere authoritarians has crumbled away with the passing of the expansionist Marxist-Leninist totalitarians. Without ever losing sight of our preference for peaceful change, we need to reassess, carefully and thoroughly, the usefulness of propping up strongmen in the name of stability, when to do this is to flout the aspirations of long-suppressed peoples and forget our national principles. Muslims in autocratic Pakistan are dangerous to us, but those in democratic India are not. . . .

Try Freedom

In the Middle East, everything has been tried except freedom. Confronted over the years with Arab Communists, Islamic extremists, and every manner of dictator, American policy-makers have juggled the imperatives of countering Soviet expansionism, fighting terrorism, and protecting world commerce in oil. Through it all, the region has remained beset by abject failure. Yet we need not despair and turn isolationist. We must rather accept that the world itself has changed since the Cold War; and in our own national interest, we must make sure that our policies evolve with it. September 11 thrust before us the infiltration of terrorist sleeper cells into the West, the appeasement of murderous Islamists by Arab dictators, and the terrorism on the West Bank. In the process, we lost the easy option of propping up the status quo—and the Islamic world lost the privilege of being different.

"Even if the United States . . . vigorously
pursued political reform in the region,
democratic results would be highly
unlikely."

The United States Cannot Impose Democracy on the Middle East

Marina Ottaway, Thomas Carothers, Amy Hawthorne, and
Daniel Brumberg

In the following viewpoint four scholars criticize the idea
that the United States could create an upsurge in Middle
East democracy by toppling Iraqi leader Saddam Hussein.
They contend that numerous internal obstacles make any
quick democratic transformation of that region a fantasy.
The United States must balance democracy promotion with
other important U.S. interests, including garnering help in
the war on terrorism, finding a solution to the Israeli-
Palestinian conflict, and maintaining access to oil. Marina
Ottaway is the author of several books on comparative politics. Thomas Carothers is the author of *Aiding Democracy*
Abroad: The Learning Curve. Amy Hawthorne is a specialist
in Arab politics. Daniel Brumberg is a professor of government at Georgetown University.

As you read, consider the following questions:

1. What experiences with democracy promotion in other
   countries do the authors describe?
2. What three main issues complicate the achievement of
   democracy in the Middle East, according to the authors?

From within the Bush administration and on the editorial pages of America's major newspapers, a growing chorus of voices is expounding an extraordinarily expansive, optimistic view of a new democratizing mission for America in the Middle East. The rhetoric has reached extraordinary heights. We are told that toppling [Iraqi leader] Saddam Hussein would allow the United States to rapidly democratize Iraq and by so doing unleash a democratic tsunami across the Islamic World. Some believe that a pro-democracy campaign in the Middle East could produce a democratic boom comparable in magnitude and significance to the one produced by the end of the Cold War.

It is good that the question of democracy in the Middle East is finally receiving serious attention. Although the United States has, over the years, offered tepid encouragement for political reform in the Arab world and funded some democracy aid programs there, past efforts were timid, erratic, and not reinforced at senior diplomatic levels. For far too long, Washington coasted on the complacent and erroneous assumption that the stability of the autocratic regimes of the Middle East could at least protect U.S. national security. Now the pendulum has swung. U.S. officials no longer see these regimes as bulwarks against Islamic extremists, but consider them responsible for the discontent that fuels terrorism and, in the case of Saudi Arabia, for the financing of extremist groups. But obstacles to democracy in the Middle East are many and go well beyond the autocratic nature of the present regimes to span a host of economic, sociopolitical, and historical factors. These realities do not mean the Middle East will never democratize or that the United States has no role to play. But they do mean that the path will be long, hard, and slow and that American expectations and plans should be calibrated accordingly.

Democratizing Iraq

It is hard not to feel the attraction of the tsunami idea—the tantalizing notion that with one hard blow in Iraq the United States can unleash a tidal wave of democracy in a region long known for resistance to such change. But can it? The United States can certainly oust Saddam Hussein and install a regime that is less repressive domestically and less hostile to U.S. interests. But democracy will not soon be forthcoming.

Experience in other countries where the United States has forcibly removed dictators or helped launch major post-conflict democratic reconstruction indicates a strong need for caution. In Haiti, for example, the 1994 U.S. invasion and the subsequent large-scale reconstruction effort have not led to democracy but instead political chaos, renewed repression, and dismal U.S.-Haiti relations. In post-Dayton Bosnia,[1] the truly massive international reconstruction effort has produced peace and some socioeconomic gains, but only a tenuous political equilibrium that even six years later would collapse if international forces pulled out. . . . It should be noted that all these countries are small, making even forceful intervention manageable. Iraq, with its 23 million inhabitants, would require an intervention on a totally different scale.

The example of Afghanistan[2] is especially sobering. Despite widespread optimism of the initial post-Taliban period and the Bush administration's ringing promises to lead the democratic reconstruction, the political situation in Afghanistan today [in October 2002] is troubled and uncertain. The administration's failure to back up its promises with a genuine commitment to Afghanistan's reconstruction will badly undercut similar promises made about Iraq.

Like Afghanistan, Iraq is a country torn by profound ideological, religious and ethnic conflicts. Before democratization can even begin, the United States would have to assemble a power-sharing agreement among ethnic Kurds, Shiites, and Sunni Muslims. Because no obvious leader is waiting in the wings and the exiled Iraqi opposition is chronically divided, Washington would have to provide the political and, most importantly, military and security infrastructure necessary for holding a new government together. In short, the United States would have to become engaged in nation building on a scale that would dwarf any other such effort

---

1. America and its NATO allies have stationed peacekeeping troops in Bosnia since the 1995 Dayton Accords ended a three-year war in that multiethnic state. 2. The United States military helped Afghan insurgents topple the Taliban regime in late 2001. America subsequently supported the accession of Hamid Karzai as president of Afghanistan in 2002 and continued to station peacekeeping troops in that country.

since the reconstruction of Germany and Japan after World War II. And it would have to stay engaged not just years, but decades, given the depth of change required to make Iraq into a democracy. Thus far the Bush administration has given no indication that it is ready to commit to such a long-term, costly endeavor. All this does not mean that Iraq can never become democratic. But the idea of a quick and easy democratic transformation is a fantasy.

Far-Fetched Notions

Equally doubtful is the idea that a regime change in Iraq would trigger a democratic tsunami in the Middle East. The notion that the fabled "Arab street" would respond to the establishment of a U.S.-installed, nominally democratic Iraqi regime by rising up in a surge of pro-democratic protests, toppling autocracy after autocracy, and installing pro-western, pluralist regimes is far-fetched. No one can predict with any certainty what the precise regional consequences of a U.S. action would be, but they would likely have as many or more negative than positive effects on the near-term potential for democracy.

For example, an invasion would very likely intensify the anti-Americanism already surging around the region, strengthening the hands of hard-line political forces. Autocratic Arab regimes that refused to support the American war effort could benefit from a wave of Arab nationalism and find their position strengthened, at least for a period. Domestic advocates of reform would come under suspicion as unpatriotic. Conversely, by supporting the invasion, several autocratic regimes, including Saudi Arabia and Egypt, might win a reprieve from any new U.S. pressure to democratize.

The formation of a new, more moderate regime in Iraq would unlikely have the inspirational effect some predict. Many Arabs, rather than looking to Iraq as a model, would focus on the fact that Iraq was "liberated" through western intervention, not by a popular Iraqi movement. One powerful current in today's regional discourse emphasizes liberation from excessive western interference in Arab affairs more than liberation from undemocratic leaders.

As to possible ramifications for the future of Palestine,

Ariel Sharon's government in Israel would likely view an American invasion of Iraq as an invitation to skirt the [Palestinian] statehood issue. Unless the Bush administration shows the political will to push now for a two-state solution—a very unlikely scenario given the close links between Israeli hard-liners and administration hawks—victory in Iraq would more likely postpone than advance the creation of a democratic Palestine.

Domino democratization does sometimes occur, as in Latin America and Eastern Europe in the 1980s and 1990s. But while external influences may increase the chance of an initial change in government, what happens next depends on internal conditions. This was certainly the case in the former Soviet Union, where what at first seemed like a wave of democracy petered out in the face of deep-seated domestic obstacles. Today most former Soviet republics are autocracies.

Middle East Realities

Even if the United States ousted Saddam Hussein and vigorously pursued political reform in the region, democratic results would be highly unlikely. Such a policy would certainly shake up the region, but the final outcome in each country would owe much more to domestic factors than to the vigor of U.S. and European reformist zeal. One of the lessons of more than a decade of democracy promotion around the world is that outsiders are usually marginal players. They become the central determinant of political change only if they are willing to intervene massively, impose a de facto protectorate, and stay for an indefinite, long term. No matter what happens in Iraq, such forceful intervention is unthinkable in most Middle East countries.

The Middle East today lacks the domestic conditions that set the stage for democratic change elsewhere. It does not have the previous experience with democracy that facilitated transitions in Central Europe. Even Egypt, which in the early part of the twentieth century had a national bourgeoisie committed to the values of liberal democracy, opted for autocracy fifty years ago. Quite a few countries in the region—Algeria, Egypt, Jordan, and Morocco among them—are liberalized autocracies whose leaders have skillfully used a measure of state-monitored political openness to promote reforms that appear pluralistic but function to preserve autocracy. Through controlled elections, divide-and-rule tactics, state interference in civil society organizations, and the obstruction of meaningful political party systems, these regimes have created deeply entrenched ruling systems that are surprisingly effective at resisting democratic change.

Nor has the Middle East experienced the prolonged periods of economic growth and the resulting dramatic changes in educational standards, living standards, and life styles that led Asian countries like Taiwan and South Korea to democratic change. The picture is instead one of socioeconomic deterioration. Even in the richest oil-producing countries, oil export revenues are no longer sufficient to subsidize rapidly growing populations at previous levels. The population of Saudi Arabia, for example, was less than six million in 1974 at the time of the first oil boom, but it is now sixteen million and growing at one of the highest rates in the world. Through state control of the economy, furthermore, regimes have purchased the support, or at least the quiescence, of key sectors of the citizenry.

Moreover, countries of the Middle East do not benefit from a positive "neighborhood effect," the regional, locally grown pressure to conform that helped democratize Latin America. On the contrary, neighborhood norms in the Middle East encourage repressive, authoritarian regimes.

Three Complicating Factors

Beyond these daunting obstacles, at least three issues complicate the achievement of democracy in the Middle East:

Islamism. The issue is not whether Islam and democracy are incompatible in an absolute sense. Like Christianity and Judaism, Islam is far too complex a religion, with too many schools of thought, for the question even to make sense. Rather, the issue is the existence in all Middle Eastern countries, and indeed in all countries with a substantial Moslem population, of both legal and clandestine political movements that use illiberal interpretations of Islam to mobilize their followers. Since these "Islamist" movements enjoy considerable grassroots support and local authenticity, they are most likely to benefit from democratic openings. Truly free and fair elections in any country of the Middle East would likely assure Islamist parties a substantial share of the vote, or possibly even a majority, as would have happened in Algeria in 1992 had the elections not been cancelled. Democratization ironically raises the possibility of bringing to power political parties that might well abrogate democracy itself. This is a different version of the old Cold War–era fears: communist parties in Western Europe and elsewhere would come to power through elections only to impose rad-

The Democracy Dilemma

American policymakers have long grappled with the so-called "democracy dilemma" in the Arab world: How should the United States promote political liberalization without threatening core U.S. interests in the Middle East? These interests include maintaining Israel's security and well-being, ensuring reliable access to petroleum reserves in the Gulf, preventing terrorism and the spread of weapons of mass destruction, and supporting U.S. investment. . . .

Many recognize that the lack of political freedom in the Arab world . . . may endanger U.S. interests in the long term. Repression and exclusion from meaningful political participation sow the seeds of hopelessness, extremism and violent upheaval. And as the connection between economic development and good governance becomes increasingly clear, the U.S. is concerned that the Arab world's sclerotic political systems are inhibiting the region's integration into the global economy.

Yet supporting genuine democratic change may not only provoke tension with Arab regimes whose cooperation is essential to the achievement of U.S. interests, it also risks bringing to power leaders who would actively reject American values. Across the region, free elections might replace current regimes, whether monarchies or secular republics, with some kind of Islamist leadership. The U.S. considers this a worse option since many Islamists reject U.S. influence in the Middle East. Throughout the Arab world, with a choice between a less-than-democratic status quo and the potential outcome of a democratization process—a power transfer to an anti-U.S. Islamist-oriented government—the U.S. has preferred the former.

Amy Hawthorne, *Foreign Service Journal*, February 2001.

ical change. However, continuing to exclude or marginalize Islamist political participation would doom democracy by silencing a voice that resonates with an important segment of the public. Doing so would only provide governments with a justification for maintaining excessive controls over the entire political sphere, thereby stunting the development of other popular forces. Many governments, such as those in Algeria, Jordan, Lebanon, Morocco, Turkey, and Yemen, have tried to skirt this dilemma by giving Islamists a chance to participate in politics while at the same time preventing them from actually assuming political power, but this solution also augurs poorly for democracy.

Conflict with Israel. Resentment against the state of Israel, particularly against the Israeli occupation of the West Bank and Gaza, creates a measure of solidarity between Arab leaders and their citizens that is exploited regularly by autocrats to deflect attention from their own shortcomings. Until there is a two-state solution of the Israeli-Palestinian conflict that gives security and dignity to both parties, resentment will infuse all aspects of Arab politics and obscure the question of democracy.

Perceptions of the United States. There is a widespread perception in the Middle East that the Bush administration is embracing the cause of democracy promotion not out of real commitment, but because doing so provides a convenient justification for American intervention in Iraq and the acceptance of the Israeli reoccupation of the West Bank. Unconditional support of Israel, combined with the Sharon government's publicly stated objective of deferring Palestinian statehood, feeds a widespread feeling that the U.S. government cannot be trusted. America's long support of Arab autocracies adds to this perception, thus undermining its credibility as an advocate of change in the Middle East.

Beyond the Mirage

The United States should promote democracy in the Middle East recognizing that quick change is a mirage. The goals must be initially modest, and the commitment to change long term. . . .

A serious program of long-term support for Middle East

democracy would need to follow these guidelines:

• *Do not reflexively attempt to marginalize Islamist groups.* Differentiate instead between the truly extremist organizations that must be isolated because they are committed to violence and those amenable to working legally to achieve their goals. Develop strategies to encourage political processes in which moderate Islamists, along with other emerging forces, can compete fairly and over time gain incentives to moderate their illiberal ideologies. To do this, the United States needs to acquire a much better understanding of the relevant organizations in each country. It will not be easy and it entails some risk. But the only means of containing dangerous extremist groups without perpetuating wholesale repression is to open the door of legal political activity to the more moderate organizations.

• *Do not overemphasize support for westernized nongovernmental organizations and individuals with impeccable liberal credentials but little influence in their societies.* Democracy promoters need to engage as much as possible in a dialogue with a wide cross section of influential elites: mainstream academics, journalists, moderate Islamists, and members of the professional associations who play a political role in some Arab countries, rather than only the narrow world of westernized democracy and human rights advocates.

• *Don't confuse a "sell America" campaign with democracy promotion.* The U.S. government has launched a major public relations campaign to burnish America's image in the Arab world. Whatever the value of this much-discussed effort, it has little to do with the politically nuanced task of pressuring governments on human rights and institutional reforms, and of supporting key civil groups and the like. Movement toward democracy and movement toward a more positive view of American culture and society are not synonymous.

• *Do not support lackluster institutional reform programs—such as with stagnant parliaments and judiciaries—in lieu of real political reform.* Push the liberalized autocracies of the region, such as in Bahrain, Egypt, Kuwait, Jordan, and Lebanon, beyond the superficial political reforms they use to sustain themselves. This will require pressuring such states to undertake true political restructuring, allow the development of political parties, and open up more space for political contestation.

• *Account for major differences in political starting points and potential for political change. Shape policies accordingly.* Be clear about the goal in each country: regime change, slow liberalization, and democratization are not the same thing. Policies to achieve one goal are not necessarily appropriate for the others. In particular, a sudden regime change would probably make democratization a more remote prospect for many countries because it would too quickly tip the balance in favor of the groups that are best organized and enjoy grassroots support, Islamist organizations in most cases. . . .

America's Limited Leverage

The idea of instant democratic transformation in the Middle East is a mirage. The fact that the Bush administration has suddenly changed its mind about the importance of democracy in the Middle East has not changed the domestic political equation in any country of the region. Furthermore, the United States has limited leverage in most Arab countries. In other regions, the United States, together with Europe and international organizations, often used the lever of economic assistance to force political reform on reluctant governments. But oil-rich countries do not receive aid. Poor countries in the region do, but the United States can hardly afford to use this aid as a weapon for political reform without jeopardizing other interests. The United States already wants a lot from Arab states. It wants help in the war on terrorism. It wants their oil. It wants cooperation in finding a solution to the Israeli-Palestinian conflict. It wants access to military installations to wage war on Iraq. It cannot afford to antagonize the very regimes whose cooperation it seeks. The United States will be forced to work with existing regimes toward gradual reform—and this is a good thing. If a tidal wave of political change actually came to pass, the United States would not be even remotely prepared to cope with the resulting instability and need for large-scale building of new political systems.

"U.S. dependency on Middle East oil can be greatly reduced, if not eliminated, through domestic energy conservation."

The United States Should Reduce Its Dependency on Middle East Oil

Part I: *Ellsworth American*; Part II: *Christian Century*

The United States imports more than half the oil it consumes, 20 percent of which comes from the Middle East. In the following two-part viewpoint, the editors of the *Ellsworth American* and the *Christian Century* argue that because of America's economic dependence on imported oil, the country has been compelled to support corrupt regimes, and has been hampered in its ability to support peace in the region. The authors call for serious measures to reduce oil consumption, such as higher gasoline taxes and stricter fuel-efficiency regulations for automobiles and sport utility vehicles (SUVs). The *Ellsworth American* is a weekly newspaper based in Maine. The *Christian Century* is a national liberal Christian publication.

As you read, consider the following questions:

1. How much of the world's oil reserves lie within the Middle East, according to the editors?
2. What possible scenarios do the editors of the *Ellsworth American* describe concerning Saudi Arabia?
3. What specific recommendations on energy conservation do the editors of the *Christian Century* make?

I

Well over half of all the proven oil reserves in the world sit beneath the sands of one of the most volatile and unpredictable regions of the world—the area surrounding the Persian Gulf. The developed and developing nations of the world, and most particularly the United States, rely almost totally on oil for transport and a multitude of other uses. Without it, our planes would not fly, our cars, trucks, buses and trains would not run, even our ships would not sail. The generation of electricity would be sharply curtailed, millions of homes would be left without heat, and our manufacturing industries would collapse. Our economy, and others, would grind to a halt.

Some will say that we need not worry since oil-exporting nations, such as Saudi Arabia, which by itself sits on a fourth of all proven oil reserves, and the buyers of its oil are mutually dependent. One needs a supply, the other a market. While the current Saudi regime is regarded as an ally of the United States, its stability is far from assured. Recent history illustrates that there are fundamentalist revolutionaries such as the Taliban within the Islamic world who would willingly consign their subjects to abject poverty to bring the West to its knees. The Middle East is a breeding ground for terrorists of the sort who launched the September 11 [2001, terrorist] attacks on America. The possibility that nuclear weapons already may be in the hands of those terrorists or the governments who overtly or covertly support them is a risk that can be ignored only at our own peril. Several Middle East countries, including Saudi Arabia, are vulnerable to those revolutionaries. Once in power, they easily could cause short-term or long-term disruptions in the supply of oil, either by sharply increasing prices, shutting off exports or even destroying the oil fields.

America's Oil Addiction

In the face of such huge risk, neither our national leaders nor our citizens seem willing to make the choices—choices that would be far less painful than those wrought by any major disruption in oil supplies—that are needed to reduce, even modestly, America's addiction to oil.

Given current and projected consumption levels over the next few decades, dependence on Middle East oil will increase, not decrease. Many of the big fields outside the embrace of OPEC [Organization of Petroleum Exporting Countries] are entering a period of decline or nearing depletion. The cost of finding and developing other non-OPEC reserves is huge, and growing.

What United States citizens and their government must do is to embrace every conceivable conservation measure for the short term and implement energy efficiency for the long term. At this point, neither is happening in any meaningful way.

Studies suggest that America could reduce fuel use on the highways by as much as 20 percent with technologies already available. But the partisan Congress has no willingness to challenge automobile companies and the American public, either by mandating significant increases in fuel economy laws or by boosting taxes on gasoline and other petroleum fuels. Government investment and support for developing alternative energy sources is minimal at best.

The President's [George W. Bush] answer to the problem is to tap oil reserves beneath the Arctic National Wildlife Refuge in Alaska, but its effect on our consumption of imported oil would be nearly negligible.

Leaders within Congress and the Bush administration doubtless recognize the national security implications posed by our dependence on OPEC and Middle East oil. Now they must somehow find the will to do something about it—before time runs out.

II

The U.S.'s approach to the Middle East frequently seems less policy than fated inevitability. The U.S. requires oil from that region for its survival, therefore it underwrites despotic and corrupt regimes, and bears the consequences of those alliances. Yet neither the need nor the alliances are written in the stars.

Energy Conservation

U.S. dependency on Middle East oil can be greatly reduced, if not eliminated, through domestic energy conservation.

More specifically, the U.S.'s need for Middle East oil would plummet if Americans chose to reduce their consumption of gasoline. Writing in *Foreign Affairs* (hardly an organ of the Green movement), Amory and Hunter Lovins have claimed that if Americans "had simply bought new cars that got 5 mpg more than they did, [the U.S.] would no longer have needed Persian Gulf oil."

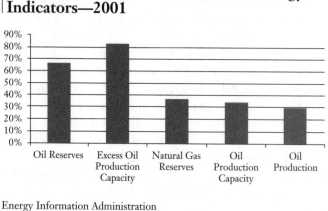

Middle East as a Percent of World Energy Indicators—2001

Energy Information Administration

Energy efficiency has increased in many sectors of American industry and domestic life—from home heating and cooling systems to innovative light bulbs. But fuel economy for vehicles has actually dropped from 26.2 mpg in the 1980s to a current average of 24.7 mpg. Raising federal taxes on gasoline and requiring vehicles to meet higher fuel-efficiency standards would help reverse this trend.

Americans pay some of the lowest gasoline taxes in the Western world. A little over a quarter of the price of gasoline at the pump goes to federal, state and local taxes. In Canada that figure is around 42 percent, and in Europe taxes can account for more than 75 percent of the price paid at the pump. Although gas prices over $2.00 a gallon are front-page news in the U.S., Europeans have been paying between $3.00 and $5.00 per gallon for years.

Increasing the federal tax on gasoline would help pay for big budget items that will continue to emerge from the

September 11 crisis and the war on terrorism, and would act as an incentive for Americans to drive less or purchase more energy efficient vehicles, or both.

However, in a country with poor public transportation, in which many workers must drive considerable distances to work, an increased federal gas tax would disproportionately affect lower-income households. For this reason, a bump up in gas taxes must be modest. Greater emphasis must be placed on achieving increased fuel efficiency for the vehicles Americans drive.

Fuel Efficiency Standards Must Be Raised

Closing the SUV loophole would be a step in the right direction. Starting in 1975, when fuel-efficiency standards were being set for vehicles, light trucks used primarily in agriculture and construction were granted lower targets than automobiles. Those targets now are 27.5 mpg for autos and 20.7 mpg for light trucks. Since 1975, however, the category "light truck" has come to include gas guzzling SUVs and vans that now account for more than half of all new car sales in the U.S. (Currently the average mileage for SUVs, vans and pickups is 18 mpg.) A standard tailored for working trucks now applies to vehicles that haul mainly groceries and soccer balls. Bringing this class of vehicles up to the same standard of efficiency as the one that currently exists for autos (not an unreasonable goal) could save as much as 1 million barrels of oil per day.

High-efficiency hybrid gas-electric cars like the Toyota Prius (49 mpg) and Honda's Insight (67 mpg) offer alternatives to the behemoths cruising America's highways. So does the development of light rail systems linking regional urban areas. These and other options for increased energy conservation would benefit the environment that sustains us all, and would free the U.S. from its dependency on Middle East oil. Released from that dependency, the U.S. may become a truly independent and honest broker of general peace in the region.

Americans displayed an immediate willingness to sacrifice their blood to aid fellow citizens following the September 11 attacks. It's time to sacrifice, for the common good, the profligate use of another viscous liquid.

"Politically correct, misguided energy schemes will not make America more independent."

Calls to Reduce America's Dependency on Middle East Oil Are Unrealistic

Henry Payne and Diane Katz

Henry Payne is an editorial cartoonist and writer for the *Detroit News*. Diane Katz is an editorial writer for the *Detroit News*. In the following viewpoint they respond to the argument that America must reduce oil and gasoline consumption to reduce its dependency on Middle East oil. Oil is produced throughout the world, Katz and Payne write, nullifying the ability of Middle East nations to manipulate global supplies. In addition, the authors criticize conservation programs such as mandated fuel-efficiency standards in automobiles, as well as proposals to develop hydrogen-powered cars, arguing that these actions are costly and will not achieve the goal of reducing economic dependence on the Middle East.

As you read, consider the following questions:
1. What has happened to oil prices since September 11, 2001, according to Katz and Payne?
2. What would raising automobile fuel-efficiency standards accomplish, according to the authors?
3. What problems exist with replacing gasoline with hydrogen fuel cells, according to Katz and Payne?

Any crisis in the Middle East inevitably prompts Washington to scapegoat the automobile as a threat to national security. The dust had barely settled on lower Manhattan last fall [following the September 11, 2001, terrorist attacks] before calls went forth—from pundits and pols across the spectrum—to relinquish our "gas-guzzlers" in the name of energy independence.

But just as the Cassandras will dominate media coverage of energy, so will Middle Eastern oil continue to fuel America's vehicles for the foreseeable future. Simple economics, geography, and consumer choice all demand it.

A Dangerous Addiction?

Since Sept. 11, Washington has mobilized to end our "dangerous addiction" to foreign energy sources. Senators John Kerry and John McCain are proposing dramatic increases in federal fuel-economy standards. The . . . Natural Resources Defense Council is insisting that we could cut gasoline consumption by 50 percent over ten years—if only the feds would mandate what and where we drove.

Even the "oil men" in the Bush administration have advocated doling out millions in research subsidies for hydrogen fuel cells that supposedly would replace the internal-combustion engine. The project, Energy Secretary Spencer Abraham announced in January [2002], is "rooted in President [George W.] Bush's call to reduce American reliance on foreign oil."

In fact, the price of oil has declined since Sept. 11, as it consistently has for decades, and with producers scattered all over the world, no single nation or region can stop the flow.

But supporters of a comprehensive energy policy seem undeterred by these realities. "Logic," [columnist] Robert Samuelson writes in the *Washington Post*, "is no defense against instability. We need to make it harder for [Middle Easterners] to use the oil weapon and take steps to protect ourselves if it is used. Even if we avoid trouble now, the threat will remain."

Past efforts to attain a petroleum-free utopia, however, have largely failed. For example, despite three decades of federal fuel-economy standards, oil imports as a share of

U.S. consumption have risen from 35 to 59 percent.

A market-based solution, such as a gas tax, is the most obvious approach to cutting consumption, but even environmentalists concede that proposing one would spell political suicide. Moreover, gas taxes are an expensive solution and come with no guarantee of energy independence. The European Union, for example, taxes gas up to $4 per gallon— and still imports over half its oil.

So instead of enraging consumers at the pump, Washington has largely relied on backdoor taxes.

Fuel-Economy Standards

The regulatory regime known as CAFE (Corporate Average Fuel Economy) was hatched in the wake of the oil-price shocks of the early 1970s, when sedans still made up most of the nation's fleet. Instead of the redesigned smaller, lighter, and less powerful vehicles, however, consumers flocked to minivans, small trucks, and sport utility vehicles, which are held to a lower CAFE standard (20.7 mpg versus the 27.5 mpg required for cars).

Today, both passenger cars and light trucks are more efficient than ever, having improved 114 percent and 56 percent, respectively, since 1974. But gasoline is so cheap, despite continuing Middle Eastern crises, that on average Americans are driving twice as many miles as in years past.

A . . . study by H. Sterling Burnett of the National Center for Policy Analysis found that raising CAFE standards by 40 percent—as Kerry and others recommend—would not "reduce future U.S. dependence on foreign oil." CAFE's only function is to keep regulators busy calculating elaborate formulas for determining compliance in which manufacturers then look for loopholes. (CAFE requires that a manufacturer's trucks meet an average standard of 20.7 mpg. Thus DaimlerChrysler AG, for example, designates its popular PT Cruiser as a "truck" in order to offset the low mpg of its large SUVs, such as the Dodge Durango.)

Worse, stricter CAFE standards would surely undermine the very economic security that proponents vow to protect. The profits of U.S. automakers—and tens of thousands of UAW [United Auto Workers] jobs—depend on sales of

SUVs and light trucks. According to an analysis by Andrew N. Kleit, a professor at Pennsylvania State University, the Kerry CAFE proposal would reduce the profits of General Motors by $3.8 billion, of Ford by $3.4 billion, and of DaimlerChrysler by $2 billion. Foreign manufacturers, which largely specialize in smaller vehicles, would see a profit increase of $4.4 billion.

Limits of Hydrogen

Evidently hoping to shield automakers from a CAFE assault—and to win PR points for expanded domestic drilling—the Bush administration has embraced the latest alternative-fuel fad: the hydrogen fuel cell.

The Bush plan replaces the Partnership for a New Generation of Vehicles, [former vice president] Al Gore's vain attempt to produce an affordable, emissions-free family sedan capable of 80 mpg by 2004. Over eight years, Washington pumped more than $1.5 billion into the program—in addition to the $1.5 billion sunk into it by the Big Three. In its annual review of the project last August [2001], the National Research Council judged the super-car goals to be inherently "unrealistic."

The Bush plan has drawn broad political support. Former Clinton chief of staff John Podesta cheers, "The next step is hydrogen-powered fuel-cell vehicles. But the only way to get these vehicles out of the lab and onto the road is with incentives and requirements aimed at producing 100,000 vehicles by 2010, 2.5 million by 2020."

But the 100-year dominance of conventional internal-combustion engines over alternatives is no accident. A quick primer on the complexities of hydrogen power helps explain why.

Hydrogen's status as the new darling of the sustainable-energy movement is understandable. Its promise lies first in its performance: Unlike ethanol, it supplies more energy per pound than gasoline. When used to power an automobile, its only emission is water—making it especially attractive to an industry already under pressure from clean-air and global-warming rules. And hydrogen is one of the most plentiful elements on the planet.

The trouble is, hydrogen always comes married to an-other element—as in methane gas or water.

Most fuel-cell technology today relies on hydrogen ex-tracted from methane, in a process that emits large quanti-ties of greenhouse gases. And as *Car and Driver* magazine's technical analyst, Patrick Bedard, explains, domestic sources of methane are "[t]oo limited to serve any significant de-mand for automobiles." A study by the Argonne National Laboratory concluded that the U.S. would have to look to foreign sources—primarily in Russia and Iran, and in other Middle East nations.

Goodbye, oil dependence. Hello, methane dependence.

No Oil Crisis

The global view suggests, in fact, that there is no supply cri-sis. We know there's a lot more oil worldwide now than in the 1970s. Using increasingly advanced probes and sensors, surveys that once estimated total global reserves at 650 bil-lion now find more than a trillion barrels. . . .

Buying oil is much easier today, too. Then and now, the Middle East oil cartel sat on roughly two thirds of known re-serves, but in 1970 its members sold directly to cus-tomers—and could punish them individually. Today oil is sold on an international market mediated by thousands of middlemen and futures exchanges around the world, a sys-tem that has done much to undermine OPEC's [Organiza-tion of Petroleum Exporting Countries] clout. "They can't cut off our oil supply, they can only cut off oil supply," says Professor William Hogan of Harvard. "It's a very blunt po-litical weapon, so they stopped using it as a weapon."

Tony Emerson et al., *Newsweek*, April 8, 2002.

Given these hurdles, attention is turning instead to elec-trolysis—the extraction of hydrogen from water, which is readily obtainable along America's ample coasts. Electrolysis is, however, the most energy-intensive process of any fuel al-ternative; studies differ on whether it would consume more carbon-based fuels than the use of hydrogen would save. What is certain, points out Stanford University professor John McCarthy, is that "the advantage of hydrogen, if you have to burn carbon fuels (coal, oil, or gas) to manufacture it, would be negligible."

In other words, McCarthy explains, the unspoken truth about hydrogen is that "it is a synonym for nuclear power.". . . .

Ironically, many of the political voices now embracing hydrogen fuel are the same ones that have prevented the construction of a single new U.S. nuclear plant in 25 years. . . .

Gasoline Remains the Answer

For now, the answer is still gasoline. Compared with the technical barriers to developing alternative fuels, there already exist numerous market mechanisms to mitigate potential oil shortages. As suggested by Donald Losman, a National Defense University economist, these include: stockpiling, futures contracts, diversifying the supplier base, and relaxing the restrictions that currently mandate some 13 different fuel blends in 30 cities.

Dramatic improvements in fuel efficiency also could be achieved if Washington allowed automakers to market diesel-powered vehicles. In Germany, for example, Volkswagen mass markets the 80-mpg Lupo, which is powered by a direct-injection diesel engine. But that's anathema to American greens who insist—without evidence—that diesel's particulate emissions are dangerous to public health. All fuels require trade-offs, of course. But politically correct, misguided energy schemes will not make America more independent. Gasoline remains by far the best deal we have.

Periodical Bibliography

The following articles have been selected to supplement the diverse views presented in this chapter.

Gawdat Bahgat "Oil and Militant Islam: Strains on U.S.-Saudi Relations," *World Affairs*, Winter 2003.

Michael Barone "Remaking the Middle East," *U.S. News & World Report*, December 2, 2002.

Joseph A. Cari Jr. "From the Center (Proposed Marshall Plan for the Middle East)," *Wilson Quarterly*, Spring 2002.

Robert Dreyfuss "The Thirty Year Itch," *Mother Jones*, March/April 2003.

Economist "A Delicate Balance; America and the Arab World," May 4, 2002.

Economist "Zigzagging; America and the Conflict," April 6, 2002.

Frank J. Gaffney Jr. "U.S. Would Sell Out Israel by Pushing for Land-for-Peace Deal," *Insight on the News*, April 15, 2002.

Adam Garfinkle "The Impossible Imperative? Conjuring Arab Democracy," *The National Interest*, Fall 2002.

Reuel Marc Gerecht "Appeasing Arab Dictators," *Weekly Standard*, April 8, 2002.

Christopher Hitchens "Single Standards," *Nation*, May 13, 2002.

Lawrence F. Kaplan "Neutrality Act—The Limits of American Influence," *New Republic*, April 15, 2002.

Alfred M. Lilienthal "The Israel Quagmire (Thoughts for the U.S. Citizen)," *Vital Speeches*, December 15, 2001.

Johanna McGeary "Looking Beyond Saddam," *Time*, March 3, 2003.

Michael B. Oren "Does the United States Finally Understand Israel?" *Commentary*, July/August 2002.

David Pryce-Jones "Oslo and Other Illusions," *National Review*, December 9, 2002.

Michael Renner "Oil & Blood," *World Watch*, January/February 2003.

Jerry Taylor "Oh No! That '70s Show: Against Carterism in Energy Policy," *National Review*, March 25, 2002.

Kenneth T. Walsh et al.	"Time to Step In," *U.S. News & World Report*, April 15, 2002.
Wilson Quarterly	"Debating Preemptive War," Winter 2003.
Fareed Zakaria	"How to Save the Arab World," *Newsweek*, December 24, 2001.
Stephen Zunes	"Problems with Current U.S. Policy," *Foreign Policy in Focus*, May 20, 2002.

CHAPTER

Is Peace Between Israel and the Palestinians Possible?

Chapter Preface

For much of the 1990s, what became known as the "Oslo process" created a sense of optimism for many that peace between Israel and the Palestinians was indeed possible. Such optimism has been replaced in the new millennium by disillusionment as peace negotiations have stalled and Israel has been racked with renewed violence and terrorist attacks.

The Oslo process began in February 1993, when representatives from Israel and the Palestine Liberation Organization (PLO) participated in secret talks in Oslo, Norway. These talks focused on implementing eventual Palestinian self-rule by withdrawing Israeli troops from the Gaza Strip and the town of Jericho (areas occupied by Israel following the 1967 Six-Day War). A newly created Palestinian Authority (PA), led by Yasser (Yasir) Arafat, was to govern these areas. The Palestine Liberation Organization in turn was to renounce its previous goal of destroying the Jewish state of Israel. In September 1993 Arafat and Israeli prime minister Yitzhak Rabin met in Washington, D.C., to sign this historic Oslo agreement. This agreement was supplemented by the Oslo II accords, signed in September 1995, and the 1998 Wye River Memorandum, both of which gave more Israeli-occupied West Bank territory over to full or limited Palestinian rule and reaffirmed PA commitments against terrorist activity against Israel. These agreements, as well as a separate 1994 peace treaty between Israel and Jordan, increased hopes for peace in the Middle East.

The Oslo process has been continually beset with problems that threaten to derail it, however. In 1994 violence broke out in the West Bank and Gaza as Jewish settlers resisted the government's efforts to hand territory over to the Palestinians. In November 1995 Rabin was assassinated by an Orthodox Jew unhappy with the Oslo accords. Palestinian militants, some of whom opposed the Palestinian Authority's recognition of Israel, committed terrorist attacks, including some suicide bombings, against Israel, although such terrorist attacks diminished somewhat after the 1998 Wye agreement.

In the summer of 2000, American president Bill Clinton

attempted to bring Arafat and Israeli prime minister Ehud Barak together to hammer out a final peace agreement, but negotiations failed to bridge differences over several key issues, including control of Jerusalem and the right of Palestinian refugees to return to Israel. In September 2000, with peace negotiations at an impasse, a new wave of violence swept through Israel after Palestinians protested a visit by Israeli political leader Ariel Sharon to a Jerusalem site holy to both Jews and Muslims. After Sharon was elected prime minister in February 2001, Israel escalated its military actions against suspected Palestinian terrorists. Israel has reoccupied much of the territory that it had handed over to the Palestinian Authority in previous years and has engaged in aggressive police and military action against suspected terrorists. Palestinian militants have committed numerous acts of terrorism against Israelis, such as the suicide bombing of a bus in Haifa on March 5, 2003, that left fifteen dead. Between September 2000 and February 2003, approximately nineteen hundred Palestinians and seven hundred Israelis perished in either terrorist or military actions.

The violence that has occurred in the years following the signing of the Oslo agreement has caused many to conclude that the Oslo process has reached a dead end. The viewpoints in this chapter examine what prospects remain for peace between Israelis and Palestinians. The enduring hostilities between the two, as evidenced by the breakdown of the Oslo peace process, certainly makes optimism difficult to maintain.

"Palestinians are ready to end the conflict. We are ready to sit down now with any Israeli leader."

A Negotiated Peace Between Israel and the Palestinians Is Possible

Yasir Arafat

Yasir (Yasser) Arafat was elected president of the Palestinian Authority in 1996. Prior to that he had already come to personify Palestinian resistance to Israel as chairman of the Palestine Liberation Organization, which he has led since 1964. The following viewpoint was published in 2002 when he was under heavy criticism for failing to curtail Palestinian terrorist attacks against Israelis. In it, Arafat condemns terrorism and sets forth his vision of Middle East peace, which he states must include the creation of a sovereign Palestinian state out of territory occupied by Israel since the 1967 war, and the sharing of Jerusalem as the capital of two states, Palestine and Israel. He argues that the Palestinians remain willing to negotiate with Israeli leaders to achieve such a peace.

As you read, consider the following questions:

1. What step did the Palestine National Council take in 1988, according to Arafat?
2. What does Arafat list as the main demands of the Palestinians?
3. What criticism does Arafat make of Israeli prime minister Ariel Sharon?

For the past 16 months [since 2000], Israelis and Palestinians have been locked in a catastrophic cycle of violence, a cycle which only promises more bloodshed and fear. The cycle has led many to conclude that peace is impossible, a myth borne out of the ignorance of the Palestinian position. Now is the time for the Palestinians to state clearly, and for the world to hear clearly, the Palestinian vision.

But first, let me be very clear. I condemn the attacks carried out by terrorist groups against Israeli civilians. These groups do not represent the Palestinian people or their legitimate aspirations for freedom. They are terrorist organizations and I am determined to put an end to their activities.

The Palestinian Vision

The Palestinian vision of peace is an independent and viable Palestinian state on the territories occupied by Israel in 1967, living as an equal neighbor alongside Israel with peace and security for both the Israeli and Palestinian peoples. In 1988, the Palestine National Council adopted a historic resolution calling for the implementation of applicable United Nations resolutions, particularly, Resolutions 242 and 338.[1] The Palestinians recognized Israel's right to exist on 78 percent of historic Palestine[2] with the understanding that we would be allowed to live in freedom on the remaining 22 percent under Israeli occupation since 1967. Our commitment to that two state solution remains unchanged, but unfortunately, also remains unreciprocated.

We seek true independence and full sovereignty: The right to control our own airspace, water resources and borders; the right to develop our own economy, to have normal commercial relations with our neighbors, and to travel freely. In short, we seek only what the free world now enjoys and only what Israel insists on for itself: the right to control our own destiny and to take our place among free nations.

1. Resolution 242, passed in 1967, called for Israel to return land seized in the 1967 war and for the nations to respect each other's right to exist within secure boundaries. Resolution 338, passed in 1973, called for a cease-fire of the Yom Kippur War and implementation of Resolution 242.   2. The territory of "historic Palestine" refers to that held by Great Britain under a League of Nations mandate from 1920 to 1948, and which was partitioned by the United Nations into Jewish and Arab states in 1947.

In addition, we seek a fair and just solution to the plight of Palestinian refugees who for 54 years have not been permitted to return to their homes.[3] We understand Israel's demographic concerns and understand that the right of return of Palestinian refugees, a right guaranteed under international law and United Nations Resolution 194, must be implemented in a way that takes into account such concerns. However, just as we Palestinians must be realistic with respect to Israel's demographic desires, Israelis too must be realistic in understanding that there can be no solution to the Israeli-Palestinian conflict if the legitimate rights of these innocent civilians continue to be ignored. Left unresolved, the refugee issue has the potential to undermine any permanent peace agreement between Palestinians and Israelis. How is a Palestinian refugee to understand that his or her right of return will not be honored but those of Kosovar Albanians, Afghans and East Timorese have been?

A Reconciliation Between Peoples

There are those who claim that I am not a partner in peace. In response, I say Israel's peace partner is, and always has been, the Palestinian people. Peace is not a signed agreement between individuals—it is reconciliation between peoples. Two peoples cannot reconcile when one demands control over the other, when one refuses to treat the other as a partner in peace, when one uses the logic of power rather than the power of logic. Israel has yet to understand that it cannot have peace while denying justice. As long as the occupation of Palestinian lands continues, as long as Palestinians are denied freedom, then the path to the "peace of the brave" that I embarked upon with my late partner Yitzhak Rabin,[4] will be littered with obstacles.

The Palestinian people have been denied their freedom for far too long and are the only people in the world still living under foreign occupation. How is it possible that the entire

3. During the 1948 war in which Arab states attacked Israel, only to have Israel successfully defend itself and occupy more land than originally assigned by the United Nations, more than one-half million Palestinians became refugees. 4. Israeli prime minister Yitzhak Rabin, who shared a Nobel Peace Prize with Arafat after the two signed the Oslo peace accords, was assassinated by an Israeli extremist in 1995.

world can tolerate this oppression, discrimination and humiliation? The 1993 Oslo Accord, signed on the White House lawn, promised the Palestinians freedom by May 1999.

Breen. © 2002 by Copley News Service. Reproduced by permission.

Instead, since 1993, the Palestinian people endured a doubling of Israeli settlers, expansion of illegal Israeli settlements on Palestinian land and increased restrictions on freedom of movement. How do I convince my people that Israel is serious about peace while over the past decade, Israel intensified the colonization of Palestinian land from which it was ostensibly negotiating a withdrawal?

Condemning Terrorism

But no degree of oppression and no level of desperation can ever justify the killing of innocent civilians. I condemn terrorism. I condemn the killing of innocent civilians, whether they are Israeli, American or Palestinian, whether they are killed by Palestinian extremists, Israeli settlers, or by the Israeli government. But condemnations do not stop terrorism. To stop terrorism, we must understand that terrorism is simply the symptom, not the disease.

The personal attacks on me currently in vogue may be highly effective in giving Israelis an excuse to ignore their own role in creating the current situation. But these attacks do little to move the peace process forward and, in fact, are not designed to. Many believe that Ariel Sharon, Israel's prime minister, given his opposition to every peace treaty Israel has ever signed, is fanning the flames of unrest in an effort to delay indefinitely a return to negotiations. Regrettably, he has done little to prove them wrong. Israeli government practices of settlement construction, home demolitions, political assassinations, closures and shameful silence in the face of Israeli settler violence and other daily humiliations are clearly not aimed at calming the situation.

The Palestinians have a vision of peace: it is a peace based on the complete end of the occupation and a return to Israel's 1967 borders, the sharing of all Jerusalem as one open city and as the capital of two states, Palestine and Israel. It is a warm peace between two equals enjoying mutually beneficial economic and social cooperation. Despite the brutal repression of Palestinians over the last four decades, I believe when Israel sees Palestinians as equals, and not as a subjugated people upon whom it can impose its will, such a vision can come true. Indeed it must.

Ready to Negotiate

Palestinians are ready to end the conflict. We are ready to sit down now with any Israeli leader, regardless of his history, to negotiate freedom for the Palestinians, a complete end of the occupation, security for Israel and creative solutions to the plight of the refugees while respecting Israel's demographic concerns. But we will only sit down as equals, not as supplicants; as partners, not as subjects; as seekers of a just and peaceful solution, not as a defeated nation grateful for whatever scraps are thrown our way. For despite Israel's overwhelming military advantage, we possess something even greater: the power of justice.

"*All attempts to negotiate an end to the Arab-Israeli conflict have merely illustrated the destructive consequences of sacrificing justice to diplomacy.*"

Peace Negotiations Between Israel and the Palestinians Are Worthless

Robert Tracinski

Robert Tracinski argues that peace negotiations between Israel and the Palestinians are futile because the Palestinian people and Arab nations want nothing less than to destroy Israel. Past efforts at negotiations ended in failure after Palestinian promises to renounce violence and terrorism were not fulfilled, he argues, and there is no reason to believe future diplomatic efforts will succeed. He concludes that the only way to achieve lasting peace is to destroy terrorists, not negotiate with them. Tracinski is the editorial director of the Ayn Rand Institute in Irvine, California.

As you read, consider the following questions:

1. How is President Bush's "road map" similar to past Middle East peace plans, in Tracinski's view?
2. What criticism does the author make of Palestinian leader Mahmoud Abbas?
3. What is the ultimate goal of the Palestinians, according to Tracinski?

Despite the big smiles, strong handshakes and profuse waving to the cameras by President [George W.] Bush, [Israeli leader] Ariel Sharon and [Palestinian leader] Mahmoud Abbas in Jordan this week [June 4, 2003], the "road map"[1] to a resolution of the Arab-Israeli conflict is doomed to failure. Why? For the same reason that every Middle East peace plan of the past has failed—because there is no "road map" for achieving peace by negotiating with terrorists.

The new plan consists, as usual, of a sequence of substantive concessions by the victim of terrorism. Israel is to withdraw its military cordon around the staging areas of Palestinian terrorism, relinquish lands crucial to its defense, and recognize a provisional state run by the same old gang of killers. In return, the Palestinians are only required to "declare" an end to violence and take "visible efforts"—whatever that means—to restrain terrorists.

This is not a trade of concessions from which both sides benefit. It is a unilateral surrender to extortion.

In fact, Bush's "road map" is just a retread of previous peace plans. A decade ago, under the Oslo accords,[2] the Palestinians pledged to renounce violence and recognize Israel's right to exist. Then, too, land was to be "traded" for peace—but the Palestinian attacks only escalated. Yet the provisions of the "new" road map are essentially identical to those of the disastrous Oslo deal. Why does anyone expect a different outcome now?

Questioning Palestine's Leadership

Negotiating with terrorists is supposed to work, this time, because of a mere change in personnel. President Bush made his road map conditional on the appointment—by arch-terrorist Yasser Arafat—of a Palestinian leader "not compromised by terror." Thus, Arafat appointed a longtime deputy, Mahmoud Abbas, as the Palestinian Authority's new public face. But Abbas is far from "uncompromised." He is a long-time leader in

1. The "road map," formulated by the United States, Europe, Russia, and the United Nations, was presented to Israeli and Palestinian leaders in April 2003. It outlines steps for the creation of a Palestinian state existing next to Israel in the West Bank and Gaza Strip.   2. A series of peace negotiations and agreements made in the 1990s that collapsed in 2000.

Arafat's PLO [Palestine Liberation Organization], and his vaunted opposition to terrorism consists of such statements as: "We are not saying to stop the intifada"—the violent Palestinian uprising—but that "it should be directed."

Israel's Prime Minister Says Terrorism Must First Cease

Israel must defeat terrorism; it cannot negotiate under fire. Israel has made painful concessions for peace before and will demonstrate diplomatic flexibility to make peace again, but it requires first and foremost a reliable partner for peace. In 1977, when Egyptian President Anwar el-Sadat came to Jerusalem, he told the people of Israel, "No more wars." From that point onward, the threat of violence was removed from the Egyptian-Israeli relationship as both negotiated their 1979 Treaty of Peace. King Hussein of Jordan followed the same pattern in 1994. This elementary commitment to permanently renouncing violence in the resolution of political differences has unfortunately not been kept by the present Palestinian leadership.

Ariel Sharon, *New York Times*, June 9, 2002.

The only thing that is supposed to make Abbas a "partner for peace" is that he isn't personally responsible for killing anyone. But if [famed organized crime leader] Al Capone's accountant were appointed as the new negotiator for the mob, would he be a leader "not compromised by crime"? Of course not—and for the same reason, Abbas is just another front man for the Palestinian terrorist establishment. . . .

The Futility of Negotiating with Terrorists

There is a reason we keep getting the same failed peace plan, with the same results. Nothing else is possible, once we accept the vicious policy of negotiating with terrorists.

Legitimate diplomacy can only take place between those who are open to settling their differences through persuasion and who recognize each other's right to live. Yet for decades the Palestinians have consistently adopted brute force and mass murder as their primary means of pursuing their "diplomatic" goals. And their ultimate goal has never changed: they seek the destruction of Israel.

All attempts to negotiate an end to the Arab-Israeli conflict have merely illustrated the destructive consequences of sacrificing justice to diplomacy. Justice demands that one judge rationally the character and conduct of those one deals with, rewarding the good and punishing the evil. To insist on diplomacy as an unqualified virtue—regardless of the nature and conduct of one's foe—does not save lives or resolve conflicts; it merely rewards and emboldens the aggressors. Why should they end terrorism, when it proves, time and time again, to be an effective means of extorting concessions?

This is why it would have been absurd for America to negotiate with [the terrorist group] al Qaeda, the Taliban [Afghanistan's ruling regime that sponsored al Qaeda], or [Iraqi leader] Saddam Hussein. It is also why America should not pressure Israel, our loyal ally in a treacherous region, to negotiate with its terrorist enemies.

One Road to Peace

Peace requires, not the accommodation of the terrorists' demands, but the total and ruthless elimination of the terrorists and those who support them. We should be pressuring Israel, not to surrender to terrorism, but to continue the war on terrorism—to continue it throughout Gaza and the West Bank, and to take it to the planners and suppliers of terrorism in Lebanon and Syria.

This is the only road to peace: to abandon diplomacy and destroy the terrorists.

| "*Peace requires a new and different Palestinian leadership, so that a Palestinian state can be born.*"

A New Palestinian Leadership Is a Necessary Precondition for Peace

George W. Bush

George W. Bush, who was inaugurated as America's president in 2001, is the first sitting U.S. president to publicly endorse the idea of creating an independent Palestinian state. In a June 24, 2002 address, excerpted here, Bush describes his vision of a peaceful resolution to the Israeli-Palestinian conflict. Arguing that both Palestinian terrorism and Israeli occupation are untenable, Bush contends that an end to conflict—which would include the creation of a provisional Palestinian state— depends on the selection of new leaders for the Palestinians. Existing leadership in the Palestinian Authority (created in the 1990s to administer parts of the West Bank and Gaza) has failed to contain and eradicate terrorism, Bush contends, and must be replaced. Bush also challenges Israel to take actions to achieve a stable and peaceful Palestinian state.

As you read, consider the following questions:
1. What complaints does Bush make about existing Palestinian political and economic institutions?
2. What rewards does Bush promise the Palestinians if they enact reforms?
3. What steps does Bush say Israel must take to support the creation of a Palestinian state?

George W. Bush, speech, Washington, DC, June 24, 2002.

For too long, the citizens of the Middle East have lived in the midst of death and fear. The hatred of a few holds the hopes of many hostage. The forces of extremism and terror are attempting to kill progress and peace by killing the innocent. And this casts a dark shadow over an entire region. For the sake of all humanity, things must change in the Middle East.

It is untenable for Israeli citizens to live in terror. It is untenable for Palestinians to live in squalor and occupation. And the current situation offers no prospect that life will improve. Israeli citizens will continue to be victimized by terrorists, and so Israel will continue to defend herself. And the situation of the Palestinian people will grow more and more miserable.

A New Palestinian Leadership

My vision is two states, living side by side in peace and security. There is simply no way to achieve that peace until all parties fight terror. Yet, at this critical moment, if all parties will break with the past and set out on a new path, we can overcome the darkness with the light of hope. Peace requires a new and different Palestinian leadership, so that a Palestinian state can be born.

I call on the Palestinian people to elect new leaders, leaders not compromised by terror. I call upon them to build a practicing democracy, based on tolerance and liberty. If the Palestinian people actively pursue these goals, America and the world will actively support their efforts. If the Palestinian people meet these goals, they will be able to reach agreement with Israel and Egypt and Jordan on security and other arrangements for independence.

And when the Palestinian people have new leaders, new institutions and new security arrangements with their neighbors, the United States of America will support the creation of a Palestinian state whose borders and certain aspects of its sovereignty will be provisional until resolved as part of a final settlement in the Middle East.

In the work ahead, we all have responsibilities. The Palestinian people are gifted and capable, and I am confident they can achieve a new birth for their nation. A Palestinian state will never be created by terror—it will be built through reform. And reform must be more than cosmetic change, or veiled attempts to preserve the status quo. True reform will require entirely new political and economic institutions, based on democracy, market economics and action against terrorism.

Today [June 24, 2002], the elected Palestinian legislature has no authority, and power is concentrated in the hands of an unaccountable few. A Palestinian state can only serve its citizens with a new constitution which separates the powers of government. The Palestinian parliament should have the full authority of a legislative body. Local officials and government ministers need authority of their own and the independence to govern effectively.

The United States, along with the European Union and Arab states, will work with Palestinian leaders to create a new constitutional framework, and a working democracy for the Palestinian people. And the United States, along with others in the international community, will help the Palestinians organize and monitor fair, multi-party local elections by the end of the year, with national elections to follow.

Today, the Palestinian people live in economic stagnation, made worse by official corruption. A Palestinian state will require a vibrant economy, where honest enterprise is encouraged by honest government. The United States, the international donor community and the World Bank stand ready to work with Palestinians on a major project of economic reform and development. The United States, the EU, the World Bank, the International Monetary Fund are willing to oversee reforms in Palestinian finances, encouraging transparency and independent auditing.

And the United States, along with our partners in the developed world, will increase our humanitarian assistance to relieve Palestinian suffering. Today, the Palestinian people lack effective courts of law and have no means to defend and vindicate their rights. A Palestinian state will require a system of reliable justice to punish those who prey on the innocent. The United States and members of the international community stand ready to work with Palestinian leaders to establish finance—establish finance and monitor a truly independent judiciary.

Support of Terrorism Is Unacceptable

Today, Palestinian authorities are encouraging, not opposing, terrorism. This is unacceptable. And the United States will not support the establishment of a Palestinian state until its leaders engage in a sustained fight against the terrorists and dismantle their infrastructure. This will require an externally supervised effort to rebuild and reform the Palestinian security services. The security system must have clear lines of authority and accountability and a unified chain of command.

America is pursuing this reform along with key regional states. The world is prepared to help, yet ultimately these steps toward statehood depend on the Palestinian people and their leaders. If they energetically take the path of reform, the rewards can come quickly. If Palestinians embrace democracy, confront corruption and firmly reject terror, they can count on American support for the creation of a provisional state of Palestine.

Setting Conditions

As for the Palestinians, their leaders (and those of the Arab states) have been entreating us for decades to press the Israelis on their behalf, and we have done so. But not until this summer [2002] has an American president set even minimal conditions on our mediation. What President [George W.] Bush has decided is that the United States cannot be an honest mediator so long as one of the parties to the conflict consists of mendacious murderers. If they want the United States to be their facilitator, they must abide by American terms. Otherwise, they're on their own.

Martin Peretz, *New Republic*, September 9, 2002.

With a dedicated effort, this state could rise rapidly, as it comes to terms with Israel, Egypt and Jordan on practical issues, such as security. The final borders, the capital and other aspects of this state's sovereignty will be negotiated between the parties, as part of a final settlement. Arab states have offered their help in this process, and their help is needed.

I've said in the past that nations are either with us or against us in the war on terror. To be counted on the side of peace, nations must act. Every leader actually committed to peace will end incitement to violence in official media, and publicly denounce homicide bombings. Every nation actually committed to peace will stop the flow of money, equipment and recruits to terrorist groups seeking the destruction of Israel—including Hamas, Islamic Jihad, and Hezbollah. Every nation actually committed to peace must block the shipment of Iranian supplies to these groups, and oppose regimes that promote terror, like Iraq. And Syria must choose the right side in the war on terror by closing terrorist camps and expelling terrorist organizations.

Leaders who want to be included in the peace process must show by their deeds an undivided support for peace. And as we move toward a peaceful solution, Arab states will be expected to build closer ties of diplomacy and commerce with Israel, leading to full normalization of relations between Israel and the entire Arab world.

Israel's Stake

Israel also has a large stake in the success of a democratic Palestine. Permanent occupation threatens Israel's identity and democracy. A stable, peaceful Palestinian state is necessary to achieve the security that Israel longs for. So I challenge Israel to take concrete steps to support the emergence of a viable, credible Palestinian state.

As we make progress towards security, Israeli forces need to withdraw fully to positions they held prior to September 28, 2000.[1] And consistent with the recommendations of the Mitchell Committee,[2] Israeli settlement activity in the occupied territories must stop.

The Palestinian economy must be allowed to develop. As violence subsides, freedom of movement should be restored, permitting innocent Palestinians to resume work and normal life. Palestinian legislators and officials, humanitarian and international workers, must be allowed to go about the business of building a better future. And Israel should release frozen

---

1. On September 28, 2000, Israeli politician Ariel Sharon made a controversial visit to a Jerusalem site holy to both Muslims and Jews, sparking a renewed wave of Palestinian violence. In response, Israel's military reoccupied parts of Gaza and the West Bank that had previously been under limited Palestinian self-rule.   2. A bipartisan commission headed by former U.S. senator George Mitchell.

Palestinian revenues into honest, accountable hands.

I've asked Secretary [of State Colin] Powell to work intensively with Middle Eastern and international leaders to realize the vision of a Palestinian state, focusing them on a comprehensive plan to support Palestinian reform and institution-building.

Ultimately, Israelis and Palestinians must address the core issues that divide them if there is to be a real peace, resolving all claims and ending the conflict between them. This means that the Israeli occupation that began in 1967 will be ended through a settlement negotiated between the parties, based on U.N. Resolutions 242 and 338,[3] with Israeli withdrawal to secure and recognize borders.

We must also resolve questions concerning Jerusalem, the plight and future of Palestinian refugees, and a final peace between Israel and Lebanon, and Israel and a Syria that supports peace and fights terror.

Peace Is Possible

All who are familiar with the history of the Middle East realize that there may be setbacks in this process. Trained and determined killers, as we have seen, want to stop it. Yet the Egyptian and Jordanian peace treaties with Israel remind us that with determined and responsible leadership progress can come quickly.

As new Palestinian institutions and new leaders emerge, demonstrating real performance on security and reform, I expect Israel to respond and work toward a final status agreement. With intensive effort by all, this agreement could be reached within three years from now. And I and my country will actively lead toward that goal.

I can understand the deep anger and anguish of the Israeli people. You've lived too long with fear and funerals, having to avoid markets and public transportation, and forced to put armed guards in kindergarten classrooms. The Palestinian

---

3. Resolution 242, passed after the 1967 war, called for the return of territories occupied in that conflict and the recognition of all states in the Middle East to exist in secure and recognized boundaries. Resolution 338, passed in 1973, called for a cease-fire in the 1973 war between Egypt and Israel and the implementation of Resolution 242.

Authority has rejected your offer at hand, and trafficked with terrorists. You have a right to a normal life; you have a right to security; and I deeply believe that you need a reformed, responsible Palestinian partner to achieve that security.

I can understand the deep anger and despair of the Palestinian people. For decades you've been treated as pawns in the Middle East conflict. Your interests have been held hostage to a comprehensive peace agreement that never seems to come, as your lives get worse year by year. You deserve democracy and the rule of law. You deserve an open society and a thriving economy. You deserve a life of hope for your children. An end to occupation and a peaceful democratic Palestinian state may seem distant, but America and our partners throughout the world stand ready to help, help you make them possible as soon as possible.

If liberty can blossom in the rocky soil of the West Bank and Gaza, it will inspire millions of men and women around the globe who are equally weary of poverty and oppression, equally entitled to the benefits of democratic government.

Universal Hopes

I have a hope for the people of Muslim countries. Your commitments to morality, and learning, and tolerance led to great historical achievements. And those values are alive in the Islamic world today. You have a rich culture, and you share the aspirations of men and women in every culture. Prosperity and freedom and dignity are not just American hopes, or Western hopes. They are universal, human hopes. And even in the violence and turmoil of the Middle East, America believes those hopes have the power to transform lives and nations.

This moment is both an opportunity and a test for all parties in the Middle East: an opportunity to lay the foundations for future peace; a test to show who is serious about peace and who is not. The choice here is stark and simple. The Bible says, "I have set before you life and death; therefore, choose life." The time has arrived for everyone in this conflict to choose peace, and hope, and life.

"Palestinian reforms will not end the conflict, because Palestinian politics is not the source of the conflict."

A New Palestinian Leadership Is Not a Necessary Precondition for Peace

Wendy Pearlman

In a June 24, 2002, speech, U.S. president George W. Bush stated that progress toward a peaceful resolution of the Israel/Palestinian conflict was dependent on the Palestinian people freely electing new leadership that would crack down on terrorist acts. The idea that new Palestinian leadership is a necessary precondition for peace is questioned in the following viewpoint by Wendy Pearlman, in which she describes her involvement in translating a constitution for the Palestinians. The obstacles to peace are not the lack of Palestinian democratic or free-market institutions, she argues, but Israel's occupation of Palestinian territory and oppression of the Palestinian people. Pearlman is the author of *Occupied Voices: Stories of Loss and Longing from the Second Intifada*.

As you read, consider the following questions:

1. What event happened about the time Pearlman was finishing her work on the Palestinian constitution?
2. Why does the author believe that Palestinian democracy is irrelevant to settling the Israeli/Palestinian conflict?
3. What actions by Israel are necessary to achieve peace, according to Pearlman?

Wendy Pearlman, "What Bush Doesn't Know About Palestine," *Boston Globe*, June 30, 2002. Copyright © 2002 by Globe Newspaper Company. Reproduced by permission of the author. Wendy Pearlman also wrote *Occupied Voices: Stories of Loss and Longing from the Second Intifada*, published by Nation Books, June 2003.

President [George W.] Bush's [June 24, 2002] speech on Palestinian reforms included several astute observations. The president was right to note that the "Palestinian Legislature has no authority and power is concentrated in the hands of an unaccountable few." Palestinian legislators, after all, are trapped under military curfew. Power over all aspects of Palestinians' lives is in the hands of the Israeli prime minister, who is unaccountable to international law, no less to the 3 million Palestinian civilians who suffer an unrelenting siege.

And the president was also right to remark, "the Palestinian people lack effective courts of law and have no means to defend and vindicate their rights." The Israeli army, after all, has rounded up thousands of Palestinians without charge or trial. They endure inhuman conditions and languish in Israeli prisons indefinitely.

But the president was misinformed when he told the Palestinians to draft a democratic constitution. The Palestinians already have such a constitution. I know, because I translated it.

Palestine's Constitution

[Palestinian leader] Yasser Arafat established a Constitution Committee in 1999, long before either George Bush or [Israeli prime minister] Ariel Sharon came to power and assumed the right to tell Palestinians how to run their affairs. After months of research and debate, the Committee completed a draft in September 2000. Two friends and I, all three of us students of Arabic sharing an apartment in Cairo, were asked to translate the draft. We eagerly agreed.

For days on end, we hovered around my laptop, meticulously considering every word we translated. As modern twenty-something women, we were determined to make the Palestinian constitution even more democratic than the American one by rendering the English text gender-neutral. Not unlike male politicians and academics everywhere, however, the members of the Palestinian Constitution Committee eventually reinserted the he's that we had taken such pains to circumvent.

So I've reviewed every "for," "if," and "but" of the Palestinian Constitution, and I can say that it's not too bad. It provides for regular elections, separation of powers, and civil rights. It addresses the rights of Palestinian refugees, and it pledges religious tolerance. Granted, the constitution is far from perfect. Palestinian human rights activists have called attention to loopholes that grant the executive branch the wide discretion that it enjoys throughout the developing world. More than grounds for invalidating the current draft, however, this debate illustrates that democratic dialogue is alive and well in Palestinian civil society.

Change Must Come from Within

If we are serious about reform in the Palestinian Authority, then we must allow the Palestinians and the Arabs to deal with [Yasser] Arafat. Credible alternative Palestinian leadership will not step forward in response to a perceived American-Israeli demand for Arafat's removal. Change must come from within. . . .

The United States must lead a diplomatic process to break the endless cycle of violence and get to the end game—an independent Palestinian state and security for Israel. We cannot wait until Palestine is a full-blown Jeffersonian democracy before getting on with a peace process.

Chuck Hagel, *Washington Post*, July 19, 2002.

My friends and I became completely absorbed in the constitution of the Palestinian state-to-be in order to meet our Sept. 30, 2000, deadline.

Renewed Violence

It was only after we had submitted our translation, therefore, that we switched on the news and discovered that Palestine was in flames. Two days before, Ariel Sharon had visited the Al-Aqsa mosque. Clashes had ensued between Palestinian protesters and Israeli police the next day. According to the Palestinian Red Crescent, some 60 Palestinians were killed and 2,500 injured during the week following Sharon's visit. Within a month, another 125 Palestinians would be killed. The 126th to die was this intifada's first suicide bomber. The rest is history.

The three of us spent weeks in our Cairo apartment consumed by the news from Palestine. Listening to the reports about the bombing of neighborhoods, demolition of homes, and countless funerals, we would exclaim, "How can this happen? The Palestinians have a constitution!" We knew then what our president still does not understand. A Palestinian constitution means little as long as the Israeli occupation continues.

Palestinian reforms will not end the conflict, because Palestinian politics is not the source of the conflict. The violence will not end until Israel takes its soldiers and settlers and leaves the West Bank and Gaza, once and for all.

Democracy in Palestine Is Beside the Point

President Bush's call for democracy in Palestine, therefore, is not wrong as much as it is beside the point. It does not matter how the Palestinians choose their leaders when Israel retains the power to besiege, arrest, or assassinate them. It does not matter what free-market institutions the Palestinians develop as long as Israel can [bring] commerce, not to mention all daily life, to a screeching halt.

Israel is wreaking havoc in Palestinian towns and refugee camps with impunity, and the White House's solution is to audit the PNA [Palestine National Authority]? Perhaps the president got the Enron and Middle East files mixed up. His speech reads more like a prescription for reforming American finance than a vision for a just resolution to the Palestinians' 50-year struggle for statehood.

The Palestinians already have a constitution; they don't need another one. What they need is to be treated like a people.

*"The fence would be no uglier than the
reality it seeks to control."*

A Fence Separating Israelis and Palestinians Can Create Peace

Richard Cohen

In 1996 Israel's internal security minister, Moshe Shahal, proposed the creation of a fence that would separate Israel from Palestinians in the West Bank. Since then, a growing number of Israelis have supported this idea, and construction of such a fence was started in 2002. In the following viewpoint, *Washington Post* columnist Richard Cohen evaluates whether a "separation fence" is desirable. Such a structure, he argues, would help prevent attacks against Israel and help quell conflict in the region. Without such a fence, he contends, Israel will remain vulnerable to suicidal terrorists.

As you read, consider the following questions:
1. What oxymoron does Cohen use to begin the article?
2. What does the author state he cannot understand about Palestinians?
3. What comparison does Cohen make between the West Bank and Gaza?

An oxymoron is a contradiction in terms. Here are some humorous ones: military justice, airline food. Here's one that's not so funny: Israeli suicide bomber.

The absurdity of the term alerts you instantly to the nature of the Palestinian-Israeli struggle. It's a clash of cultures. One side could never use suicide bombers; the other serves them up on almost a daily basis. One side has soldiers who weep over the bodies of their dead comrades; the other has fighters who transform death into a political statement so that every funeral is a rally.

A Separating Fence

Ehud Barak, the former Israeli prime minister, is among those who recommend that a fence be erected to separate the two peoples. It is a capital idea—not a long-term solution, not a peace plan and, of course, not a beautiful sight for the world's TV cameras. Such a fence could separate Palestinians from Jews on the West Bank and those areas of it—the Jerusalem suburbs, for instance—that are destined to remain part of Israel for the foreseeable future. The fence would be no uglier than the reality it seeks to control.

This fence would take its place with its historical predecessors—the Great Wall of China or the one the Roman Emperor Hadrian had built across the north of England. It ran 73 miles and was designed to keep out the "barbarians"—a word that nowadays you have to put in quotation marks, since it is forbidden to consider one culture inferior to another. So without getting into value judgments, let us just stipulate that Palestinian and Israeli cultures are different—and that difference requires a fence.

The difference is encapsulated in the chirpy remark of Khalil Takafka, whose daughter, Andaleeb, had just blown up herself and six others at Jerusalem's Mahane Yehuda market. "I am happy," he said. "All girls should do it." His daughter was 20.

I understand. I understand the political situation, the frustration, the humiliation of the Israeli occupation. I have seen it firsthand. I understand the lack of hope, how dim the future is and the hate for the Israelis, who not only have the biggest guns but a swaggering know-how. I understand.

But I do not understand the celebration over the loss of life—the newspaper notices placed by the proud family of the martyrdom of their son or daughter. I do not understand the lack of bitter regret or grudging reluctance to accept the tactic and, instead, a joyful embrace of suicide-cum-homicide, even when the victims are children, pregnant women or the old. The best—the only—thing that can be said of such tactics is that they work. Indeed, they do.

An Israeli Writer Endorses Separation

Since neither [the Palestinians] nor we are at present capable of reaching [a peace agreement] . . . regarding the permanent border, it is imperative that we set this border ourselves, temporarily, and withdraw from part of the territories, including the many remote settlements that preclude any possibility of drawing this border.

A border will protect us better against destructive suicide bombers, and will assist the saner elements in the Palestinian camp to stop them before they reach us, thus restricting the vicious cycle of their terror and our counter-attack. Unilateral withdrawal will make curfews, closures and roadblocks unnecessary, along with the daily suffering they cause the Palestinian population, and will prevent loss of life among the settlers and the soldiers charged with protecting them.

This partial, unilateral withdrawal will also debunk the false myth that the Arabs have subscribed to since the early days of Zionism, the myth of the Jew coming to rob their lands from the Nile to the Tigris. The image of the borderless Jew will become that of the Israeli within borders.

I am not so naive as to think that this will bring immediate peace. . . .

But this path will enable us at least to free ourselves partially from the suicidal Palestinian embrace while we wait for them to come to their senses. There are some indications that this is happening; the seeds of Palestinian self-criticism give us hope.

Avraham B. Yehoshua, *Jerusalem Evening Post*, July 19, 2002.

So the fence. There is one between Israel and the Gaza Strip. Anyone who has been there can tell you that the West Bank is Eden by comparison. Gaza is poor. Gaza is a mess. In Gaza, 78 percent of the residents approve of suicide bombings. Yet few suicide bombers have come from Gaza. The reason? The fence.

Conventional wisdom has it that Israel is the dominant power in the region. Conventionally speaking, that's true. But in an interview with my *Washington Post* colleague Lee Hockstader, a senior Hamas official identified Israel's Achilles' heel. "Anyone reading an Israeli newspaper can see their suffering," said Ismail Haniya. Jews "love life" more than any other people, he said.

Well, I don't know about any other people, but I do know that Jews would never send their young out to blow themselves up and kill innocent people in the process. I do know that they are culturally incapable of such behavior—although, for sure, here and there a crazed zealot exists. . . .

Good Fences Make Good Neighbors

Occupation powers do tough, mean things, and Israel has done them. Israel ought to get out of the West Bank, get out of the settlements—and get a prime minister who at least believes in the peace process and is not a walking, talking provocation to the Palestinians.

But as quickly as it can, it ought to build that fence, unilaterally disengaging from the Palestinians. What Robert Frost said about a New England wall applies to a Middle East fence. It would make for good neighbors.

*"Israel must not be tempted by the fiction
of security behind a wall."*

A Fence Between Israelis and Palestinians Will Not Create Peace

David Grossman

Responding to months of conflict and terrorist attacks, some Israeli leaders have proposed the option of "unilateral separation" between Israelis and Palestinians. They argue that by enforcing such a separation with walls, fences, and surveillance systems between Israel and areas under the limited self-rule of the Palestinian Authority, terrorist attacks could be prevented and conflict reduced. On June 17, 2002, construction began on a 217-mile fence between Israel and the West Bank. In the following viewpoint, Israeli author and peace activist David Grossman argues that although a secure border between Israel and Palestine is necessary, constructing this wall without first reaching a peace agreement with the Palestinians will provide only a temporary illusion of peace and security for Israel. The fence will only encourage those on both sides of the conflict to give up any efforts to reach a negotiated peace, and may cause increased unrest among Israel's Arab citizens, he contends.

As you read, consider the following questions:
1. What military problems does Grossman foresee arising from the security fence?
2. How is Israel hurting itself in peace negotiations by constructing a wall, according to the author?
3. Why do many Israelis support a fence, according to Grossman?

As you read this [in July 2002], a fence is going up to separate Israel from Palestinians. For now, it is defined as temporary, for defensive purposes only. It encompasses, on its Israeli side, most of the settlements Israel has established in the occupied territories. It is not intended to determine the future border between Israel and the Palestinian Authority.

"Good fences make good neighbors," wrote the poet Robert Frost. Israel and Palestine are certainly not good neighbors, and there is an urgent need, both in practice and in principle, to establish a border between them. I mean a border with defensive and barrier devices, open only at crossings established by mutual consent. Such a border will protect the two sides from each other, help stabilize their relations and, especially, require them to internalize, once and for all, the concept of a border. It's a vague, elusive and problematic concept for both, since they've lived for the last 100 years without clear boundaries, with constant invasion, each within, on top of, over and under the other.

A Temporary Illusion of Security

Yet it is very dangerous to establish such a border fence right now, unilaterally, without a peace agreement. It is yet another precipitate action aimed at giving the Israeli public a temporary illusion of security; its main effect will be to supply Israelis with a counterfeit replacement for a peace process.

There may well come a time—after both sides have attempted another serious and sincere move toward peace—when Israel will conclude that there really is no chance of peace in this generation. In such a case, Israel will have to withdraw from the occupied territories, evacuate almost all the settlements, shut itself behind a thick wall and prepare for an ongoing battle.

From my conversations with Palestinian leaders, however, I am convinced there still is a chance for peace. Most Israelis disagree. "There's no one to make an agreement with!" they say. "Even [former Israeli prime minister] Shimon Peres and the leaders of the left say that they are no longer willing to talk with [Palestinian leader Yasser] Arafat, and in the meantime Israel must defend itself against terror somehow!"

But even if we assume that Yasir Arafat is not a negotiating partner—by the way, it certainly hasn't been proved that [Israeli prime minister] Ariel Sharon is a partner—we need to examine the practical implications of building a barrier fence without an agreement. It is clear to everyone that such a fence will not prevent, for example, the Palestinians' firing rockets and mortars from their territory into Israel. The Israeli Army will have to operate beyond the fence, in order to defend isolated Israeli settlements that will remain on the other side. It takes little imagination to realize what military complications this will bring.

The fence will not provide an appropriate military response to the complex situation in Jerusalem, in which Jews and Arabs rub shoulders each day. Quite the opposite. An attempt to detach East Jerusalem from the rest of the Palestinian territories is liable to turn the Arab city's inhabitants to the use of terror, which they have mostly resisted so far.

The distress Israelis feel is plain and comprehensible. It derives from the inhuman cruelty of the suicide bombings and from the feeling that there is no way out, given the huge support for terrorism among Palestinians. But this distress cannot overcome my sense that the Israeli infatuation with the fence is the product of a psychological need. It is not a well-considered policy.

Sacrificing Negotiating Positions

In establishing a fence unilaterally, Israel is throwing away the best card it has. It will be discarding this trump without receiving anything in return from the Palestinians. Last month [June 2002] in London, I heard Yasir Abed Rabbo, the Palestinian information minister, say in a conversation with Israelis from the peace camp that if Israel withdraws behind a fence, Palestinians will spend a day celebrating that most of the occupation has ended, and the next day will continue the intifada, in order to obtain the rest of their demands.

Those other demands are well known: Israeli withdrawal from 100 percent of the territories Israel occupied in the 1967 war; evacuation of all the [Jewish West Bank] settlements; Arab Jerusalem as the capital of Palestine; and acceptance of the principle of the Palestinian refugees' right of return within Israel proper.

Yet there is today a good chance of resolving all these issues in negotiations. . . . But if the demands of Palestinians are not resolved in negotiations, the fighting will continue. In fact, Palestinians may fight more fiercely if they feel their terror has forced Israel into a new ghetto.

A Palestinian View

To Palestinians, the proposals for unilateral separation are just another form of maintaining the Israeli occupation on certain parts of the Palestinian territories. They are also perceived as a way for Israel to unilaterally determine the future of the relationship between the two sides—boxing Palestinians in on "their" side, without access to resources and divided by Israeli settlements and areas of control. . . .

Those who hope that plans for separation would move us closer towards peace, or even calm the currently fierce struggle against occupation and the Israeli violence used to maintain that occupation, will be sorely mistaken. Plans for unilateral separation leave certain parts of the Palestinian territories under occupation, do not solve the issue of Jerusalem and do not bring closure to the problem of the Palestinian refugees. These are major components of the conflict that must be addressed and agreed upon with the support of international legality and in a way that is acceptable to both sides.

What proponents of unilateral separation hope is that if the two peoples become invisible to one another, their conflict will diminish. But the conflict cannot be taken care of by shutting the door on Palestinians.

Ghassan Khatib, *bitterlemons.org*, April 2, 2002.

Because it is so important, let me say it again: the establishment of a fence without an agreement means Israel will give up most of the occupied territories without the Palestinians giving up the right of return.

Palestinians in Israel

The establishment of a fence without peace also means that the fence will have to extend into the West Bank to encompass most of the settlements. But in building the fence to include the settlements, Israel will have to take in many Palestinian towns and villages that lie close to the settlements and to the roads that lead to them. According to some estimates, this will involve about 150,000 Palestinians. If we add the Arabs of East Jerusalem, the number of Palestinians on the Israeli side of the fence may well reach 400,000.

These people will not be Israeli citizens. Israel does not want them. They will have no clear legal status and will not be able to participate in elections. Does anyone seriously believe they will not turn to terrorism? When that happens, they will be inside the fence, not outside it, and they will have unobstructed passage to Israel's city centers. Or will Israel confine them behind yet another, second fence?

Israel correctly fears giving Palestinians the right of return to within its borders. So it is hard to understand how Israel could be prepared to take in hundreds of thousands of hostile Palestinians by building a fence.

Another question: How will Israel's Arab citizens feel? They are about a sixth of the population. Many have ties to families in the Palestinian Authority lands. Will these ties be severed by the fence? Will Israel not be increasing the bitterness and frustration of this one-sixth of the citizenry, and will not this lead Israeli Arabs to adopt even more extreme positions at a time when their connection to their country has been growing more tenuous?

The fence's major drawing power for most Israelis is that it has never been tried. So it can be believed in, for a while.

The Luxury of Despair

But the border between Israel and Palestine can be set only through full agreement by both sides. Such an agreement seems impossible today, but we cannot allow ourselves the luxury of despairing of it. I think it's better to wait and live for a few more years without this fence of illusions. This wall will declare our absolute despair of reaching a peace agreement in our generation, of integrating a normal Israel into the region around it.

A wall will allow the extremists—who are all too numerous—to argue that there will be no one to talk to in the future. Putting the other out of sight will only make dehumanization easier and justify a more extreme struggle.

Israel must not be tempted by the fiction of security behind a wall. Instead, it must invest its energy in the recommencement of negotiations. If Mr. Arafat is unacceptable to Mr. Sharon and Mr. Bush, let those leaders explain to us how they can create a better situation. Until they can do so, they bear the responsibility—no less weighty than Mr. Arafat's responsibility—for the immobility, the insensibility and the despair on both sides.

Periodical Bibliography

The following articles have been selected to supplement the diverse views presented in this chapter.

Hady Amr	"How Can Bullets and Bombs Bring Peace? Palestinians Have Cause for Grievance, but the World Won't Listen Until They Return to Nonviolent Protest," *Newsweek*, March 11, 2002.
David Arnow	"Voices of Reconciliation in a Time of Hatred," *Tikkun*, March/April 2001.
Shlomo Avineri	"Irreconcilable Differences: The Best Solution to the Israeli-Palestinian Conflict Might Be No Solution at All," *Foreign Policy*, March 2002.
Mubarak Awad and Abdul Aziz	"The Road to Arab-Israeli Peace," *Tikkun*, January/February 2001.
Aluf Benn	"The Last of the Patriarchs," *Foreign Affairs*, May/June 2002.
Current Events	"Mideast Meltdown: Fighting Intensifies Between Israelis and Palestinians," April 5, 2002.
Economist	"The Dangers of Leaving It to Sharon; America, Israel, and the Palestinians," February 2, 2002.
Yuval Elizur	"Israel Banks on a Fence," *Foreign Affairs*, March/April 2003.
Mordechai Gafni	"Do Not Ask Israel to Atone," *Tikkun*, January/February 2001.
Ronald L. Hatchett	"The Importance of the Saudi Peace Plan," *World & I*, June 2002.
Tony Judt	"The Road to Nowhere," *New York Review of Books*, May 9, 2002.
James Kitfield	"The Ties That Bind, and Constrain: The Mideast," *National Journal*, April 20, 2002.
Anthony Lewis	"Is There a Solution?" *New York Review of Books*, April 25, 2002.
Johanna McGeary	"The Four Sticking Points: Peace Will Never Be Achieved Unless Israel and the Palestinians Compromise on Some Extremely Tough Issues," *Time*, April 22, 2002.
Jerome Slater	"What Went Wrong?" The Collapse of the Israeli-Palestinian Peace Process," *Political Science Quarterly*, Summer 2001.

Time   "Israel's Last-Ditch Peace Plan: Exhausted by Violence, Israel's Politicians Consider a Radical Move. Is It Time for Economic Separation?" November 6, 2000.

James M. Wall   "Numb About Israel," *Christian Century*, March 27, 2002.

For Further Discussion

Chapter 1

1. Efraim Karsh argues that Palestinians and outsiders have different conceptions of the word *occupation*. Why does he consider it important to clarify the differing meanings of such terms as *occupation* and *occupied territories*? Do you agree that such delineation is necessary? Explain.

2. William O. Beeman's argument that Middle East conflict is in part created by the United States and other nations is presented in the context of assessing America's "war on terrorism" following the September 11, 2001, attacks. What does he recommend the United States do to respond to the attacks? Do you agree or disagree with his view that military attacks would not work?

3. The authors of this chapter discuss several causes of tension and potential conflict in the Middle East. After reading this chapter, what do you believe is the predominant source of conflict in the region? Support your answer with evidence from the viewpoints.

Chapter 2

1. Ray Takeyh argues that future Islamic democracies may well contain elements of Western democracies, but they would also be different in important ways; for example, Islamic democracies may impose more limits on individual freedoms. Takeyh argues against a "single universal standard" of human rights. Do you agree or disagree with this position? Could an Islamic nation adopt just some elements of Western democracies and still be considered true democracies? Defend your answer.

2. After reading the articles by Takeyh and Milton Viorst, do you think that the Middle East will be more democratic in ten years? In fifty? Or are such predictions inherently suspect? Explain, citing examples from both texts.

3. Martin Kramer contends that fundamentalist Islam's drive for power often mobilizes its adherents for violent conflict. Muhammad M. El-Hodaiby argues that a Muslim who participates in violence is committing a sin because Islamic tenets explicitly reject violence. Kramer was the director of a Middle Eastern studies program at an Israeli university; El-Hodaiby is a leader of the Muslim Brotherhood in Egypt. Does knowing

their backgrounds influence your assessment of their arguments? Explain your answer.

Chapter 3

1. Leon T. Hadar argues that the United States has no compelling reason to intervene to end the Arab-Israeli conflict. Is his contention addressed in Sherwin Wine's article? What, if any, American national interests do you believe may justify American intervention in the Middle East? Defend your answer.

2. After reading the articles by Wine and Hadar, how much influence do you believe the United States has in the Middle East? Could the United States impose a peace agreement to end the Arab-Israeli conflict if it really wanted to? Explain.

3. Both Victor Davis Hanson and Marina Ottway and her coauthors argue that building democracy in the Middle East will be a long and difficult process. What is their main area of disagreement? Who do you believe makes the more convincing argument? Defend your answer.

4. After reading the viewpoints by the *Ellsworth American* and *Christian Century*, and by Diane Katz and Henry Payne, do you think America's dependency on Middle East oil is a serious problem? Explain, citing from the viewpoints.

5. After reading the viewpoints in this chapter, identify what you believe to be America's leading interests and concerns in the Middle East. Which do you consider most important? Defend your rankings.

Chapter 4

1. Many of the arguments against Israeli-Palestinian peace negotiations focus on the credibility of Yasir (Yasser) Arafat. Arafat contends that such personal attacks are not relevant nor are they conducive to the peace process. Do you believe such personal attacks raise a legitimate point, given Arafat's position as leader of the Palestinians? Explain your answer.

2. Some critics of George W. Bush argue that the demands he makes on the Palestinians are not balanced by equivalent demands on Israel. After reading the viewpoints by Bush and by Wendy Pearlman, do you agree with this assessment? What additional demands, if any, on either Palestine or Israel, would you consider as a precondition to peace talks?

3. What comparison does Richard Cohen make between the Israelis and the Palestinians? Do you agree or disagree with his assessment of the nature of the Palestinian people? Why or why not?

4. After reading the arguments of Cohen and David Grossman, do you believe a separation fence would be a feasible short-term solution for the Israeli-Palestinian conflict? A good long-term solution? What would you consider to be the major advantages and disadvantages of unilateral separation?

Chronology of Events

1897	Theodor Herzl convenes First Zionist Congress, which designates Palestine as an appropriate Jewish homeland. Less than 10 percent of Palestine's population is Jewish.
1914–1918	World War I. Arab nationalists cooperate with Britain against Turkey. Turkey's Ottoman Empire collapses.
1917	British foreign secretary A.J. Balfour declares Britain's support for a national homeland for the Jewish people in Palestine, a declaration that conflicts with promises to the Arabs.
1920–1948	Britain rules Palestine under agreement with the League of Nations. The British mandate approves limited immigration for Jews.
1921	Military officer Reza Khan rules Iran after a coup and begins a secularization campaign that abolishes many Islamic customs. Faisal I, with British support, is made king of Iraq, which is composed of three former Ottoman Empire provinces.
1922	At the Uqair Conference, the modern borders of Iraq, Saudi Arabia, and Kuwait are drawn by representatives of the British government.
1927–1938	Oil is discovered in commercial quantities in northern Iraq, Bahrain, Saudi Arabia, and Kuwait.
1928	The Muslim Brotherhood is established in Egypt as a movement of fundamentalist reform among Sunni Muslims.
1929–1939	Arabs rebel against British rule; Arabs fight Jews for the right to live in Palestine.
1939–1945	World War II. Six million Jews are killed by Nazi Germany. Jewish population in Palestine swells to 608,000 by 1946.
1941	British and Soviet forces, concerned that Reza Khan is allied with Adolf Hitler, invade Iran and depose the monarch, replacing him with his son, Muhammed Reza Khan Pahlavi.
November 1943	Lebanon achieves independence, with government posts given to members of each of the main religious groups.
November 29, 1947	United Nations (UN) General Assembly votes to partition Palestine into Jewish and Arab states with Jerusalem being an international city. Arabs refuse.

May 14, 1948	David Ben-Gurion proclaims the state of Israel, which is immediately attacked by five Arab states. Israel defeats the coalition, and takes more land than originally assigned. More than 500,000 Palestinians flee Israel.
1952	Officers of the Egyptian army overthrow King Farouk and replace him with their leader, Gamal Abdel Nasser.
1953	U.S. and British intelligence forces organize a coup against democratic reformer Muhammed Mossadeq that restores the Shah of Iran, Muhammed Reza Pahlavi, to power. He allows a consortium of foreign companies to operate Iran's oil industry.
July 1956	The U.S. and Britain refuse to support a loan to Egypt to build the Aswan High Dam; in retaliation, Nasser seizes control of the Suez Canal. After Britain freezes Egyptian assets held in England, Egypt closes the canal.
October 1956	The Israelis, with military aid from Britain and France, invade Egypt. They take the Gaza Strip and the Sinai Peninsula, which they later return in a peace settlement.
1958	Faisal II, who had succeeded Faisal I as king of Iraq, is assassinated. Abdul Karim Kassem installs himself as military dictator of Iraq.
August 1959	Jordan offers citizenship to all Palestinian refugees.
January 1961	Iran, Iraq, Kuwait, and Saudi Arabia found the Organization of Petroleum Exporting Countries (OPEC).
May 1964	Palestine Liberation Organization (PLO) is established.
May 1967	Nasser orders UN emergency forces to withdraw from the Sinai, declares a state of emergency in the Gaza Strip, and closes the Strait of Tiran to shipping to and from Israel. Israel and the U.S warn Egypt to remove the blockade.
June 5–10, 1967	Six-Day War. Israel attacks Egypt, Jordan, and Syria and captures the Sinai, Gaza Strip, West Bank, and Golan Heights.
November 22, 1967	UN Security Council Resolution 242 calling for peace in the Middle East is adopted. The resolution asks that Israel return land acquired in the Six-Day War and that Arabs respect Israel's boundaries.
1969	Yasser Arafat and Fatah (the largest Palestinian group) take over the PLO and give it a more assertive role.

1970	Nasser dies and Vice President Anwar Sadat takes over leadership of Egypt.
1970–1971	Jordanian civil war. King Hussein crushes Palestinian guerrillas and invading troops. Palestinians move offices from Jordan to Beirut, Lebanon.
October 6, 1973	Yom Kippur War. Egypt and Syria launch a two-front surprise attack on Israeli forces in the Sinai Peninsula and the Golan Heights.
October 18, 1973	First day of five-month Arab oil embargo cutting off or sharply curtailing oil exports to countries that support Israel.
November 11, 1973	Egypt and Israel agree to a cease-fire.
October 1974	The UN grants the PLO observer status and allows it to participate in debates on the status of Palestinian refugees.
April 1975	In Lebanon, Christian Phalangists attack Palestinians, touching off large-scale confrontations between Christians and Muslims. Syria participates on the side of the Muslims.
November 1977	Sadat makes the first visit of an Arab leader to Israel to promote renewed peace talks. In exchange for peace, Israel offers to return Sinai to Egypt and allow limited Palestinian self-rule in the Israeli-occupied areas of the West Bank and Gaza Strip.
September 1978	Camp David summit meeting between U.S. president Jimmy Carter, Israeli prime minister Menachem Begin, and Sadat leads to an Egyptian-Israeli peace agreement and accords on the Palestinian question. Under the agreement, Israel returns all of Sinai to Egypt by 1982. Most of the Arab states, the Soviet Union, and the PLO denounce the agreements.
February 1979	After months of unrest, the government of Iran is overthrown. The Shah is replaced by Shi'ite Muslim fundamentalists led by Ayatollah Ruhollah Khomeini.
July 1979	Saddam Hussein seizes power in Iraq.
November 4, 1979	Militants storm the U.S. embassy in Tehran, Iran, and hold fifty-two Americans hostage for the next fourteen months.
September 1980	Iran makes air attacks on Iraqi towns. A few weeks later, Iraq invades Iran, beginning the eight-year Iran-Iraq war.
1981	Jewish settlements and housing construction on the West Bank begin.

June 1981	Israel bombs a nuclear reactor in Iraq "to prevent another Holocaust." The U.S. refuses to deliver promised military equipment to Israel.
October 1981	Sadat is assassinated by members of the Egyptian army. Vice President Hosni Mubarak takes over the government.
December 1981	Israel annexes the Golan Heights in Syria. The UN Security Council declares the annexation "null and void." Israel refuses to withdraw.
February 1982	Syrian leader Hafez Assad's troops crush a Muslim Brotherhood uprising in the city of Hama, killing more than ten thousand people.
June–September 1982	Israel invades Lebanon; it occupies Beirut and demands that the PLO leave the city. U.S. Marines help oversee the PLO evacuation. The PLO establishes its headquarters in Tunisia.
April 18, 1983	Sixty-three people are killed in the bombing of the U.S. embassy in Beirut.
May 17, 1983	Lebanon and Israel sign an agreement to withdraw Israeli forces from Lebanon. Israel refuses to withdraw completely until Syria also withdraws.
October 23, 1983	A pro-Iranian suicide bomber drives an explosives-laden truck into U.S. Marine headquarters in Beirut, killing 241 people.
January 1984	The administration of U.S. president Ronald Reagan officially lists Iran as a supporter of international terrorism and cuts arms sales to Iran.
May 16, 1985	Journalist Terry A. Anderson is kidnapped and held hostage in Lebanon. He becomes the longest-held American hostage of the eighteen kidnapped by various Islamic groups in Lebanon between 1982 and 1991. Of these eighteen hostages, three died or were killed in captivity, one escaped, six were released before 1987, two were released in 1990, and the remaining six were released in 1991.
June 1985	Shi'ite gunmen hijack TWA flight 847 and hold its 153 passengers hostage. They kill a U.S. Navy passenger. Most passengers are released except for 39 Americans, who are taken to Beirut. Iranian officials help negotiate freedom for the Americans.
October 7, 1985	Four Palestinians hijack the Italian ship *Achille Lauro* and hold 400 hostages. They kill Leon Klinghoffer, an elderly American Jew.
April 14, 1986	Reagan, arguing that Libyan leader Muammar Qaddafi supports anti-American terrorism, orders the bombing

of Libyan cities Tripoli and Benghazi. Dozens of Libyans die as many homes are hit, including Qaddafi's.

November 1986   The U.S. government reveals that it covertly sold arms to Iran and diverted profits to the Nicaraguan Contra resistance in Central America. The scandal becomes known as the Iran-Contra affair.

December 1987   Four Palestinians are killed when an Israeli army truck rams their car after they attempt to run a military road-block in Gaza. During their funeral, Israeli troops clash with mourners. The event marks the beginning of the widespread Palestinian uprising that comes to be called the *intifada*. Hundreds of demonstrators are killed over the next five years in clashes between Israelis and Palestinians.

July 3, 1988   U.S. Navy ship patrolling the Persian Gulf accidentally shoots down Iranian commercial airliner, killing 290.

August 1988   Iran and Iraq accept UN peace terms and announce a cease-fire. The eight-year war leaves more than one million casualties. 100,000 Kurds flee to Turkey amidst reports that Iraq is attacking them with poison gas.

November 1988   Palestine National Council (PNC) meets in Algiers and votes to accept UN Security Council Resolutions 242 and 338, which call for Arab recognition of Israel and Israeli withdrawal from territories occupied since 1967. Jordan severs legal and administrative ties to the West Bank. Responsibility for the West Bank's economic and municipal functions shifts to the PLO.

December 1988   The U.S. establishes a "diplomatic dialogue" with the PLO after Arafat renounces terrorism and states that he accepts the right of "Palestine, Israel, and other neighbors" to exist in peace.

February 1989   Iranian leader Khomeini calls for Muslims to execute Indian-born British author Salman Rushdie, whose novel *The Satanic Verses* Khomeini calls blasphemous.

June 3, 1989   Iranian leader Khomeini dies in Tehran.

April 2, 1990   Iraqi president Saddam Hussein claims Iraq possesses advanced chemical weapons and threatens to destroy half of Israel if it launches any preemptive strike against Iraq.

August 2, 1990   Iraq invades Kuwait. The emir of Kuwait flees to Saudi Arabia. The UN Security Council passes Resolution 660 condemning the invasion and demanding Iraq's unconditional withdrawal from Kuwait.

August 6, 1990	The UN Security Council passes Resolution 661, which imposes a trade embargo and economic sanctions on Iraq.
August 7, 1990	U.S. president George H.W. Bush, after consulting with the leaders of Great Britain, the Soviet Union, Japan, Egypt, and Saudi Arabia, sends U.S. forces to Saudi Arabia to protect it from a potential Iraqi invasion.
November 29, 1990	The UN Security Council passes Resolution 678 authorizing the use of "all necessary means" to force Iraq from Kuwait if Iraq does not withdraw before January 15, 1991.
January 16, 1991	Allied coalition forces launch massive air attacks on Iraq. Israel declares a state of emergency and imposes a curfew in the occupied territories.
January 18, 1991	Iraq attacks Israel with Scud missiles, causing light casualties. The U.S. responds by sending troops to operate Patriot anti-missile systems in Israel.
February 23, 1991	The U.S.-led multinational coalition launches a ground offensive against Iraqi troops.
February 27, 1991	Bush declares victory over Iraq and announces the liberation of Kuwait.
April 1991	The UN Security Council passes resolutions establishing a formal cease-fire between Iraq and the UN coalition and condemning Iraq's suppression of Kurds and Shi'ites. It also passes Resolution 687, requiring Iraq to destroy its weapons of mass destruction. A Special Commission on Iraq (UNSCOM) is formed to monitor Iraq's compliance with Resolution 687.
July 4, 1991	After four days of clashes around Sidon, Lebanon, the PLO agrees to withdraw from its only military base near Israel.
October 30, 1991	International Middle East peace conference is convened in Madrid, Spain. The event marks the first open and direct negotiations between Israel, Syria, Jordan, Lebanon, and the Palestinians. No treaties or agreements are signed. The participants agree to meet for further talks.
July 1992	Yitzhak Rabin is elected prime minister of Israel. He pledges to promote peace and to limit construction of new Jewish settlements in the occupied territories.
August 1992	The UN Security Council establishes "no-fly" zones in northern and southern Iraq in response to continued Iraqi air strikes on Shi'ite rebels. The areas are patrolled by U.S.-led UN troops.

February 1993	Israeli and Palestinian officials begin secret talks in Oslo, Norway. Israel agrees to withdraw from most of Gaza and the West Bank city of Jericho. Arafat's Palestinian Authority is to administer these areas. The final status of the occupied territories is to be determined over the next several years.
February 26, 1993	The World Trade Center in New York City is bombed, leaving six dead and thousands injured. A group of Middle Eastern Islamic militants, later convicted of the bombing, claim the attack was in revenge for U.S. support of Israel.
July 25, 1993	Israel begins a week-long air and artillery assault on 70 villages in southern Lebanon, killing more than 100 Lebanese and driving 300,000 refugees northward. The assault is in retaliation for rocket attacks on Israeli settlements by the pro-Iranian Hezbollah militia, stationed in Lebanon.
September 1993	Rabin and Arafat sign letters proclaiming that the PLO recognizes the right of Israel to exist in peace and security and that Israel acknowledges the PLO as the representative of the Palestinian people. In Washington, D.C., Rabin and Arafat officially sign the historic peace accords agreed to at Oslo.
1994	The Palestinian National Authority (PNA) is formed to govern the semi-autonomous Palestinian state. Violence breaks out as Jewish settlers resist efforts to turn land over to the PNA.
October 1994	54,000 U.S. troops are sent to the Middle East after Iraq again threatens to invade Kuwait. Iraq subsequently withdraws its troops from the Kuwaiti border.
September 1995	The Israeli-Palestinian Oslo II interim agreements are signed. Oslo II divides the West Bank into three areas: one section that is to be governed by the PNA, another section that is granted limited Palestinian self-rule, and a third area to remain under Israeli rule.
November 1995	A car bomb explodes outside an army training building in Riyadh, Saudi Arabia, killing five Americans and two Indians. The Saudi government captures and executes Muslim terrorists implicated in the bombing.
November 4, 1995	Yitzhak Rabin is assassinated by an ultra-right Israeli extremist. Shimon Peres takes over as Israel's prime minister.
May 1996	Benjamin Netanyahu is elected prime minister of Israel.
June 25, 1996	A truck bomb explodes outside a military apartment building in the Khobar Towers complex in Dhahran,

Saudi Arabia, killing 19 U.S. airmen and injuring hundreds. Shi'ite terrorists are suspected in the bombing.

September 1996   Violence breaks out in Jerusalem after Israeli authorities open a tunnel near a Muslim holy site. More than 70 people die as a result of clashes involving protestors, Palestinian police, and Israeli soldiers. The U.S. launches 44 cruise missiles into Iraq in response to Iraqi attacks on Kurds in the north. The UN extends the southern no-fly zone closer to Baghdad.

January 1997   Israeli and Palestinian officials sign the Hebron agreement, in which Israel agrees to withdraw its forces from most of the West Bank city of Hebron and to resume Israeli military redeployment throughout the West Bank.

February 1997   Netanyahu announces the beginning of massive construction of Israeli settlements in the West Bank. Violent clashes occur between Palestinian protestors and Israeli troops, stalling peace negotiations.

October 1997   Iraq orders U.S. members of the UN weapons-inspection team to leave the country and threatens to shoot down any U.S. spy planes used for inspections. The remaining UNSCOM team leaves Iraq in support of their U.S. colleagues. After Russian diplomats intervene, the inspectors are allowed to return in November.

January 1998   Iranian president Muhammad Khatami, a political moderate, invites the U.S. to engage in a cultural dialogue and exchange with Iran.

August 7, 1998   U.S. embassies in Nairobi, Kenya, and Dar es Salaam, Tanzania, are simultaneously bombed, killing 257 and injuring thousands. Investigators suspect Osama bin Laden, a Saudi Arabian dissident said to be residing in Afghanistan. Bin Laden is also possibly linked to the 1993 World Trade Center bombing and bombings in Riyadh, Saudi Arabia.

August 22, 1998   The U.S. launches military strikes on suspected terrorist-related facilities in Afghanistan and Sudan in retaliation for the August 7 embassy bombings.

October 1998   At the Wye River Conference Center in Maryland, U.S., Israeli, and Arab leaders sign the Wye Memorandum, in which Israel grants Palestinians more control over the West Bank in exchange for guarantees of security and antiterrorism measures from Palestinian authorities.

December 1998   The Palestinian National Council revokes clauses in its founding charter that call for Israel's destruction.

December 15, 1998	In response to repeated Iraqi threats to suspend cooperation with UN weapons inspectors, the U.S. launches four days of air strikes on Iraq. At the end of the operation, Saddam Hussein permanently terminates cooperation with weapons inspectors.
February 7, 1999	King Hussein of Jordan dies. His son, Abdullah, takes the throne.
May 1999	Ehud Barak is elected prime minister of Israel.
October 1999	Saudi women attend the session of the Consultative Council, an advisory body of the Saudi Arabian government, for the first time.
May 2000	Israel withdraws its troops from southern Lebanon.
June 2000	Syrian president Hafiz al-Assad dies and is succeeded by his son, Bashar.
August 2000	Yasser Arafat and Ehud Barak, meeting with U.S. president Bill Clinton at Camp David, Maryland, try to negotiate a final peace settlement, but talks break down over the status of Jerusalem.
September 28, 2000	Israeli Parliament member Ariel Sharon visits a Jerusalem site holy to both Jews and Muslims with a 1,000-member armed guard. Palestinians respond with violence, sparking a new *intifada*.
October 12, 2000	A suicide terrorist attack damages the American naval ship USS *Cole* off the coast of Yemen and kills seventeen.
January 21–27, 2001	Peace negotiations between Israelis and Palestinians take place at the resort town of Taba, Egypt. Prime minister Barak calls off the talks on the eve of Israeli elections without any official agreements being reached.
February 2001	Ariel Sharon is elected prime minister of Israel.
February 15, 2001	The United States and Great Britain carry out bomb attacks aimed at Iraq's air defense network. The bombings have little international support.
April 2001	Iran and Saudi Arabia sign a major security accord to combat terrorism, drug trafficking and organized crime.
April 30, 2001	The Mitchell Commission, an American group headed by former senator George Mitchell, releases its report on the Israeli/Palestinian conflict. The document, calling for a cease-fire as well as a monitoring mechanism to watch over the growth of Israeli settlements and Israeli enclosures of Palestinians, becomes the basis for repeated new calls for peace.

September 11, 2001	Terrorists crash American jet planes into the World Trade Center in New York and the Pentagon in Washington, D.C. It is later discovered that the terrorists were all from Saudi Arabia and other Middle East nations.
October 2001	The Israeli tourism minister is killed by Palestinian terrorists. Citing the inadequate response of the Palestine National Authority, Israeli troops enter and occupy Palestinian areas in the West Bank.
January 5, 2002	Israel captures a Palestinian ship loaded with fifty tons of missiles, rockets, and other munitions off its coast; it accuses the Palestinian Authority of purchasing these weapons from Iran.
January 29, 2002	Two Middle East nations, Iran and Iraq, are named by President George W. Bush as part of an "axis of evil" for supporting terrorism and pursuing weapons of mass destruction.
March 9, 2002	Eleven Israelis are killed at the Moment Café in Jerusalem by a suicide bomber.
March 27, 2002	Twenty-eight Jews are killed at a Passover seder in Netanya by a suicide bomber.
March 29–May 2, 2002	In an effort to restore calm and prevent further violence, Sharon orders tanks into the West Bank. Israeli forces barricade Yasser Arafat in his government compound in Ramallah. Tanks level much of the compound, but stop short of taking Arafat captive. After over a month, the siege ends, and tanks withdraw from the West Bank. A UN investigation into the reported massacre of Palestinian noncombatants in a Jenin refugee camp is abandoned after Israel refuses to cooperate.
April 2002	Egypt, responding to Israel's crackdown on Arafat, downgrades its relations with Israel.
April 2, 2002	More than 200 Palestinian militants and bystanders take refuge in the Church of the Nativity in Bethlehem in order to escape Israeli military incursions in the West Bank. After five weeks of negotiations, the captives are allowed to leave the church; 13 of the gunmen are sent into exile, and 26 are handed over to Palestinian authorities.
June 2002	President George W. Bush calls for Israeli withdrawal and Palestinian statehood, pending reforms and new political leadership in the PNA. Israel reoccupies the entire West Bank except for the city of Jericho.

September 2002	Iran begins construction of its first nuclear reactor with Russian technical help over the objections of the United States.
September 12, 2002	President George W. Bush addresses the United Nations and calls on that body to enforce its disarmament resolutions against Iraq.
September 24, 2000	The United Nations Security Council passes a resolution that calls on Israel to withdraw from Palestinian towns.
November 8, 2002	Resolution 1441, which gives Iraq a final chance to disarm or face "serious consequences," is passed unanimously by the United Nations Security Council.
December 7, 2002	Iraq submits documentation required by UN Resolution 1441 in which it claims it disposed of all weapons of mass destruction.
January 2003	Elections return Israel's prime minister Ariel Sharon to power.
February–March 2003	Israel launches military incursions into Gaza in response to terrorist attacks.
March 7, 2003	UN chief inspector Hans Blix submits report to UN Security Council stating that Iraq has partially but not completely cooperated in weapons disarmament.
March 10, 2003	The PLO's central council, meeting in Ramallah, approves Arafat's proposal to name Abu Mazen as the PNA's new prime minister, and condemns violence against civilians.
March 14, 2003	President George W. Bush unveils a "road map" to peace that would result in the creation of a Palestinian state on land held by Israel by 2005.
March 18, 2003	In a televised address, President Bush gives Saddam Hussein 48 hours to leave Iraq or face invasion.
March 20, 2003	An American-led coalition begins military action against Iraq.

Organizations and Websites

The editors have compiled the following list of organizations concerned with the issues debated in this book. The descriptions are derived from materials provided by the organizations. All have publications or information available for interested readers. The list was compiled on the date of publication of the present volume; the information provided here may change. Be aware that many organizations take several weeks or longer to respond to inquiries, so allow as much time as possible.

American-Israeli Cooperative Enterprise (AICE)
2810 Blaine Dr., Chevy Chase, MD 20815
(301) 565-3918 • fax: (301) 587-9056
e-mail: mgbard@aol.com • website: www.us-israel.org

AICE seeks to strengthen the U.S.-Israel relationship by emphasizing values the two nations have in common and developing cooperative social and educational programs that address shared domestic problems. It also works to enhance Israel's image by publicizing novel Israeli solutions to these problems. It publishes the book *Partners for Change: How U.S.-Israel Cooperation Can Benefit America*. Its website includes the Jewish Virtual Library, a comprehensive online encyclopedia of Jewish history.

American Jewish Committee (AJC)
PO Box 705, New York, NY 10150
(212) 751-4000 • fax: (212) 838-2120
e-mail: PR@ajc.org • website: www.ajc.org

AJC works to strengthen U.S.-Israel relations, build international support for Israel, and support the Israeli-Arab peace process. The committee's numerous publications include the *AJC Journal*, the report *Muslim Anti-Semitism: A Clear and Present Danger*, and the papers "Iran and the Palestinian War Against Israel" and "The Arab Campaign to Destroy Israel."

Americans for Middle East Understanding (AMEU)
475 Riverside Dr., Room 245, New York, NY 10115-0245
(212) 870-2053 • fax: (212) 870-2050
e-mail: info@ameu.org • website: www.ameu.org

AMEU's purpose is to foster a better understanding in America of the history, goals, and values of Middle Eastern cultures and peoples, the rights of Palestinians, and the forces shaping U.S. policy in the Middle East. AMEU publishes *The Link*, a bimonthly newsletter, as well as books and pamphlets on the Middle East.

Center for Middle Eastern Studies
University of Texas, Austin, TX 78712
(512) 471-3881 • fax: (512) 471-7834
e-mail: cmes@menic.texas.edu
website: http://menic.utexas.edu/menic/cmes

The center was established by the U.S. Department of Education to promote a better understanding of the Middle East. It provides research and instructional materials, and publishes three series of books on the Middle East: the Modern Middle East Series, the Middle East Monograph Series, and the Modern Middle East Literatures in Translation Series.

Foundation for Middle East Peace
1763 N St. NW, Washington, DC 20036
(202) 835-3650 • fax: (202) 835-3651
e-mail: info@fmep.org • website: www.fmep.org

The foundation assists the peaceful resolution of the Israeli-Palestinian conflict by making financial grants available within the Arab and Jewish communities. It publishes the bimonthly *Report on Israeli Settlements in the Occupied Territories* and additional books and papers.

Institute for Palestine Studies (IPS)
3501 M St. NW, Washington, DC 20007
(202) 342-3990 • fax: (202) 342-3927
e-mail: ips@ipsjps.org • website: www.ipsjps.org

The Institute for Palestine Studies is a private, nonprofit, pro-Arab institute unaffiliated with any political organization or government. Established in 1963 in Beirut, the institute promotes research, analysis, and documentation of the Arab-Israeli conflict and its resolution. IPS publishes quarterlies in three languages and maintains offices all over the world. In addition to editing the *Journal of Palestine Studies*, the institute's U.S. branch publishes books and documents on the Arab-Israeli conflict and Palestinian affairs.

Jordan Information Bureau
2319 Wyoming Ave. NW, Washington, DC 20008
(202) 265-1606 • fax: (202) 667-0777
e-mail: JordanInfo@aol.com
website: www.jordanembassyus.org/new/jib/indexjib.shtml

The bureau provides political, cultural, and economic information on Jordan. It publishes fact sheets, speeches by Jordanian officials, and government documents, many of which are available on its website.

Middle East Forum
1500 Walnut St., Suite 1050, Philadelphia, PA 19102
(215) 546-5406 • fax: (215) 546-5409
e-mail: info@meforum.org • website: www.meforum.org
The Middle East Forum is a think tank that works to define and promote American interests in the Middle East. It supports strong American ties with Israel, Turkey, and other democracies as they emerge. It publishes the *Middle East Quarterly*, a policy-oriented journal. Its website includes articles, summaries of activities, and a discussion forum.

Middle East Institute
1761 N St. NW, Washington, DC 20036-2882
(202) 785-1141 • fax: (202) 331-8861
e-mail: mideasti@mideasti.org
website: www.themiddleeastinstitute.org
The institute's charter mission is to promote better understanding of Middle Eastern cultures, languages, religions, and politics. It publishes numerous books, papers, audiotapes, and videos as well as the quarterly *Middle East Journal*. It also maintains an Educational Outreach Department to give teachers and students of all grade levels advice on resources.

Middle East Media Research Institute (MEMRI)
PO Box 27837, Washington, DC 20038-7837
(202) 955-9070 • fax: (202) 955-9077
e-mail: memri@memri.org • website: www.memri.org
MEMRI translates and disseminates articles and commentaries from Middle East media sources and provides analysis on the political, ideological, intellectual, social, cultural, and religious trends in the region.

Middle East Policy Council
1730 M St. NW, Suite 512, Washington, DC 20036-4505
(202) 296-6767 • fax: (202) 296-5791
e-mail: info@mepc.org • website: www.mepc.org
The Middle East Policy Council was founded in 1981 to expand public discussion and understanding of issues affecting U.S. policy in the Middle East. The council is a nonprofit educational organization that operates nationwide. It publishes the quarterly *Middle East Policy Journal*.

Middle East Research and Information Project (MERIP)
1500 Massachusetts Ave. NW, Washington, DC 20005
(202) 223-3677 • fax: (202) 223-3604
website: www.merip.org

MERIP is a nonprofit, nongovernmental organization with no links to any religious, educational, or political organizations in the United States or elsewhere. Its mission is to educate the public about the contemporary Middle East with particular emphasis on U.S. foreign policy, human rights, and social justice issues. It publishes the bimonthly *Middle East Report.*

United States Department of State, Bureau of Near Eastern Affairs
U.S. Department of State
2201 C St. NW, Washington, DC 20520
(202) 647-4000
website: www.state.gov/p/nea

The bureau deals with U.S. foreign policy and U.S. relations with the countries in the Middle East and North Africa. Its website offers country information as well as news briefings and press statements on U.S. foreign policy.

Washington Institute for Near East Policy
1828 L St. NW, Suite 1050, Washington, DC 20036
(202) 452-0650 • fax: (202) 223-5364
e-mail: info@washingtoninstitute.org
website: www.washingtoninstitute.org

The institute is an independent, nonprofit research organization that provides information and analysis on the Middle East and U.S. policy in the region. It publishes numerous books, periodic monographs, and reports on regional politics, security, and economics, including *PeaceWatch*, which focuses on the Arab-Israeli peace process, and the reports *Democracy and Arab Political Culture* and *Radical Middle East States and U.S. Policy.*

Websites

Bitterlemons.org
www.bitterlemons.org

This website presents Israeli and Palestinian viewpoints on the Palestinian-Israeli conflict and peace process as well as related regional issues of concern.

Ha'Aretz Online

www.haaretzdaily.com

This is an online edition of one of the leading Israeli newspapers published in English.

Islamic Republic News Agency

www.irna.com

This agency of the government of Iran provides links to news articles and current affairs about that nation and the Middle East.

MidEastWeb

www.mideastweb.org

MidEastWeb is a website founded by people from different nations who are active in peace education efforts. Its website features articles and opinions about events in the region, as well as maps and a history of the conflict in the Middle East.

Saudi Arabia Ministry of Information

www.saudinf.com

This official Saudi government site has links to thousands of pages of information on the Kingdom of Saudi Arabia.

Bibliography of Books

Lila Abu-Lughod, ed.   *Feminism and Modernity in the Middle East.* Princeton, NJ: Princeton University Press, 1998.

Gilbert Achcar   *The Clash of Barbarisms: September 11 and the Making of the New World Disorder.* New York: Monthly Review Press, 2002.

Karen Armstrong   *Jerusalem: One City, Three Faiths.* New York: Knopf, 1996.

Naseer Aruri, ed.   *Palestinian Refugees: The Right of Return.* London, UK: Pluto, 2001.

Christiane Bird   *Neither East nor West: One Woman's Journey Through the Islamic Republic of Iran.* New York: Pocket Books, 2001.

Yossef Bodansky   *The High Cost of Peace: How Washington's Middle East Policy Left America Vulnerable to Terrorism.* Roseville, CA: Prima, 2002.

Daniel Brumberg   *Reinventing Khomeini: The Struggle for Reform in Iran.* Chicago: University of Chicago Press, 2001.

Roane Carey, ed.   *The New Intifada: Resisting Israel's Apartheid.* New York: Verso, 2001.

Noam Chomsky   *The Fateful Triangle: The United States, Israel and the Palestinians.* London, UK: Pluto Press, 2000.

Toby Dodge and Steven Simon, eds.   *Iraq at the Crossroads: State and Society in the Shadow of Regime Change.* New York: Oxford University Press, 2003.

John L. Esposito and John O. Voll, eds.   *Islam and Democracy.* New York: Oxford University Press, 1996.

Norman G. Finkelstein   *Image and Reality of the Israel-Palestine Conflict.* New York: Verso, 2001.

Deborah J. Gerner, ed.   *Understanding the Contemporary Middle East.* Boulder, CO: Lynne Reinner, 2000.

Victor Davis Hanson   *An Autumn of War: What America Learned from September 11 and the War on Terrorism.* New York: Anchor, 2002.

Birthe Hanssen   *Unipolarity and the Middle East.* Richmond, Surrey, UK: Curzon, 2000.

Nathanial Harris   *Israel and Arab Nations in Conflict.* New York: Raintree/SteckVaughan, 1999.

Dilip Hiro   *Iraq: In the Eye of the Storm.* New York: Thunder's Mouth Press, 2002.

Dilip Hiro	*Neighbors, Not Friends: Iraq and Iran After the Gulf Wars.* New York: Routledge, 2001.
Laurel Holliday	*Children of Israel, Children of Palestine: Our Own True Stories.* New York: Pocket Books, 1999.
Albert Hourani	*A History of the Arab Peoples.* Boston: Harvard University Press, 1997.
Mehran Kamrava	*Democracy in the Balance: Culture and Society in the Middle East.* Chappaqua, NY: Chatham House, 1998.
Martin Kramer	*Ivory Towers on Sand.* Washington, DC: Washington Institute for Near East Policy, 2001.
Walter Laqueur and Barry Rubin, eds.	*The Israel-Arab Reader: A Documentary History of the Middle East Conflict.* New York: Penguin USA, 2001.
David W. Lesch, ed.	*The Middle East and the United States: A Historical and Political Reassessment.* Boulder, CO: Westview Press, 2003.
Bernard Lewis	*The Middle East: A Brief History of the Last 2000 Years.* New York: Scribner, 1996.
Bernard Lewis	*What Went Wrong: The Clash Between Islam and Modernity in the Middle East.* New York: Harperperennial, 2003.
Philip Mattar, ed.	*The Encyclopedia of the Palestinians.* New York: Facts On File, 2000.
Mahmood Monshipouri	*Islamism, Secularism, and Human Rights in the Middle East.* Boulder, CO: Lynne Rienner, 1998.
Benny Morris	*Righteous Victims: A History of the Zionist-Arab Conflict, 1881–2001.* New York: Vintage, 2001.
Michael B. Owen	*Six Days of War: June 1967 and the Making of the Modern Middle East.* Novato, CA: Presidio, 2003.
Kenneth M. Pollack	*The Threatening Storm: The Case for Invading Iraq.* New York: Random House, 2002.
Milan Rai	*War Plan Iraq: Ten Reasons Against War with Iraq.* New York: Verso, 2002.
Edward W. Said	*The End of the Peace Process: Oslo and After.* New York: Vintage, 2000.
Elaine Sciolino	*Persian Mirrors: The Elusive Face of Iran.* New York: Free Press, 2000.
David K. Shipler	*Arab and Jew: Wounded Spirits in a Promised Land.* New York: Penguin, 2002.

Avi Shlaim	*The Iron Wall: Israel and the Arab World.* New York: W.W. Norton, 2001.
Charles D. Smith	*Palestine and the Arab-Israeli Conflict.* New York: Bedford/St. Martin's, 2000.
Shibley Telhami	*The Stakes: America and the Middle East.* Boulder, CO: Westview, 2002.
Harlan Ullman	*Unfinished Business: Afghanistan, the Middle East and Beyond—Defusing the Dangers That Threaten American Security.* New York: Citadel Press, 2002.

Index

in supply of, 130
U.S. addiction to, 130–31, 135–36
Oslo process, 99, 143
Ottaway, Marina, 119
Ottoman Empire, 13

Pakistan, 115
Palestine
  number of Jews in, 18
  partitioning of, 18, 35–36
Palestine Authority (PA), 143
Palestine Liberation Organization
  (PLO), 40–41, 143
Palestine National Council, 146
Palestinians
  are not persecuted under Israeli
    occupation, 37
  constitution of, 162–63
  fence separating Israelis from,
    166–68
    illusion of security with, 170–71
    is ineffective, 172–73
    Palestinian view on, 172
    pursuing negotiations instead of,
      173–74
    sacrifices negotiation positions,
      171–72
  nationhood for, rejection of, 36–37
Partnership for a New Generation
  of Vehicles, 137
Payne, Henry, 134
Pearlman, Wendy, 161
Peretz, Martin, 157

Rabbo, Yasir Abed, 171
Rabin, Yitzhak, 143
refugees, Palestinian, 18, 147

Saudi Arabia, 59, 130
Seitz, Charmaine, 53
September 11 terrorist attacks, 47, 61
Sharon, Ariel
  peace process and, 106, 149, 152
  visit of, to Al-Aqsa mosque,
    163–64
Sh'i' Da'wa Party, 79
Shi'i movements, 78–79
Shiites, 67
Six-Day war, 41, 67
Society of Muslim Brethren, 74–75
suicide bombings, 43, 79, 166–67
Syrian Arab Republic, 52

Takeyh, Ray, 60
Tenet, George, 105

terrorism
  Israeli-Palestinian conflict and, 23,
    155–56
  Israeli-Palestinian peace process
    and, 42–43, 152–53, 157–58
  Arafat's condemnation of, 148
Tracinski, Robert, 150
Turkey, 52

United Nations
  Development Programme
    (UNDP), 58
  partitioning of Palestine and, 18,
    35–36
  Security Council Resolution 242,
    21, 24, 36
  Security Council Resolution 446,
    22
  Security Council Resolution 465,
    22
United States
  aid to the Middle East, 94
  energy conservation and, 131–33
  Israeli-Palestinian peace process
    and, 155, 156
  Middle East resentment of, 110–11
  military involvement in the Middle
    East, 94
  oil addiction of, 130–31, 135–36
  reasons for interest in the Middle
    East, 94–95
  resistance to foreign control by,
    15–16
  role in Israeli-Palestinian conflict
    expectations vs. reality for,
      105–106
    necessary intervention and,
      101–102
    resisting interventionist urge for,
      106–107
  role in Iraq, conflicting opinion
    on, 109
  see also democracy, U.S. promotion
    of

violence
  following Oslo peace agreements,
    143
  following Sharon's Al-Aqsa
    mosque visit, 163–64
  Iranian Islamic Revolution and,
    78–79
  Islamic fundamentalism fosters,
    70–80
    con, 81–91

202